KANT'S CRITIQUE
OF
PURE REASON

A Commentary for Students

KANT'S CRITIQUE OF PURE REASON

A Commentary for Students

BY

T. E. WILKERSON

CLARENDON PRESS · OXFORD
1976

Oxford University Press, Ely House, London W. 1

GLASGOW NEW YORK TORONTO MELBOURNE WELLINGTON
CAPE TOWN IBADAN NAIROBI DAR ES SALAAM LUSAKA ADDIS ABABA
DELHI BOMBAY CALCUTTA MADRAS KARACHI DACCA
KUALA LUMPUR SINGAPORE HONG KONG TOKYO

CASEBOUND ISBN 0 19 824548 3
PAPERBACK ISBN 0 19 824549 1

© *Oxford University Press 1976*

*Printed in Great Britain by
Butler & Tanner Ltd
Frome and London*

PREFACE

ELEVEN years ago I first began to struggle through the *Critique of Pure Reason* under the infinitely sympathetic eye of Professor P. F. Strawson. Ever since that time I have felt the need for a commentary designed specifically for second- and third-year undergraduates approaching Kant for the first time, and indeed for intelligent laymen of similar competence. Their needs are extremely complex. They need to understand Kant's relation to the great rationalist and empiricist philosophers with whom they are already acquainted. They will want their work on Kant to improve their grasp of modern epistemology. They will want explanations of Kant's elaborate and rather pretentious technical terms and of his rhetorical idiosyncrasies. If they are not to be utterly confused they will need to be reminded of the distinction between exposition and reconstruction, between what Kant actually said and certain interesting views inspired by what he said. Perhaps most important of all, they will not be satisfied with a sketchy introduction to the first *Critique* but will expect to be stimulated to a more profound examination of Kant and Kantian problems.

This book is an attempt to cater for those needs. Indeed both in form and in content it reflects my own experience of initiating undergraduates into the mysteries of the first *Critique*. My debt to Professor Strawson, both as my teacher and as the author of *The Bounds of Sense*, is obvious throughout. But this book is in no sense the *Prolegomena* to his *Critique*, for his aims and many of his views are different from mine. I have learned and borrowed a great deal from many other commentators, some of whom are mentioned in the Bibliography. But I share Strawson's and Bennett's assumption that Kant is of great interest and significance to modern analytical philosophers, even though some of his views are superficially repellent or historically parochial. I also share their obvious distaste for the philosophical sycophancy that still disfigures so much work on Kant. There can be no doubt that Kant is an extremely important and fertile philosopher whom we neglect at our peril. But he is by no means incapable of descending to nonsense, falsehood, or triviality.

My thanks are due to a number of people. Rita Lee typed with her usual extraordinary efficiency, Vera Peetz made valiant efforts to improve my understanding of mathematics, my wife tolerated many fits of preoccupation and absentmindedness, and my baby daughter was comparatively quiet. Perhaps my greatest debt is to successive generations of finalists at Keele and Nottingham, who forced me both to wrestle with the *Critique* continuously for a long period, and to make it comprehensible to them.

The editors of *The Philosophical Quarterly* and of *Kant-Studien* have kindly allowed me to use in Chapter 10 material from my 'Transcendental Arguments' (1970) and 'Transcendental Arguments Revisited' (1975) respectively. I am also grateful to Macmillan and Co., Ltd, and to St Martin's Press, Inc., for permission to quote from N. Kemp-Smith's translation of the *Critique of Pure Reason*.

The text only contains sufficient bibliographical information for readers' immediate purposes. Complete references will be found in the Bibliography.

Nottingham, 1975   T. E. W.

CONTENTS

PART V   THREE PROBLEMS

PART I

INTRODUCTION

Varsonofiev relaxed and said with a tired smile: 'Important questions always have long, tortuous answers . . .'

(A. Solzhenitsyn, *August 1914*, Ch. 42)

I

KANT'S ENTERPRISE

1. THE CRITICAL PHILOSOPHY

It is probably still true that, except for the *Groundwork*, Kant's work has been neglected by modern analytical philosophers. They can be pardoned for concentrating on that book, for it is very much shorter and somewhat clearer than his other important works, and is regarded by many as the most striking exposition of a deontological account of ethics. But the concentration is rather unfortunate for three reasons. First, the *Groundwork* certainly does not contain all Kant's work on ethics, and he has very many interesting things to say elsewhere, notably in the *Critique of Practical Reason*. Second, Kant insisted in the *Critique of Pure Reason* that a great deal of general philosophical spadework has to be done before we can start to attack the special problems of ethics. And it is difficult to understand the extravagant complexity of his ethical views unless one first examines the spadework in the first *Critique*. Third, Kant's major philosophical advances were made in epistemology and the philosophy of mind. I would not consider it an exaggeration to say that much of his epistemology and philosophy of mind is right and important, but that most of his ethical views are disastrously wrong. For example in the first *Critique* we find a very plausible objection to phenomenalism in any form, an objection which had no currency in the long and sometimes tiresome discussion of sense-data during the last fifty years or so. It is rather disconcerting also to find a defence of phenomenalism in the first *Critique*, but I shall explain the inconsistency later.

If you dip into the first *Critique* it is clear why Kant's epistemology has been neglected. A man of unusual honesty, Kant himself said of it, 'It will be misjudged because it is misunderstood, and misunderstood because men choose to skim through the book and not to think through it—a disagreeable task, because the work is dry, obscure, opposed to all ordinary notions, and moreover long-winded' (*Prolegomena*, p. 261). Indeed the *Prolegomena to Any Future Metaphysics* were written to correct some of the misunderstanding by presenting the doctrines of the first *Critique* in a summary form. But it would be foolish to exaggerate the difficulty of the first *Critique*. Admittedly Kant has some rather unfortunate literary habits. The text is full of additions and revisions, and he is not always careful to ensure that the revised version is consistent. He cheerfully contradicts himself. And even in Kemp-Smith's very elegant translation the prose is tortuous and pedestrian. But these are for the most part difficulties of form, and the content of the book is probably no more difficult than the work of the more eloquent Hume.

Kant himself was in many ways an unremarkable man. He spent his entire life in Königsberg, now Kaliningrad, a University town and busy port in East Prussia. He appears to have had no spectacular experiences, vices, virtues, or passions, save perhaps an obsession about telling the truth,[1] a profound fear of varicose veins,[2] and a rather Lutheran interest in the state of his bowels.[3] But his philosophical career was quite extraordinary. He was born in 1724 and was therefore only a few years younger than Hume. From our point of view he published little of philosophical interest until 1781, when he was fifty-seven. For much of his career he was practising and teaching later strains of Leibnizian rationalism, together with various other disciplines still considered to be the province of the philosopher, such as astronomy and natural history. For example he gave an account of the influence of the moon on the tides, arrived independently at a Laplacean account of the origin of the solar system, and noticed the physiological similarities between many animals.

But then he suddenly entered an enormously fertile period which yielded the first *Critique* (1781), the *Prolegomena* (1783), the *Groundwork* (1785), the *Critique of Practical Reason* (1788), the *Critique of Judgement* (1790), and many other works. The most remarkable fact about these works is that they are in no sense the final results of a life's work, for they represented a radical change in Kant's philosophical outlook. It seems that during the 1760s and 1770s Kant became increasingly dissatisfied with the rationalist tradition within which he had been working all his life. What exactly inspired the dissatisfaction is not entirely clear, for the evidence is rather inconclusive, and Kant himself gives slightly different accounts in different places. But there are probably two important factors. One was that he noticed certain apparent contradictions or 'antinomies' in traditional rationalist metaphysics, contradictions he examined in the Transcendental Dialectic of the first *Critique*. The

---

[1] According to Plessing it was common for poor unmarried mothers in Königsberg to bring paternity suits against prosperous burghers, whether they were the fathers or not, in an attempt to extort handsome maintenance. It is interesting that Kant was never a victim of such a scheme, and it is tempting to conclude that his reputation for absolute honesty made him a very unprofitable target for slanderous accusations. A more prosaic and historically more plausible explanation would be that he was very poor for much of his career. Cf. Letter from F. V. L. Plessing, 3 Apr. 1784 (Zweig, pp. 117–18).

[2] Cf. Abbott, p. xliv.   [3] Cf. Letter to Marcus Herz, 20 Aug. 1777 (Zweig, pp. 87–8).

second was that he began to feel the influence of empiricism, particularly
the influence of Hume: 'I openly confess my recollection of David Hume
was the very thing which many years ago first interrupted my dogmatic
slumber and gave my investigations in the field of speculative philosophy
a quite new direction' (*Prolegomena*, p. 260). The 'recollection' was not
very extensive, for Kant was probably only acquainted at first hand with
the first *Enquiry*. But there were empiricist philosophers in Germany, and
he must have been acquainted with and impressed by Humean criticism
of rationalist metaphysics. 'If we take in our hand any volume; of divinity
or school metaphysics, for instance; let us ask, *Does it contain any abstract
reasoning concerning quantity or number?* No. *Does it contain any experimental reasoning concerning matter of fact and existence?* No. Commit it
then to the flames: for it can contain nothing but sophistry and illusion'
(first *Enquiry*, XII; Selby-Bigge, p. 165).

We might say that, among other things, Hume was struggling to make
a clear distinction between *a priori* and experimental inquiries. It might
seem obvious to us (at least to those of us unimpressed by Quine's attack
on the analytic/synthetic distinction) that certain claims can only be
established *a priori*, by careful analysis of certain expressions, and that
other claims can only be established experimentally. For example we can
only establish *a priori* that bachelors are unmarried, or that a cat is an
animal. It would be absurd to observe bachelors in an effort to discover
whether they are unmarried, or to observe cats in an effort to discover
whether they are animals. On the other hand *a priori* speculation is powerless to show that the earth revolves around the sun, or that hydrogen
is combustible in oxygen. Such claims can only be established or refuted
by experiment, by observation.

But the distinction between *a priori* and *a posteriori* truths, between
a priori and experimental inquiries, was certainly not obvious in the eighteenth century. (Indeed even in the nineteenth century theologians made
wholly *a priori* objections to Darwin's account of evolution; conversely
J. S. Mill seriously entertained the possibility that truths of logic are high-
level empirical generalizations.) The great rationalists with whom Kant
was acquainted had an absurdly ambitious view of the scope of *a priori*
speculation. They thought that in principle we could establish absolutely
any facts about the world *a priori*. Not merely did they not understand
the importance of experiment, of observation, in enlarging our knowledge
of the world, they very definitely scorned experimental methods. They
believed that empirical observation could only yield a very muddy and
inferior picture of the world, and that we must resort to *a priori* reflection
if we are to reveal the real structure of the things around us.

Kant's 'recollection of David Hume' evidently made him dissatisfied with the method of rationalist metaphysics, the bland assumption that our knowledge of the world can and should be enlarged wholly *a priori*. He was not concerned to show that the stratospheric claims about God, the soul, freedom, etc., were *false*; he was rather inclined to think that we have no *right* to make the claims at all. And he was inclined to think that we have no right to make them, because he was beginning to appreciate the significance of one main strand of the empiricist tradition, namely the doctrine that we can only make substantive claims about the world if it is in principle possible to establish or refute them directly or indirectly by sense-experience. Much of rationalist metaphysics is unacceptable in principle because it consists of claims wholly divorced from sense-experience, claims about objects that are not objects of a possible experience.

In the Introduction and Prefaces to the first *Critique* (esp. A2/B6 ff.) Kant expresses his dissatisfaction in the language of faculties as follows. Rationalist or 'dogmatic' metaphysicians use the faculty of reason to come to general metaphysical conclusions about God, the soul, the extent and nature of the universe, and so on. But we cannot use our reason until we have examined its credentials, until we have decided which deliverances of reason can count as knowledge, and which cannot. In other words we must first answer a host of questions about philosophical method, about what counts as genuine knowledge and what does not. By neglecting the vital preliminary methodological questions we have not merely 'run every risk of error' (A3/B7), but have actually produced philosophical views that are vacuous.

So one of Kant's main aims in the first *Critique* is to provoke 'the downfall of all dogmatic metaphysics' (*Prolegomena*, p. 367), to limit very considerably the scope of *a priori* speculation, to establish the limits of metaphysical inquiry. He is impressed by the Humean claim that we can only make substantive claims about the world if they can in principle be established or refuted in sense-experience. But it is obvious as the *Critique* proceeds that he does not accept Hume's wholesale rejection of metaphysics. The only field of *a priori* inquiry that Hume seems to allow is an investigation of 'relations between ideas', including most notably logic and mathematics, 'abstract reasoning concerning quantity and number'. Any other kind of *a priori* speculation is 'sophistry and illusion'. But Kant thinks he can steer a middle course between over-ambitious rationalist 'enthusiasm' and philosophically ascetic Humean 'scepticism' (B128). He thinks he can leave room for legitimate *a priori* knowledge of the world without again embarking on the vacuous metaphysical fantasies of traditional rationalism. He wants to gain some substantive *a priori* knowledge of the world, while conceding to Hume that such knowledge must be very intimately connected with sense-experience.

2. SPECIFIC PHILOSOPHICAL PROBLEMS

It is clear then why the *Critique of Pure Reason* is called the *Critique of Pure Reason*. It is meant to be a preliminary account of what reason can and cannot attempt in the way of *a priori* metaphysical speculation. It is Cartesian in spirit, in the sense that it purports to settle the vital methodological problem concerning criteria of knowledge before attempting to solve any specific philosophical problems. But if you were to start to read the *Critique of Pure Reason* on the assumption that it is a critical study of philosophical method, you would be rather puzzled. For Kant only begins directly to attack problems about the nature and status of metaphysics at a fairly late stage of the proceedings, in the Transcendental Dialectic. The earlier sections of the *Critique* look much more like a discussion of a number of specific philosophical problems, all of which would have been of common interest then, and some of which are of great interest now. Indeed the main interest for us is probably Kant's discussion of the specific philosophical problems, rather than his discussion of the general methodological issue.

But the preoccupation with method is never far below the surface, for two connected reasons. First, Kant wants to expose the vacuous metaphysics of traditional rationalism. To do that he must first develop his own positive account of knowledge, must establish for example that we can only make knowledge-claims about spatio-temporal objects which obey causal laws. And to do that he must discuss specific problems about space, time, and causality. Second, as I have just pointed out, although he is impressed by Hume's attack on rationalist metaphysics, he thinks that we can and should leave room for some *a priori* knowledge of the world. The earlier sections of the *Critique* are devoted to an examination and justification of that *a priori* knowledge. For example according to Kant we can and do know *a priori* that objects are spatial, temporal, causal, etc. So although Kant's discussion of specific philosophical problems is of great intrinsic interest, we should not lose sight of its strategic role in the general plan of the first *Critique*, in establishing a clear distinction between genuine and spurious *a priori* knowledge-claims.

It is perhaps important in passing to note that Kant was a very poor scholar in the narrow sense of 'scholarship'. I said that the specific problems he discusses were of great interest then, for they had been discussed by Descartes, Leibniz, Locke, Berkeley, Hume, and many other philosophers. But Kant's references to other people's views are often misleading, and sometimes just straightforwardly wrong. On both historical and textual grounds it seems unlikely that he had read many of his great predecessors at first hand. Even his acquaintance with Leibniz was largely second-hand, through the work of such Leibnizian disciples as Wolff or Baumgarten. Of course Kant had some excuse for his sins of omission, for some philosophical works available to us, notably some of Leibniz's, had not then been published, and others, such as those of Locke, Berkeley, and Hume, may not have been widely circulated on the Continent. Even so, one cannot help feeling that Kant was rather careless in expounding other philosophers' views. Indeed, as we shall see, he occasionally expounded his own views incorrectly, misstating the most elementary points.

To return to the matter in hand, I said that although Kant is constantly preoccupied with a general methodological problem, he discusses a number of specific philosophical problems of great interest. Although there are very many of them, four are of special note, for they form the core of the first main sections of the *Critique*, the Transcendental Aesthetic and the Transcendental Analytic, and they are of special interest to modern philosophers. The first is a problem about the nature of space and time. At that time there were two prevailing and competing views. Disciples of Leibniz thought of space and time as essentially relational, as a set of relations between objects. According to them it made no sense to talk of space and time in complete isolation from objects spatially and temporally related. If there were no objects there would be no space and no time. In contrast Newtonians regarded space and time as logically independent individuals, infinitely extended, which contained objects but which were independent of them. That is, even if there were no objects there would still be space and time, empty space and empty time. Formally Leibnizians regarded space and time as logically *secondary*, dependent entirely on there being various objects spatially and temporally related, whereas Newtonians regarded space and time as logically *primary*, perfectly capable of existing in the complete absence of any objects.

The second problem concerns our concept of a person. People are in many respects like trees and tables and chairs, for they have physical bodies. But they also have rather peculiar properties which are not shared by tables and chairs, for they think, have sense-impressions, memories, images, pains, and so on. And the fact that they have these peculiar properties makes it rather difficult to formulate precise criteria of personal identity. What makes Smith today the same person as Smith five years ago? We talk of people, but what exactly is a person? We talk of being self-conscious, but of what are we conscious when we are self-conscious? I am not going to attempt to answer these questions now. I want only to point out that the two approaches to these problems that should be borne in mind are Descartes's and Hume's. According to Descartes a person is essentially a non-physical substance attached to a physical body.

Strictly a person is not a material object at all, but rather a non-physical object attached to a material object. In a sense the Cartesian position is a neat solution of the problem of personal identity, but at the cost of introducing extremely mysterious non-physical soul-substances. Hume very laudably refuses to embrace a mysterious solution, but fails to solve the problem. He looks for a Cartesian soul-substance but complains that he cannot find it. Whenever he introspectively starts the search, perceptions inevitably bar the way, and so he abandons the search as wholly fruitless. But to abandon the search is to be left with no criterion of personal identity, no way of tying up the 'bundle of perceptions'. We have no way of guaranteeing that all my experiences form a single series, that all Jones's experiences form a second, that all Smith's form a third, and so on. The best Hume can do is to tie each bundle by identifying various relations between all the experiences in the bundle, notably the relations of resemblance and causality. But sadly the relations of resemblance and causality do not yield a foolproof plan for distinguishing one bundle, and hence one person, from another.

The third problem, the nature of causality, also takes us back to Hume. Classical rationalists failed to distinguish clearly between causal and logical connections, and regarded causal connections as necessary rather than contingent. Hume simply denied that there could be necessary connections between what he would call 'distinct existences', or between what we would call distinct events. He suggested that 'A causes B' could best be interpreted to mean 'A-type events precede and are constantly conjoined with B-type events'. It is possible, he admitted, that we are strongly tempted to think that cause and effect are necessarily connected, but the temptation is to be resisted, for we have been misled by a curious psychological association of ideas. As we acquire more and more experience of A-type events causing B-type events, we tend to associate the two, and as soon as we perceive a new A-type event we immediately think of a B-type event (and vice versa). The purely psychological association of ideas of A-type events with ideas of B-type events is then projected on to the world and mistaken for a necessary connection between the events themselves. But in fact cause and effect are only contingently connected, and we can easily conceive of our causal laws being quite other than they are. If you hit a piece of glass with a hammer it breaks, but we can easily conceive of its behaving quite differently. As far as logic is concerned the glass might open to admit the advancing hammer, or disappear from view, or turn into a cabbage.

The fourth problem is rather difficult to state without anticipating some of the discussion of Kant's views on it. I shall therefore tend to state it from his point of view. The problem is to determine the status of the most general truths of mathematics and physics, which for Kant meant Euclidean geometry and simple arithmetic on the one hand, and Newtonian physics on the other. What is the status of such general truths as that $2+2=4$, or that a triangle's interior angles equal two right angles, or that action and reaction are equal? Are they necessary truths established by *a priori* argument, or are they contingent truths to be proved experimentally? Certainly these are fairly recurrent philosophical problems, at least as far as mathematics is concerned. In the case of mathematics we might state the problem with Kantian *naïveté* as follows. Either the general truths of mathematics are essentially *a priori*/necessary/analytic truths or they are essentially *a posteriori*/contingent/synthetic truths. But neither alternative seems very attractive (cf. B14–15). It does not seem very attractive to say that mathematical truths are logical truths, because we have a rather naïve feeling that logic can never enlarge our knowledge. Far from telling us anything new, a logical truth merely juggles with what we know already. 'Analytic judgements ... are ... those in which the connection of the predicate with the subject is thought through identity' (A7/B10). But many mathematical theorems tell us all sorts of new and interesting things. For example Pythagoras's theorem starts with a very unambitious assumption about a right-angled triangle, yet finishes with a very exciting new fact about the relation between the square on the hypotenuse and the squares on the other two sides. So presumably we do not want to say that mathematical truths are analytic, instances of logical truths. But the other alternative, that they are synthetic or contingent or *a posteriori* truths, seems equally unattractive. For it would follow that, like any other synthetic or contingent truths, they are verifiable only by experience, and open to falsification. That is, we should not be surprised if we discovered that occasionally $2+2=5$ or $6\frac{1}{2}$ or 482, or that the interior angles of a triangle sometimes equal 179°, or 500°, or 92° ... etc.

I have expressed the problem rather tendentiously, but Kant's account of mathematics and of the analytic/synthetic distinction suggests very strongly that he thought of the problem in precisely the terms I used. I shall discuss his account of mathematics later on, in Chapters 2 and 8, and will be content for the moment to make two points. First, Kant thought that in one crucial respect mathematics and physics are similar disciplines. He thought that the most general claims of Newtonian physics, such as 'action and reaction are equal and opposite' or 'the quantity of matter is constant, whatever physical or chemical changes occur', have the same status as mathematical theorems, such as '$2+2=$ 4' or 'the interior angles of a triangle equal two right angles'. That is, he thought that the most general claims of physics, like the theorems of mathematics, are necessary truths. It is a rather bizarre view to our ears, for it seems obvious that physics and mathematics are quite different disciplines, that physics is an empirical or experimental discipline whose results are falsifiable. Kant would certainly agree that the majority of physics is empirical, for he would agree that specific physical hypotheses are empirical and falsifiable. But he would insist that certain basic assumptions, such as the principle of the conservation of matter, or the principle that every event has a cause, are necessary truths which could not be falsified.

Second, we must note that Kant also thought that the problem about the status of mathematics and physics is central to his whole enterprise. The first *Critique* is constructed, superficially at least, round a discussion of mathematics, physics, and metaphysics. He wants to contrast the genuine knowledge yielded by mathematics and physics with the vacuous claims of traditional metaphysics. He wants to show against the rationalists that their attempts to gain substantive *a priori* knowledge of the world fail miserably. But he wants to show against Hume that two important disciplines can yield legitimate substantive *a priori* knowledge of the world, namely mathematics and physics.

3. THE GENERAL ENTERPRISE

So we now have a general idea of the philosophical background of the first *Critique*. Kant's general inspiration seems to have been a dissatisfaction with rationalist metaphysics, a feeling that rationalists were confused about the criteria of knowledge, about what should count as good metaphysics, what as bad. He thought that the absence of a critique of reason itself vitiated much of rationalist thought and led inevitably to contradiction. But at the same time he was not very attracted by standard empiricist alternatives, by the scepticism of Hume. And in the main sections of the *Critique* he reveals a keen interest in at least four main problems of great interest to us now, namely the problem of the nature of space and time, the problem of personal identity, the problem of causality, and the problem of the status of the theorems of mathematics and the most general truths of physics.

We can at last start to look in more detail at the *Critique* itself. Kant tells us that the 'proper problem of pure reason is contained in the question: How are *a priori* synthetic judgements possible?' (B19). Unfortunately as it stands that very famous question is very difficult to understand. Kant helps us a little by explaining that it divides into a number of more specific questions, of which the three most important for our purposes are, How is pure mathematics possible?, How is pure science of nature possible?, How is metaphysics, as science, possible? (B20, 22). But even

with our background knowledge of Kant's enterprise it is still very un-
clear what those questions mean. It is perhaps clear how the references
to mathematics, pure natural science (or physics), and metaphysics have
crept in. After all, one of his main concerns is to compare the status of
mathematics and physics on the one hand, with that of metaphysics on
the other. The concern influences his literary plans so much that he writes
the *Critique* in three main sections, the Transcendental Aesthetic (concerned with mathematics), the Transcendental Analytic (concerned with
physics), and the Transcendental Dialectic (concerned with metaphysics). Moreover, instead of talking about the status of those three disciplines we might equally well talk about their criteria of knowledge, or
their standards of evidence or proof. Kant misleads us a little by the form
of his questions, no doubt, but in asking, How is mathematics or physics
or metaphysics *possible?* he is in effect asking questions about the status
of mathematics or physics or metaphysics as *knowledge*.

But the most puzzling feature of the questions is the reference to synthetic *a priori* judgements. Let us return for a moment to my account
in the previous section of the problem about the status of mathematics.
I said that we were faced with two alternatives, neither of which is particularly attractive. On the one hand we could say that mathematical truths
are *a priori* or necessary or analytic truths, but it was then difficult to
see how they could be so informative, could extend our knowledge. On
the other hand we could say that they were synthetic or *a posteriori* or contingent, but that seemed to imply that they could be falsified. You will
notice that I have implicitly assumed that the distinction between analytic
and synthetic truths is parallel to the distinction between *a priori* and *a
posteriori* truths. Kant rejects that assumption and is therefore able to
investigate a third possibility, that mathematical truths are synthetic and
a priori. It is by no means clear what he means by 'synthetic' and '*a priori*',
and it is by no means clear whether he is entitled to talk about synthetic
a priori truths at all. With characteristic obscurity he tells us that
'Necessity and strict universality are ... sure criteria of *a priori* knowledge' (B4) and that synthetic judgements 'add to the concept of the subject a predicate which has not been in any wise thought in it' (A7/B11).
The obscurity can be forgiven because, as I explained earlier, Kant's predecessors, both rationalist and empiricist, did not clearly understand the
distinctions between the analytic and the synthetic, and between the *a
priori* and the *a posteriori*. Kant could reasonably be credited with the
first attempt to draw them. Very sympathetically understood his remarks
can be made to yield the following definitions, which will be adequate for
our present purposes. An analytic proposition is an instance of a logical
truth, a proposition whose contradictory is self-contradictory; a syn-

thetic proposition is a proposition that is not analytic. An *a priori* proposition is established independently of experience; an *a posteriori* proposition is established by experience. So a synthetic *a priori* proposition is not analytic, not an instance of a logical truth, but is established independently of experience. Kant wants to say that the general claims of mathematics, physics, and metaphysics are synthetic *a priori* propositions or, more strictly translated, synthetic *a priori* 'judgements'.

So we can at last see why Kant expresses his problem in the way he does. He is particularly interested in mathematical, physical, and metaphysical claims, he thinks that they are synthetic but *a priori*, and he is concerned to discover how they can be established. He therefore expresses his problem in the form, How are synthetic *a priori* judgements possible? And as we shall see, his general answer will be that those of mathematics and physics are possible, but that those of metaphysics are not. But I am going to suggest a slightly different way of approaching the *Critique of Pure Reason* which is much clearer and much more helpful when one is actually confronted with the text. It is the approach originally developed with considerable philosophical profit in P. F. Strawson's *Bounds of Sense*. I am going to suppose that instead of asking, How are synthetic *a priori* propositions possible?, Kant is really asking, What are the necessary conditions of a possible experience?

The cynical might suspect that we have moved from one obscure question to another, so let us break it down into a number of more specific questions. For example we know that we perceive a world of fairly solid material objects, which exist whether or not we perceive them, which are spatially and temporally related to us and to each other, and which causally act and react. Kant wants to ask whether any of these features are *necessary* to our experience. Would it make sense to talk of perceiving a world of non-spatial or non-temporal objects? Or a world that obeyed no causal laws, was completely chaotic? Or a world of Berkeleian ideas in which objects lasted no longer than perceptions of them? It appears that Kant wants to insist that many such features are *necessary* to experience, that there are many conditions that must be fulfilled if we are to have any experience at all. For example he argues that the classical Berkeleian picture of the world is absurd, and that any sort of Humean doubts about the existence of the external world are incoherent. Returning to his general interest in philosophical method, he wants to show that much of rationalist metaphysics is absurd, because it overlooks one fundamental fact about the necessary features of human knowledge.

It is always arrogant and dangerous to re-write great philosophers, despite Kant's comforting observation 'that it is by no means unusual, upon comparing the thoughts which an author has expressed in regard to his subject . . . to find that we understand him better than he has understood himself' (A314/B370). But I think that much of what he has to say in the Transcendental Aesthetic and the Transcendental Analytic makes more sense to modern readers if we suppose that he was asking, What are the necessary conditions of a possible experience? Indeed Kant would not regard that question as distinct from the question, How are the synthetic *a priori* judgements of mathematics and physics possible? For he wants to argue that experience must be of objects that conform to the general truths of mathematics and physics. To investigate mathematics and physics is to investigate the necessary conditions of a possible experience. Strawson's version of Kant's problem and Kant's version amount for Kant to the same thing.

Why then should I concentrate on Strawson's version? If the two versions amount to the same thing, why should I be so concerned to use one rather than the other? There are two main reasons. First, the notion of a synthetic *a priori* judgement is unfamiliar to modern readers. It requires a considerable psychological effort to concentrate on the possibility of synthetic *a priori* judgements. But our familiarity with the later Wittgenstein, and of course with Strawson's *Individuals*, makes it easier for us to reflect on the necessary conditions of a possible experience. Second, as I have already argued, the revised version makes much more sense of the text of the first *Critique*. Although corresponding sections of the *Prolegomena* certainly deal primarily and prominently with mathematics and physics, the Aesthetic and Analytic of the first *Critique* do not. The references to mathematics and physics are very thinly scattered, are often very contrived, and usually sit awkwardly with the other material. Despite Kant's protestations to the contrary, his references to mathematics and physics are not stitched very confidently or very prominently into the majority of the Aesthetic and Analytic. So, entirely unrepentant, I suggest that we can best understand Kant's general problem as that of articulating the necessary conditions of a possible experience.

4. TECHNICAL TERMS

Before plunging into the main sections of the *Critique* we must try to understand Kant's somewhat unfamiliar technical terms. 'It is the boast of the Germans that, where steady and continuous industry are requisite, they can carry things farther than other nations' (*Prolegomena*, p. 381), and Kant reveals a passion for a systematic and highly technical exposition of his views. The technical terms are not in themselves very difficult to understand, but they and certain extravagant doctrines associated with them tend to make the *Critique* more tedious to read than it needs to be. So I shall attempt a judicious translation of the main terms.

The first is '*a priori*' and its very common synonym, 'pure'. Kant distinguishes between *a priori* or pure features of experience, and its empirical or *a posteriori* features. He is interested only in the pure or *a priori* features; indeed it is a *Critique of Pure* and not *Empirical Reason*. Anticipating quite a lot of what follows and returning to my comments about necessary conditions of a possible experience, we can explain the meaning of 'pure' or '*a priori*' as follows. Our ordinary experience contains a number of logically trivial features. It contains perceptions of motor-cars, asparagus, books, Blackpool rock. But it would be absurd to suggest that it is *necessary* in any interesting sense that we perceive motor-cars, asparagus, books, and Blackpool rock. Those are logically *contingent* features of experience, and we can easily imagine an experience that contained none of them, for example the experience of a man brought up on a remote desert island. We can easily abstract all those features from our account of experience without obliterating the concept of experience. In contrast there appear to be other features which we cannot abstract, which are logically indispensable if we are to have anything recognizable as experience. For example it is difficult to think of experience of objects that are neither spatial nor temporal, or obey no causal laws, or last no longer than perceptions of them. These are *prima facie* necessary features of experience. And when Kant says he is interested in the pure or *a priori* features of experience, he is concerned to abstract all the trivial contingent features, such as asparagus or Blackpool rock, and expose the general necessary features, such as space, time, and causality. He often uses the word 'transcendental' to make the same point, for a *transcendental* inquiry is an inquiry into the possibility of *a priori* knowledge (A11–12/B25). Thus the Aesthetic and Analytic are Transcendental because they investigate the *a priori* features of our knowledge of objects. The Dialectic is Transcendental because it investigates *a priori* claims which traditional rationalism has mistaken for genuine knowledge.

Clearly, if we are interested in the necessary conditions of a possible experience, we are bound in Kant's historical context to be interested in experiences, states of consciousness, in perceptions, thoughts, memory-experiences, after-images, etc. Whereas Locke and Berkeley talked of ideas, and Hume of impressions and ideas, Kant talks very generally of 'representations'. A representation is more or less any state of consciousness, any mental event. Kant's use of 'representation' is not always consistent, and he sometimes uses it to refer to things that we would certainly not regard as states of consciousness at all, such as concepts. But the second fault was common to all his great philosophical predecessors and to many of his successors.

So a representation is a state of consciousness, an experience. Some of these may be after-images, some may be thoughts, some may be bodily sensations such as pain sensations, and most importantly, some will be sense-impressions, experiences that are ostensibly perceptions of the external world. Hume called sense-impressions 'impressions', modern philosophers have often called them 'sense-data', and Kant called them 'intuitions'. Regrettably his use of 'intuition' is not consistent, and he often uses 'representation' and 'intuition' interchangeably, but he obviously meant 'intuition' to mean 'sense-impression'. Incidentally it is advisable to think of 'intuition' merely as a technical term, and to ignore any possible connection with ethical or feminine intuition, or with the mathematical intuition that persuades me that $2+2=4$.

This brings us to a fundamental distinction which Kant introduces at the beginning of the Transcendental Aesthetic (A19/B33 ff.), a distinction between concepts and intuitions. We are concerned to discover with Kant's assistance the necessary conditions of a possible experience. But, says Kant, in order for a man to experience something, two complementary conditions have to be fulfilled. First, something must be given or presented to his senses, and second, he must recognize it as of a certain kind, must attribute a certain property to it. In Kantian terms he must have an intuition and he must bring that intuition under a concept. The conditions are complementary and both necessary to experience: 'neither concepts without an intuition in some way corresponding to them, nor intuition without concepts, can yield knowledge' (A50/B74). 'Thoughts without content are empty, intuitions without concepts are blind' (A51/B75). To take a simple example, if I am to have knowledge of a table, two complementary conditions must be fulfilled. First, I must have an intuition or sense-impression of the table, and second, I must bring the intuition under a concept, recognize it as a perception of a table.

Expressed in that way the distinction between intuitions and concepts is only a variation on the distinction between particular things, such as tables and chairs, and general concepts, such as the concept of colour or shape or hardness, or the distinction between particular things and their common properties. But Kant goes further by making a parallel distinction between the faculties of sensibility and understanding. Sensibility is the faculty of intuitions and understanding the faculty of concepts. Sensibility, the faculty of intuitions, produces a manifold of intuitions, a disorganized rhapsody of perceptions, while understanding organizes and unifies all the diverse intuitions, brings the manifold of intuitions under concepts. The product of the complicated two-stage process is empirical knowledge, experience.

The psychological story is not particularly interesting or attractive, but it does contain one absolutely crucial point which shows how Kant steers carefully between the Scylla of rationalism and the Charybdis of empiricism. Of course the distinction between rationalism and empiricism should be treated with considerable caution. For example it could be argued that Descartes is in some respects an empiricist, while Locke is in some respects a rationalist. But the distinction can be quite illuminating if regarded as a distinction between two accounts of knowledge. For a traditional empiricist the paradigm of knowledge is knowledge through the senses of sight, hearing, etc. He seldom refers to the intellect at all and when he does so he assigns it a rather secondary role in the acquisition of knowledge. For example 'understanding' for Locke is only responsible for reorganizing the knowledge acquired through sensation and reflection. According to Hume 'reason' is responsible for identifying 'relations between ideas', but the ideas have been acquired through the senses. In contrast a traditional rationalist insists that the paradigm of knowledge is knowledge through the reason or understanding. In so far as the senses yield knowledge at all, it is only a very dim, muddy, confused approximation to the real thing, knowledge through the reason or understanding, such as knowledge of logical and mathematical truths. When Descartes talks with the aid of his translators of 'clearly and distinctly perceiving' this or that, he is not referring to perfect vision or hearing, but to the knowledge characteristic of the understanding or reason. To put the point slightly archaically, he is referring to *con*ceiving rather than *per*ceiving.

Kant stands clearly opposed to both positions and insists that knowledge is possible only through the co-operation of both understanding and sensibility, of both our intellectual faculty and our senses. We must have both a relevant concept and a relevant intuition. The empiricists committed the mistake of trying to acquire knowledge through intuitions alone, whereas the rationalists committed the mistake of trying to acquire knowledge through concepts alone. 'Leibniz *intellectualised* appearances, just as Locke ... *sensualised* all concepts of the understanding, i.e. interpreted them as nothing more than empirical or abstracted concepts of reflection. Instead of seeking in understanding and sensibility two sources of representations which, while quite different, can supply objectively valid judgements of things only in *conjunction* with each other, each of these great men holds to one only of the two ...' (A271/B327). It is impossible to exaggerate the significance in Kant's work of his claim that knowledge requires both concepts and intuitions, both understanding and sensibility.

5. THE MAIN DIVISIONS OF THE FIRST CRITIQUE

We can now begin the systematic examination of the *Critique of Pure Reason*. Since, it appears, experience has two complementary components, the conceptual and the intuitional, we might expect that our original question, What are the necessary conditions of a possible experience?, can be treated in two parts corresponding to the two components. That is precisely what happens. The first main section, the Transcendental Aesthetic, is concerned with the contribution of sensibility to experience, with necessary or *a priori* or pure intuitions. The second main section, the Transcendental Analytic, is devoted to the contribution of understanding to experience, with necessary or *a priori* or pure concepts, otherwise known as the categories. In the third main section, the Transcendental Dialectic, Kant is concerned among other things to describe the ghastly fate that awaits a metaphysician who forgets that experience or empirical knowledge does indeed have two complementary components. He reveals the weaknesses of speculative uses of concepts to which no intuitions correspond, such as the concept of a soul, or of an infinite universe, or of God. I propose to follow most other commentators and ignore the final part of the *Critique*, the Transcendental Doctrine of Method, for there is virtually nothing of interest there that is not discussed earlier. I shall only refer to one passage in the course of discussing Kant's account of mathematics. The main outline of the first *Critique* and the corresponding sections of the *Prolegomena* is therefore as follows.

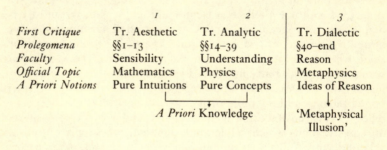

	1	*2*	*3*
First Critique	Tr. Aesthetic	Tr. Analytic	Tr. Dialectic
Prolegomena	§§1–13	§§14–39	§40–end
Faculty	Sensibility	Understanding	Reason
Official Topic	Mathematics	Physics	Metaphysics
A Priori Notions	Pure Intuitions	Pure Concepts	Ideas of Reason
	A Priori Knowledge		'Metaphysical Illusion'

PART II

TRANSCENDENTAL AESTHETIC

2

SPACE AND TIME

We can now approach the first part of Kant's answer to his general question. He insists that knowledge involves two complementary factors, the receiving of intuitions or perceptions, and their being brought under concepts. Neither intuitions alone nor concepts alone yield knowledge. In the language of faculties he insists that knowledge is the result of the co-operation of sensibility, the faculty of intuitions, and understanding, the faculty of concepts. Since we are interested in the necessary conditions of a possible experience, we are interested in the *a priori* or pure or necessary contributions of sensibility and understanding to experience. The inquiry therefore splits naturally into three parts. The first, the Transcendental Aesthetic, is concerned with the *a priori* contribution of sensibility, the faculty of intuitions; the second, the Transcendental Analytic, is concerned with the *a priori* contribution of understanding, the faculty of concepts; and the third, the Transcendental Dialectic, describes the dismal results of any attempt to gain knowledge from concepts alone, the results of forgetting that knowledge requires both concepts and intuitions.

The Transcendental Aesthetic disappoints our expectations, and gives us the very strong impression that Kant has not quite got to grips with the enterprise. One of the most striking features of the Aesthetic is the absence of argument, for it consists principally of a large number of unsupported assertions accompanied by explanatory comments. The topic for discussion, the nature of space and time, is of considerable philosophical interest, but the arguments Kant might have used to support his conclusions are very thinly scattered, and many do not appear until much later in the *Critique*. From our point of view the Aesthetic serves mainly to pick out certain philosophical problems and to suggest possible solutions. It has three main parts, a discussion of space (A22–30/B37–45), a discussion of time (A30–6/B46–53), and a number of general comments (A36–49/B53–73).

Probably the most important passages are the 'Metaphysical Expositions' or general philosophical analyses of space and time, for they contain a number of striking observations, fairly systematically presented (A22–

5/B37–40, A30–2/B46–8). Although the text is neatly divided into five paragraphs concerned with space and five with time, I would suggest that there are six doctrines of special interest. The first is the very puzzling and slightly peripheral doctrine that space and time are intuitions, not concepts. 'Space is not a . . . general concept of relations of things in general, but a pure intuition' (A24–5/B39). 'Time is not . . . a general concept, but a pure form of sensible intuition' (A31/B47). Kant confuses us by referring to space and time as concepts in several places (e.g. A22/B37, A30/B46), but his considered view seems to be that they are intuitions, features of our experience contributed by sensibility rather than understanding. I shall return briefly to that doctrine in Chapter 4. (I discuss it in more detail in 'Things, Stuffs and Kant's Aesthetic'.)

The second and third doctrines are more comprehensible and might encourage us to think that Kant shares Newton's views on space and time. The second doctrine is that space and time are infinite (A25/B39, A32/B47), and the third is that space and time are logically prior to objects, can exist in the absence of any objects. 'We can never represent to ourselves the absence of space, though we can quite well think it as empty of objects' (A24/B38). 'We cannot . . . remove time itself, though we can quite well think time as void of appearances' (A31/B46). I shall return to that doctrine in section 5, where I shall argue that the Newtonian overtones are decidedly misleading.

The fourth doctrine is that space and time are unitary, that all spaces are parts of one and the same space, all times parts of one and the same time, that every point is spatially related to every other and every instant temporally related to every other: 'we can represent to ourselves only one space; and if we speak of diverse spaces, we mean thereby only parts of one and the same unique space' (A25/B39). 'Different times are but parts of one and the same time' (A31–2/B47). That doctrine will occupy our attention in section 3.

The fifth doctrine is that there is a very intimate connection between space, time, and mathematics. I said in the previous chapter that one of Kant's aims is to show against Hume that we can have substantive knowledge of the world *a priori*, in the form of the general truths of mathematics and physics. The Aesthetic is devoted among other things to justifying the necessity of mathematics, the necessary application to experience of mathematical truths. It seems that the necessity of mathematics is guaranteed by the central role of space and time in our experience. 'The apodeictic certainty of all geometrical propositions, and the possibility of their *a priori* construction, is grounded in this *a priori* necessity of space' (A24). 'The possibility of apodeictic principles concerning the relations of time, or of axioms of time in general, is also

grounded upon this *a priori* necessity' (A31/B47). You may find it difficult to believe that in talking of 'axioms of time in general' Kant is actually
referring to arithmetic, but that and other features of his account of
mathematics will be discussed in section 4.

The sixth and by far the most important doctrine is that objects of
experience, tables and chairs, are necessarily spatial and temporal, that
we could not perceive objects at all unless they had spatial and temporal
position, that our notions of space and time are not derived from experience but are logically prior to it. They are 'pure forms of all sensible
intuition' (A39/B56) which give an essential basic structure to our experience. 'Space is a necessary *a priori* representation, which underlies all
outer intuitions' (A24/B38). 'Time is a necessary representation that
underlies all intuitions' (A31/B46). In other words, our perception of the
objects around us must be spatial and temporal. It seems that there is
one important difference between space and time, a difference between
'outer sense' and 'inner sense'. If we think about experiences in general
we are thinking about various temporal series. My experiences form one
temporal series, yours form another, Fred's form another, and so on.
Some experiences will be sense-impressions or 'intuitions' of tables and
chairs around us. But to talk of perceiving tables and chairs is to use
some notion of space, for we are aware of tables and chairs as spatially
arranged. Kant's expression for awareness of experiences in general is
'inner sense', and for awareness of external objects 'outer sense'. Thus
the important difference between space and time is that, whereas all my
experiences are temporal, only some of them, the sense-impressions, are
spatial. All experiences are of inner sense, the form of which is time, but
some of them, namely sense-impressions, are of outer sense, the form
of which is space (A26/B42, A33/B49).

As I pointed out earlier, Kant offers very little supporting argument
for his views in the Aesthetic, and that important doctrine, that objects
of experience are necessarily spatial and temporal, is no exception. Even
his formulation of the doctrine is very unfortunate, for occasionally he
seems to make the feeble and tautologous observation that we can only
perceive the spatial and temporal properties of objects if we have notions
of space and time: 'in order that certain sensations be referred to something outside me . . . and similarly in order that I may be able to represent
them as outside and alongside one another, and accordingly as not only
different but as in different places, the representation of space must be
presupposed' (A23/B38); 'neither coexistence nor succession would ever
come within our perception, if the representation of time were not presupposed as underlying them *a priori*' (A30/B46). But it is fairly clear
that he wants to make the much stronger and more striking claim that

we could not perceive any objects at all unless they were spatial and temporal. He is not merely arguing that experience of spatial and temporal things presupposes a notion of space and time, but rather that experience of any objects whatever entails that they are spatial and temporal.

I shall attempt to remedy his failure to provide supporting argument for that important doctrine by sketching an argument remotely akin to an argument in Chapter 2 of *Individuals*, in which Strawson tries to show that objects must be spatially related, or at least related in a way that is for all significant philosophical purposes spatial. We might begin by reflecting on what we mean by knowledge of objects, of tables, chairs, trees, cabbages. Part of what we mean is that we know how to identify them and re-identify them. For example we know how to identify tables, to tell a table from a handsaw, and we can tell where one table ends and a second table begins. We have ways of re-identifying tables, of telling whether this is the table I wrote on yesterday, or saw in a shop a week ago. We can identify, count, and re-identify tables. But it should strike us that there is a very close connection between the identity of an object and its spatial and temporal properties, for two things cannot be in exactly the same place at exactly the same time, cannot share exactly the same spatial and temporal properties. If *per impossibile* they did share exactly the same spatial and temporal properties, they would not be two things at all, but one. In contrast two things can share all their other properties, and we can have two chairs of exactly the same colour, texture, shape, composition, etc. In short the criteria of identity of objects seem very intimately connected with their spatial and temporal properties, but do not seem closely connected with their other properties.

Consider a simple example. Suppose I engage to prove that the chair here is not the same chair as the one over there. It is no good referring to their respective colours, for they may have the same colour; nor to their shape, for they may have the same shape; nor to their weight or composition, for they may have the same weight and be made of the same materials, and so on. The only certain way of distinguishing one from the other is to show that they are in different places at the same time. However many other similarities there may be between the two chairs, they are certainly two, because one is here and the other is over there. Similarly suppose I am confronted with a problem of re-identification. I want to decide whether this chair is the same as the chair I saw last week in a shop window. Again I might refer to its colour, shape, texture, composition, etc., but that will not be enough, for there could easily be many other chairs of exactly the same kind. The only way I can show conclusively that this chair is the same as the chair in the shop is by following the spatio-temporal route of the chairs in question. If today's chair is spatio-temporally continuous with the chair in the shop, they are one and the same chair; if not, not.

If we thread all those considerations together, we obtain a fairly plausible argument to show that objects of experience must be spatial and temporal:

1. If experience is to be possible, we must identify and re-identify objects.

2. There is a crucial connection between the identity of an object and its spatio-temporal properties.

∴ 3. Experience of objects is possible only if they are spatial and temporal.

We have given some content to Kant's claim that space and time are 'pure forms of intuition', necessary features of our perception of objects. We seem to have produced the first part of an answer to Kant's general question, What are the necessary conditions of a possible experience?

2. TRANSCENDENTAL IDEALISM

But rejoicing is premature. We may well have produced an argument to support Kant's claim that objects of experience must be spatial and temporal, but it should be treated with considerable caution for at least two reasons. First, we must remember that one of Kant's aims in the *Critique* is to dispel sceptical doubts about the existence of the external world, to prove against Hume that we can have genuine *a priori* knowledge of the world and its properties. He intends among other things to show that the existence of external objects is not merely possible or probable, but certain, indeed that it is a necessary condition of any coherent experience. If he is to execute that intention successfully he cannot merely deny the sceptical position, but must refute it. So even if we interpret Kant as claiming that objects of experience must be spatial and temporal, we cannot for the moment regard the claim with any enthusiasm. He has yet to show that there are external objects, however interesting their properties may be. That is, he has yet to justify step 1 of the argument I have just sketched.

The second reason for treating the claim with caution is much more complicated, and brings us to a complex set of doctrines which cast a gratuitous blanket of mystery and confusion over the whole of the first *Critique* and many other Critical works. Let us approach them by considering a shorthand slogan which Kant uses throughout the Aesthetic, namely that 'space and time are pure forms of intuition'. I have interpreted that slogan fairly charitably as the claim that objects of experience are necessarily spatial and temporal. But eschewing sympathy, what literally does the slogan mean? We know that 'intuition' means 'sense-impression' (though frequently in the Aesthetic Kant uses 'intuition' and 'representation' interchangeably, to mean 'experience' or 'state of consciousness'). Presumably a 'form' is some principle of arrangement, a rule of organization or relation between things. If we translate the references to forms and intuitions into more familiar terms, then Kant's slogan becomes the claim that experiences are spatially and temporally related. If we then incorporate the distinction between inner and outer sense, we are left with the claim that all experiences are temporally related and that some of them, namely sense-impressions, are also spatially related.

But something must have gone wrong, for it is downright nonsense to say that experiences are spatially related. My visual impressions of the concert are neither to the left nor to the right, neither to the top nor the bottom, of my auditory impressions. They are simply not the sort of things that have spatial properties at all. Conductors, orchestras, and members of the audience are certainly in space and are spatially related to each other, but my perceptions of them are not. One wants to say that Kant's slogan, 'space and time are pure forms of intuition', cannot make literal sense unless we neglect the important distinction between *objects*, which are spatial, and *perceptions* of objects, which are not. If we acknowledge that distinction together with Kant's distinction between inner and outer sense, Kant's slogan is seen to be a misleading ellipsis for two quite separate doctrines, namely first, that space and time are the pure forms of objects of intuition, and second, that time is also the pure form of intuitions. Or as we would say, it is an ellipsis for the doctrines first, that objects of experience, conductors, orchestras, tables, and chairs, must be spatial and temporal, and second, that experiences are temporally related to one another.

We might think that that is a very gratifying interpretation of Kant's results, that he really wanted to say that space and time are pure forms of the *objects* of intuition. And we might again rehearse the argument I sketched in the previous section. There is obviously a very intimate connection between the identity of an object and its spatio–temporal properties. No description of its colour or texture or size or shape or composition will uniquely identify it, will guarantee that it has been successfully identified or re-identified. Success can only be guaranteed by referring to its spatial and temporal properties, since two objects cannot be in exactly the same place at exactly the same time.

Thus not only do we have a gratifying interpretation of Kant's results, but more importantly we have in outline an argument to support the central doctrine that objects of experience must be spatial and temporal. But we have done no justice to the complexity of Kant's position. He would be rather unhappy with the unqualified insistence that space and time are the forms of objects for the simple and devastating Berkeleian reason that strictly there are no objects independent of our perceptions or intuitions of them. That is, just as we are beginning to make sense of the cryptic comments of the Aesthetic, he launches into a set of doctrines which he wrongly thinks to be essential to his enterprise, the doctrines of transcendental idealism. Transcendental idealism is essentially a mixture of certain rationalist doctrines and Berkeleian idealism, expressed in an elaborate psychological vocabulary. The rationalist tradition emerges in the form of a distinction between two kinds of object, things as they appear or phenomena or sensible things or appearances, and things in themselves or noumena or intelligible things. We can and do have knowledge of things as they appear or phenomena, for they are the ordinary objects of experience such as tables and chairs. We do not and cannot have knowledge of things in themselves or noumena, the things that lie behind the ordinary world of familiar everyday objects. There seems to be some sort of causal connection between things in themselves and things as they appear, but we can only have knowledge of things as they appear. So when Kant asks, What are the necessary conditions of a possible experience?, he is looking for the essential features of our knowledge of things as they appear, the spatial and temporal objects around us. There can be no knowledge of things as they are in themselves, of the non-spatial and non-temporal objects of the intelligible world.

On any standard two sets of objects constitute an absurd philosophical extravagance. But worse is still to come, for according to Kant there are strictly no things as they appear independent of our perceptions of them. Just as Berkeley insisted that strictly there are no objects, that there are only perceivers and their ideas, so Kant insists that strictly there are no things as they appear, that there are only perceivers and their 'representations'. Strictly there is no external world independent of us. It is constructed by the mind, by the joint efforts of sensibility and understanding, and 'if the subject, or even only the subjective constitution of the senses in general, be removed, the whole constitution and all the relations of objects in space and time, nay space and time themselves, would vanish' (A42/B59); 'not only are the drops of rain mere appearances, but ... even their round shape, nay even the space in which they fall, are nothing in themselves, but merely modifications or fundamental forms of our sensible intuition' (A46/B63); '... what we call outer objects are nothing but mere representations of our sensibility ...' (A30/B45).

I shall devote the whole of Chapter 9 to a detailed discussion of transcendental idealism but several comments should be made now. First, we can see why Kant talked contentedly of space and time as pure forms of intuition rather than as pure forms of objects of intuition. For his very Berkeleian utterances imply that he wants to say that strictly there is no distinction between perceptions and objects perceived. Strictly objects are collections of intuitions, collections of perceptions. Space and time do not exist independently of perceivers, but are rather 'modifications of our sensibility', forms which we project upon the world, forms according to which our minds construct the external world. Despite Kant's patronizing reference to the 'good Berkeley' (B71) he is clearly committed to claiming that 'what we call outer objects are nothing but mere representations of our sensibility', wholly dependent on a certain kind of human cognitive apparatus.

Second, we can see the very special force that the expression 'a priori' has for Kant. I have argued that his main aim is to articulate the necessary or a priori conditions of experience, that he wants to describe the logically essential features of any possible experience. But the intrusion of transcendental idealism gives a new and very different gloss to the expression 'a priori', for it heralds a stream of information about the psychologically a priori conditions of experience, the psychological story of sensibility's co-operation with understanding in the construction of 'what we call outer objects'. That is, it becomes impossible henceforth to tell whether Kant is interested in the logically a priori conditions of experience or in the psychologically a priori conditions. Indeed he seems to regard the logical and psychological stories as merely two versions of the same story. He appears to regard the question, How does the mind construct the objects of experience?, as only another version of the question, What are the logically necessary conditions of a possible experience?

Third, Kant's general criteria of knowledge make nonsense of his enthusiasm for the psychological story. He is not merely expressing the logical story in psychological terms, for it becomes clear in later sections of the Critique that the psychological operations of sensibility and understanding are prior to experience, take place in the self in itself, the noumenal self. For example the operation of the understanding is 'an act of the self-activity of the subject', as he opaquely puts it at B130. Yet he is at constant pains to insist that we do not and cannot have knowledge of things in themselves. With our human faculty of sensibility we can only have knowledge of objects that are spatial and temporal, and things in themselves are non-spatial and non-temporal. Thus throughout the Critique Kant is both at pains to prevent our having knowledge of things in themselves, and concerned to record important information about them.

3. THE UNITY OF SPACE AND TIME

I want now to discuss (albeit briefly) the unity of space and time. As we have seen, Kant appears to insist that space and time are unitary, and that the unity is necessary, not contingent: '. . . we can represent to ourselves only one space; and if we speak of diverse spaces, we mean thereby only parts of one and the same unique space' (A25/B39). 'Different times are but parts of one and the same time' (A31–2/B47). But he does not attempt to explain or justify his position, except for very brief comments later in the *Critique* (at A110 and A216/B263). It may therefore seem rather extravagant of me to devote a whole section to the unity of space and time. But the problem itself is of great modern philosophical interest, and despite Kant's very sketchy treatment it raises issues that are crucial for a full understanding of the first *Critique*.

Let us start by defining the unity of space and time. There is one space if and only if every place is spatially related to every other. Whichever two places one takes, one could in principle measure the distance between them. Similarly there is one time if and only if every instant is temporally related to every other. Whichever two instants one takes, one instant is before or after or simultaneous with the other. If there is more than one space, there are at least two places not spatially related to one another; if there is more than one time, there are at least two instants not temporally related to one another. Many modern philosophers[1] have doubted whether space and time are necessarily unitary. Some have argued that there could be two spaces, some that there could be two times, and some have argued for both.

Consider a fantasy which in all essential respects I borrow from Quinton. Suppose I fall asleep tonight in Nottingham and appear to wake up in a jungle village shortly before breakfast. I spend an exciting and interesting jungle day in the company of jungle wife and friends, eat my jungle supper, and fall asleep. I wake up in Nottingham shortly before breakfast, spend a Nottingham day in the company of Nottingham wife and friends, eat my Nottingham supper, and retire to sleep, waking shortly before breakfast in the jungle, and so on. Suppose also that my jungle experience is coherent and connected, that jungle breakfasts seem to be the right number of jungle hours after jungle suppers, that I bump into the same jungle people every jungle day, and so on. Similarly suppose that my Nottingham experience is also coherent and connected, that the same Nottingham friends and neighbours appear regularly in my Nottingham

---

[1] Cf. A. M. Quinton, 'Spaces and Times'; M. Hollis, 'Times and Spaces'; R. G. Swinburne, *Space and Time*, Chs. 2, 10.

experience, and so on. Finally suppose that the systematic splitting of my experience continues for a considerable time, that I appear to be living two wholly different lives, each internally consistent but entirely distinct from the other.

If that very exhausting experience left me any time for philosophical speculation I might draw the very daring conclusion that I am living in two spaces, or two times, or both. I might suppose that I have access to two spaces because I am apparently living in two spatial regions which are as real to me as I could wish them to be, but which have no spatial route connecting them. My 'travelling' from Nottingham to the jungle and back again does not seem literally to be travelling. Careful exploration from Nottingham reveals nothing faintly resembling my jungle village, and careful exploration from the jungle village reveals nothing even faintly resembling Nottingham. With a little elaboration the fantasy could also be made to support the claim that I am living in two times. Nottingham time is internally coherent and jungle time is internally coherent. There are Nottingham clocks in Nottingham and jungle clocks in the jungle. But I may find it impossible to correlate them, to map the two times on to a single temporal series. For example I find that I can indulge in a jungle orgy for four days without sleeping, but when I finally retire to bed I wake up in Nottingham about ten Nottingham hours after my last Nottingham supper. Nottingham events form one temporal series and jungle events form another, but I find it impossible to arrange both sets of events in a single temporal series. There seems to be no correspondence, however rough, between jungle time and Nottingham time.

Let us consider each hypothesis in turn, with the aid of various arguments from Quinton and Swinburne. First consider the hypothesis that I am living in two spaces, two spatial regions which are spatially unrelated, that there is no way, however arduous, of literally travelling from one to the other. No measuring rod, however long and however skilfully deployed, could measure the distance between them. One objection to that hypothesis is that it raises serious problems of personal identity. For what happens to my body in the fantasy? Does it remain asleep in Nottingham while I disport myself in the jungle, and remain asleep in the jungle while I am busy in Nottingham? If so, the fantasy is absurd, because it involves saying that a man has two bodies, a white Nottingham body and a black jungle body, and therefore that he is in two places at once. But the objection is not particularly damaging. On the one hand we might argue that a man could certainly have two bodies, one white and one black, one asleep and one awake. Such a situation would no doubt be unusual but it would not be absurd, and we might cheerfully modify our assumptions about personal identity to accommodate the case of a man with two bodies, a man who is in two places at once. On the other hand we might concede the general point of the objection and modify the fantasy accordingly. That is, we might suppose that my body gradually disappears from Nottingham as sleep overtakes me, and gradually appears in the jungle, perhaps a shade darker, as I wake up. It disappears from the jungle when I fall asleep and reappears in Nottingham, perhaps a shade lighter, as I wake up. Thus there would only be one body to account for at any given time.

A second objection is that it is absurdly melodramatic to interpret the fantasy as the experience of two spaces, that a much simpler and much more reasonable explanation is that I am having a very lifelike and recurrent dream. Although the dream is extremely coherent and extraordinarily protracted, it is none the less a dream. The least mystifying explanation of my strange experience is that I am leading a normal life in Nottingham, and having frequent dreams about wholly imaginary events in a jungle. Since the objects that appear in dreams are not in space in any literal sense, there is no need to conclude that I have access to two quite separate spaces. The urge to talk of a second space is no more sensible than any urge to talk seriously about Alice's Wonderland. But that objection really will not do. Its admirable tone of common sense begins to sound rather hollow as soon as one elaborates the fantasy to include similar experiences of other people. Suppose for example that my Nottingham friends also begin to report experiences in the jungle similar to my own, that their translation to and from the jungle happens just as mine does, by their falling asleep, and that their accounts of the jungle tally very closely with mine. Indeed let us suppose that we arrange in Nottingham to meet under a particular palm-tree in the jungle, and vice versa, and that we succeed in keeping our appointments. Of course we could insist that a large number of people in Nottingham are dreaming, that the striking similarity between all their dreams is entirely accidental. But surely it is much more plausible to accept that they are not dreaming at all, that they all have access to two quite separate spaces.

A third objection to the two-spaces hypothesis is that Nottingham and the jungle village must be in one and the same space but very far from each other, that careful exploration will eventually reveal a direct but very long spatial route from one to the other. The sudden movement from one place to a far distant place may force us to revise our views about maximum possible velocities, but that revision is to be preferred to the mystery of two entirely separate spaces. But the objection is easily dealt with, for we can reasonably suppose that the most careful exploration has been carried out but to no avail. Jungle geographers fail to discover any traces of Nottingham, and Nottingham geographers have no success in locating the jungle. They must finally and reasonably conclude that Nottingham and the jungle are in two quite separate spaces, spatially unrelated.

In short, we can see quite pressing grounds for disagreeing with Kant about the unity of space, for insisting that there could be more than one space. Although we might be tempted to dismiss the story initially as merely a protracted dream, we might eventually concede that it is the story of a life in two quite distinct spaces. But what of the unity of time? Could the fantasy be used to show that I am living in two quite separate times, that time is not necessarily unitary? Are there grounds for saying that events in the jungle and events in Nottingham cannot even in principle be arranged in a single temporal series? I suggested earlier that we might find no very close correspondence between the passage of time in the jungle and the passage of time in Nottingham, that I might spend four jungle days enjoying a jungle feast and yet still wake up in Nottingham approximately ten Nottingham hours after my last Nottingham supper. But that would not entail that I am living in two times. It would still be possible to arrange jungle events and Nottingham events in the same temporal series, although some events might have to be squashed or extended a little relative to others. If we are to take the two-times hypothesis seriously the fantasy must be much more bizarre than that.

I shall resort to a few visual aids in an attempt to develop the two-times hypothesis. So far I have described the fantasy as follows.

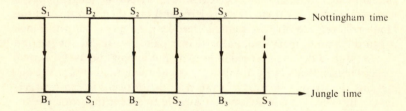

That is, I have my Nottingham supper[1], then my jungle breakfast[1], then my jungle supper[1], then my Nottingham supper[2], and so on. I never have any meal twice, never experience any event twice. I always experience Nottingham events in the order in which they actually happen in Nottingham, and always experience jungle events in the order in which they actually happen in the jungle. But that is a very simple fantasy, and would seem to indicate that jungle events and Nottingham events happen in one and the same time, for they can easily be arranged in a single temporal series. That is, jungle events and Nottingham events occur in the order in which I experience them. Jungle days fit neatly into Nottingham nights, and Nottingham days into jungle nights. We may have reason to talk of two spaces here but none to talk of two times.

So if the two-times hypothesis is to be taken seriously the fantasy must be developed. If there were two times there would be no step-by-step correspondence between jungle events and Nottingham events. Indeed if there were two times there would be no reason to expect the jungle events and Nottingham events to occur in the order in which I experience them. If the two times really were two, there would be nothing to prevent my turning up in the jungle before the last jungle event I witnessed. There would be nothing to prevent my turning up absolutely anywhere in the jungle, as follows.

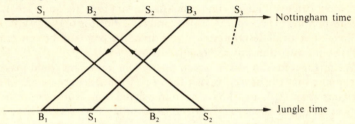

There would be nothing to prevent my experiencing jungle day two before I experience jungle day one. I might witness the funeral of the tribal chief before I witness his falling ill.

There is an even stranger possibility. If Nottingham time and jungle time were quite separate, if there were no way of arranging jungle events and Nottingham events in a single series, then I might even witness the same jungle event whenever I fall asleep in Nottingham. Perhaps a particular orgy is so memorable that I contrive to visit it whenever I fall asleep in Nottingham.

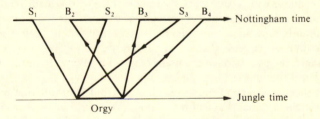

But it is at that point that the two-times hypothesis is involved in contradiction. We are supposing that all temporal links between jungle time and Nottingham are severed, and that I may therefore witness the same jungle event again and again. We must of course insist that I engage in exactly the same activities on each 'visit', or our notion of personal identity would be undermined immediately. There would be too many of me at the orgy. Moreover it is reasonable to assume that I will remember all previous visits, for a man normally remembers his recent and more striking experiences. But if we attempted to describe the orgy, and in particular the man who is engaged in moving to and fro between Nottingham and the jungle, we will be involved in contradiction. We must say that I remember the orgy, on all 'visits' but the first, and yet do not remember it, on the first 'visit'. And we must say that I remember visiting only once before, because it is my second visit, and only twice before, because it is my third, and only three times before, because it is my fourth, and so on. Briefly, if jungle time and Nottingham time are quite separate, there is nothing to prevent my visiting and revisiting the orgy any number of times; but a full description of the man at the orgy will be contradictory; so the two-times hypothesis is absurd.

We might refuse to give it up so easily. One move we could make is to suppose that whenever I revisit the orgy I immediately forget all my previous visits. Although I have been translated from Nottingham to the orgy every Nottingham night for the last Nottingham week, I have forgotten every visit but the last. Hence I am not in the lamentably contradictory condition described in the previous paragraph. But that move proves far too much, for it deprives the fantasy of any philosophical interest it might have had. The fantasy was interesting precisely because it described me as apparently having a long and systematic experience of two worlds, the jungle world and the Nottingham world. Although there were apparently no connections between the two worlds, I appeared to have constant and continuing access to each in turn. But to make sense of the fantasy in those terms we must suppose that we are indeed talking of the experience of one and the same person, that we are concerned in Kant's phrase with a 'unity of experience'. One of the main reasons for thinking that it is the unified experience of one and the same man is that I apparently remember the majority of my escapades in both worlds. If at any time we suggest that I have forgotten all my previous visits to the jungle, then we remove the main reason for saying that the Nottingham I and the jungle I are the same person.

But there is a second move which will avoid contradiction and still preserve the original shape of the fantasy. We could insist that however frequently I move from Nottingham to the jungle and back again, jungle time and Nottingham time must keep roughly in step. For example if I wake in the jungle after falling asleep in Nottingham, I must wake some jungle time after the last jungle events I witnessed. When I finally retire to my jungle bed and wake in Nottingham, I must wake some Nottingham time after my last Nottingham experiences. Of course jungle time may seem a trifle squashed in relation to Nottingham time, and vice versa, for I may find that a four-day orgy in the jungle only occupies ten Nottingham hours. But jungle time and Nottingham time must keep in step, even if some steps are squashed, some extremely extended, in relation to others. But that proposal proves too much. To insist that the two times must keep in step is in effect to insist that they are one and the same time, that all jungle events and all Nottingham events could be arranged in a single temporal series. In other words, if we are to preserve the general shape of the fantasy, as an account of the unified experience of a single person, we must at least insist on the unity of time.

To sum up, Kant suggests that space and time are necessarily unitary, that all spaces are parts of one space, all times parts of one time. Our fantasy suggests very strongly that he is right about the unity of time, at least in the sense that a unified *experience* of two times is impossible. But it also suggests that he is wrong about space, for we seem to be able to make sense of the notion of two spaces that are spatially unrelated.

4. MATHEMATICS

As I explained in Chapter 1, one of Kant's recurrent concerns in the first *Critique* and in corresponding sections of the *Prolegomena* is to determine the status of mathematics, by which he meant principally Euclidean geometry and simple arithmetic. The official problem of the Aesthetic is to explain how pure mathematics is possible, and Kant refers on a number of occasions to geometry and arithmetic. He argues that space and time are pure forms of intuition, necessary contributions of sensibility to experience, and he appears to think that geometry is the mathematics of space and arithmetic the mathematics of time. It is certainly an odd position, for although it may be reasonable to think of geometry as the mathematics of space, it is difficult to see why arithmetic should be the mathematics of time. But despite the strain Kant maintains the parallel as far as possible, and he devotes one paragraph to geometry in the 'Metaphysical Exposition' of space (A24), and one to 'axioms of time in general' or arithmetic in the 'Metaphysical Exposition' of time (A31/B47). Thus in showing to his own satisfaction that experience must be spatial and temporal, Kant thinks he has shown that experience must also conform to the mathematics of space and time, to geometry and arithmetic.

I suggested in Chapter 1 that there are *prima facie* two ways of thinking of mathematical theorems, neither of which is very attractive. One is to regard them as necessary or analytic or *a priori* truths, but then we are surprised to discover how much new information they can yield. The other is to say that they are contingent or synthetic or *a posteriori* truths, but it then follows that they can be falsified in experience. But Kant suggests a compromise. He argues that they are synthetic and *a priori*. They are not analytic truths, but they are not derived from experience. In one sense of *a priori* they are *a priori*, for they are not derived from experience, but they are not logically *a priori* or logically necessary truths. Their contradictories are not self-contradictory.

Transcendental idealism is the key to understanding the claim that mathematical truths are synthetic *a priori*. According to transcendental idealism the general properties of the world around us are strictly not properties of objects but rather properties of ourselves, patterns according to which our minds construct the world. The world must be spatial and temporal precisely because our minds construct our experience spatially and temporally. Thus the expression '*a priori*' has for Kant a very special significance, for he appears to think that the inquiry into the logically *a priori* conditions of experience is irretrievably connected with an inquiry into its psychologically *a priori* conditions. In particular he guarantees the necessity of mathematics by reducing it to some kind of psychological necessity. The world must conform to the theorems of Euclidean geometry and simple arithmetic because our faculty of sensibility constructs the mathematical properties of objects and projects them upon the world. The theorems are logically synthetic but they are *a priori* in the peculiar sense I have explained, for they are functions of the human faculty of sensibility. Indeed according to Kant we cannot explain the necessity of mathematics unless we resort to transcendental idealism. If we take the realist view that space and time are properties of objects independent of any perceivers, then we 'can neither account for the possibility of *a priori* mathematical knowledge, nor bring the propositions of experience into necessary agreement with it' (A40–1/B57–8).

Kant's views are very unsatisfactory in many respects. The notion of synthetic *a priori* truth is unattractive, particularly when Kant retreats from the logically to the psychologically *a priori*. His reasons for thinking that mathematical proof is synthetic rather than analytic are unconvincing. And one contemplates with gloom the pervasive influence of transcendental idealism. But I shall return to these problems in more detail in Chapter 8.

5. KANT, LEIBNIZ, AND NEWTON

I have so far said nothing in my discussion of Kant's account of space and time about his relation to Leibniz and Newton. Indeed he only mentions Leibniz once in the Aesthetic, and Newton not at all. He certainly does not commit himself either to Leibniz's view that space and time are essentially systems of relations between objects, or to Newton's view that space and time are absolute, infinite, and logically prior to any objects. I have already pointed out that Kant makes a number of extremely Newtonian observations. 'We can never represent to ourselves the absence of space, though we can quite well think it as empty of objects' (A24/B38). 'We cannot ... remove time itself, though we can quite well think time as void of appearances' (A31/B46). 'Space is represented as an infinite *given* magnitude' (A25/B39). 'The original representation, *time*, must therefore be given as unlimited' (A32/B48). But his apparent willingness to embrace Newton is grossly misleading, and Kant's views on space and time are very far from both the traditional alternatives.

Predictably the crucial complication is transcendental idealism. Whatever their differences Leibniz and Newton would at least agree that space and time are independent of us, that even if there were no perceivers there would still be space and time. For Leibniz there would still be an independent world of objects spatially and temporally related, while for Newton there would still be absolute space and absolute time, containing inanimate objects. One would insist that space and time are relational, the other that they are absolute individuals, but both would assume that they are in a clear sense independent of perceivers. In complete contrast Kant rejects that assumption and insists that space and time are in no sense independent of perceivers, that they are neither relational properties of objects independent of us nor absolute individuals independent of us. They are 'in us', forms of our sensibility, fundamental features of the way we look at the world, forms which we project upon the world. But 'if the subject, or even only the subjective constitution of the senses in general, be removed, the whole constitution and all the relations of objects in space and time, nay space and time themselves, would vanish' (A42/B59).

Kant's steady progress away from the traditionally alternative views of space and time can be illustrated by his discussion of the problem of incongruous counterparts. Curiously the problem is not mentioned in the first *Critique* but it is discussed in some detail in several pre-Critical works and in the *Prolegomena*. Incongruous counterparts are pairs of objects that are exactly alike in every respect save that one is a perfect counterpart or mirror-image of the other. Consider for example a left and a right hand, or two similar screws, one with a left-hand thread and one with a right-hand thread, or the two right-angled triangles formed by bisecting an isosceles triangle. In each case the two objects are exactly alike, save that one is an incongruous counterpart, a perfect mirror-image, of the other.

Such examples are usually exploited against Leibniz's account of space as follows. If, as Leibniz argues, space is wholly relational, is essentially a system of relations between objects, then it ought to be possible to give a complete description of an object's spatial properties in relational terms. For example it ought to be possible to describe the size, shape, and position of the United Kingdom by describing in full its relation to all other objects and the relations of all its parts to one another: 'Birmingham is 100 miles from London and eighty miles from Liverpool, which is forty miles from Manchester, which is ... etc. etc.' Or to take a simpler example, I could describe the size and shape of a triangle by describing three lines AB, BC, and AC such that AB is three feet, BC is four feet, and AC is five feet. Obviously if the object to be described is three-dimensional or rather messy, such as a compost heap, the complete relational description will be extremely complicated. But according to Leibniz there should be no difficulty in principle in producing such a description.

But although he can in principle cater for a compost heap he will encounter serious problems in trying to cater for incongruous counterparts. Consider the two right-angled triangles formed by bisecting an isosceles triangle. I could offer a relational description of one of them: 'AB is three feet, BC is four feet, CA is five feet'. But that description applies equally to both triangles, both 'left' and 'right'. Similarly I could describe a hand in relational terms, by describing the dimensions of each finger, the distance between them, the size of the palm, and so on. But that relational description could fit both left and right hands. There is clearly some spatial difference between the two hands, or the two triangles, for although they are perfect counterparts they are not congruent. The difference cannot be explained in terms of further relational properties, for there are no further relational properties. We appear to be using a non-relational spatial concept of left and right.

I am not sure what conclusion should be drawn. It seems reasonable to conclude that we should reject a very simple Leibnizian view, the view that all spatial concepts are reducible to relational concepts. Indeed there are other objections to that simple view, such as the circularity objection. If we are only able to locate an object A by describing its relation to other objects, B, C, etc., and those in turn by their relation to A, D, E, etc., we will never succeed in locating A's position. We will only produce a circular description of the form 'A is so far from B, which is so far from C, which is so far from D, which ... which is so far from A'. To succeed in locating anything at all we must regard at least one point as fixed, a point which does not have to be located by reference to other points. For example we might regard the North and South Poles and Greenwich as fixed points of reference for our geographical purposes.

Hence to avoid circularity and to cater for incongruous counterparts Leibniz must concede that spatial concepts are not completely reducible to relational concepts. If he is to avoid circularity he must introduce conventional fixed points of reference, and if he is to cater for incongruous counterparts he may have to allow that we have a non-relational concept of left and right. But none of those concessions would force him into the arms of Newton, for he could still insist that space is logically secondary, dependent on there being objects spatially related. To introduce conventional fixed points of reference or to talk of a non-relational concept of left and right is not to concede that there could be completely empty space. It would make no sense to talk of any conventional fixed points, or of the left and right sides of the universe, in the complete absence of any objects.

Let us return to Kant's struggle with the problem of incongruous counterparts. In 1768, in a paper 'Concerning the Ultimate Foundations of the Differentiation of Regions in Space', he drew a decidedly Newtonian conclusion: 'the determinations of space are not consequences of the situations of the parts of matter relative to each other; rather are the latter consequences of the former. It is also clear that in the constitution of bodies differences, and real differences at that, can be found; and these differences are connected purely with *absolute and original space*, for it is only through it that the relation of physical things is possible' (Kerferd and Walford, p. 43). But in the *Inaugural Dissertation* of 1770, in which we see the first signs of the Critical philosophy, he pours scorn on the view that space is 'an *absolute* and boundless *receptacle* of possible things', dismissing it as an 'empty fabrication of the reason' which 'pertains to the world of fable' (ibid., p. 70). His preferred solution of the problem of incongruous counterparts is that 'the diversity, I mean the discongruity, can only be noticed by a certain act of pure intuition' (ibid., p. 69). It is not clear what he means. He might be suggesting that human beings have an immediate awareness of the left and right, top and bottom, of their visual fields. Perhaps our ability to distinguish incongruous counterparts is connected with our ability to recognize immediately the parts of our visual field, even when its content is completely symmetrical. For example even when I am looking at a picture in a kaleidoscope I am aware of the top and bottom, the left and the right, of my visual field.

The *Prolegomena* of 1783 yield the final, unattractive, idealist solution of the problem. 'Those who cannot yet rid themselves of the notion that space and time are actual qualities inherent in things in themselves may exercise their acumen on [the problem of incongruous counterparts]. When they have in vain attempted its solution and are free from prejudices at least for a few moments, they will suspect that the degradation of space and time to mere forms of our sensuous intuition may perhaps be well-founded' (p. 285). The disagreement with both Leibniz and Newton is complete, for they could not rid themselves of realist views about space and time. According to Kant the spatial and temporal properties of things are neither dependent on there being objects spatially and temporally related, nor dependent on there being absolute space and time. They are wholly dependent on there being perceivers with the human faculty of sensibility, whose forms of intuition are space and time, who project space and time upon the objects of experience, whose minds construct a picture of a spatial and temporal world.

6. FINAL COMMENTS

What then do we take from the Aesthetic? We do not take many arguments, for Kant seems to prefer an assertive rather than a discursive style, but he makes a number of pregnant suggestions which are in many cases argued for and elaborated later in the *Critique*. For example there is the interesting and controversial suggestion that space and time are necessarily unitary, that all spaces are parts of one space, all times are parts of one time. There are various remarks about the status of mathematics. We are introduced to the vast machinery of transcendental idealism, to the distinction between noumena or things in themselves, and phenomena or things as they appear; and Kant apparently makes the Berkeleian claim that objects of experience or phenomena are merely collections of representations, collections of perceptions, the result of the joint constructive endeavours of sensibility and understanding. Space and time are 'in us', patterns according to which our minds construct a picture of external things, and they are in no sense external to or logically independent of ourselves.

By far the most important doctrine of the Aesthetic, however, is the claim that objects of experience, tables and chairs, must be in space and time if they are to be perceived at all. It is a necessary condition of any coherent experience that we perceive objects spatially and temporally. And that doctrine is to play a central role in the general strategy of the first *Critique*, in the attempt to distinguish between genuine and spurious knowledge claims. Knowledge requires both concepts and intuitions, and sensibility, the faculty of intuitions, is spatial and temporal. In other words human beings can only make substantive knowledge claims about objects that are in space and time. Kant will argue in the Transcendental Dialectic that one of the main weaknesses of speculative rationalist metaphysics is that it consists in an investigation of objects that are non-spatial and non-temporal, objects that cannot even in principle yield intuitions, cannot be perceived by human beings.

I pointed out that Kant offers very little argument for the view that objects of experience must be spatial and temporal, and I sketched an argument that might well serve his purpose. I suggested that space and time are very intimately connected with the identity of objects, because two objects cannot be in exactly the same place at exactly the same time. I shall return to the argument in Chapter 4, and merely observe for the moment that in the Aesthetic Kant only seems to offer a *psychological* argument for the view that the objects of experience must be spatial and temporal. That is, he argues that objects must be spatial and temporal because our minds construct them so. Generally the Aesthetic introduces us to two main philosophical strands running through the whole of the *Critique*, strands which correspond to the two senses of '*a priori*' I distinguished earlier. The claim that objects of experience must be spatial and temporal is part of a general philosophical inquiry into the necessary or logically *a priori* conditions of a possible experience. Some of the doctrines of transcendental idealism are part of an inquiry into the genesis, the psychologically *a priori* conditions, of experience. Kant seems to regard the two inquiries as irretrievably connected, as virtually two versions of the same inquiry. For example his ambiguous intentions are revealed in his account of mathematics, for he reduces the necessity of mathematical truths to certain logically contingent but psychologically central features of human beings. Objects must conform to the theorems of Euclidean geometry and arithmetic because our minds construct their mathematical properties in precisely that way.

PART III

TRANSCENDENTAL ANALYTIC

3

THE ANALYTIC OF CONCEPTS

1. THE METAPHYSICAL DEDUCTION

We turn now to the second stage of Kant's attempt to discover the necessary conditions of a possible experience. We have been told that experience or knowledge requires both intuitions and concepts. The Transcendental Aesthetic examined the *a priori* contribution to experi- .ence of sensibility, the faculty of intuitions, and in the Transcendental Analytic we are promised an account of the *a priori* contribution of understanding, the faculty of concepts. Just as the Aesthetic yielded pure intuitions, space and time, so the Analytic is to yield pure concepts or categories. As usual, intention and execution do not entirely coincide. In a sense the Transcendental Analytic could stand alone, detached from Kant's elaborate and systematic plan, for it provides the most interest- ing and most important satisfaction of Kant's search for the necessary conditions of a possible experience.

For reasons which do not concern us here but which will concern us in the final section of Chapter 4, the Analytic is divided into two parts, the Analytic of Concepts (A65–130/B90–169) and the Analytic of Prin- ciples (A130–260/B169–315). In this chapter we shall be concerned with the Analytic of Concepts. Its first few pages and the few preceding pages on the 'Idea of a Transcendental Logic' (A50–65/B74–90) show Kant very much at his worst. He wants to discover the pure concepts of under- standing, the categories, and tries to take a short cut. First he makes a general psychological assumption, namely that the faculty of understand- ing, which brings intuitions under concepts, has a more general use in 'general logic'. The faculty that helps us to organize our perceptions is also the faculty responsible for inference. It has the general task of think- ing, and is then called reason, and the more specific task of thinking about objects, when it is called understanding. We have one intellectual faculty which has a general task in logic and a more specific task in making judge- ments about tables and chairs. 'Logic . . . can be treated . . . either as logic of the general or as logic of the special employment of the understanding. The former contains the absolutely necessary rules of thought without which there can be no employment whatsoever of the understanding . . .

The logic of the special employment of the understanding contains the rules of correct thinking as regards a certain kind of objects' (A52/B76).

So, Kant thinks, if we want to discover the pure concepts of the understanding, the pure concepts of objects, all we have to do is to list the concepts of general logic and then qualify them appropriately. We list the main formal features of thinking anything whatever, and we can then derive the main formal features of thinking about objects of experience. 'The functions of the understanding can . . . be discovered if we can give an exhaustive statement of the functions of unity in judgments' (A69/B94). Kant proceeds to do that, in a passage officially called 'The Clue to the Discovery of All Pure Concepts of the Understanding' and more popularly known as the Metaphysical Deduction of the Categories (A66–83/B91–116). He lists the various kinds of judgement, the concepts of general logic (A70/B95), and then derives a corresponding list of categories, pure concepts of understanding (A80/B106). Both lists consist of four sets of three.

We are entitled to treat the exercise with considerable scepticism. Whatever connections there may be between inference and our knowledge of objects, Kant's attempt to conjure the categories from the concepts of logic is disastrous. One objection I used earlier springs to mind, namely that he has offered a psychological answer to questions about the logically *a priori* conditions of experience. He has attempted to justify the categories as *a priori* concepts on the ground that they are fundamental concepts of the faculty of understanding. But that justification is of little philosophical interest because the psychologically central features of the faculty of understanding may be logically contingent features of experience.

Even if we treat the enterprise more sympathetically and ignore the extravagant manifestations of a crude faculty psychology, there is another important objection, namely that there is no reason to expect any close parallel between the concepts of logic and the concepts of experience. Indeed a careful comparison of Kant's Table of Judgements with his Table of Categories considerably diminishes any confidence one might have had in discovering a parallel. The only promising cases are the first two relational concepts in each Table, for there is a superficial connection between the notion of a categorical judgement and that of a substance, and between the notion of a hypothetical judgement and that of cause and effect. But such connections are remote and certainly liable to mislead. For example to pay too much attention to the connection between categorical subject-predicate propositions and the epistemological distinction between 'substance' and 'accident' or object and property is to invite the sort of confusion that inspired Locke's account of substance.

One is likely to expect to find two kinds of thing in the world, objects and their properties, corresponding to the two elements of the subject-predicate proposition.

Nor can we rescue Kant from his embarrassment by pointing out that he was labouring under the malign and parochial influences of Aristotelian Logic. For even had he basked in the light of modern propositional and predicate logic, the objection to his enterprise would still remain. There is no reason to suppose that the concepts we use in logic in describing and relating certain features of propositions will have anything in common with the concepts we use in experience in describing the objects around us. Indeed any parallels which do exist should be treated with caution, for they will tend to increase rather than diminish confusion.

2. TRANSCENDENTAL DEDUCTION: MAIN ARGUMENT

Thus we are left at the end of the Metaphysical Deduction precisely where we began. But we must remember the alleged results of the Metaphysical Deduction because Kant uses them in the next main section of the Analytic of Concepts, the Transcendental Deduction. That section is extremely interesting and extremely important. According to Kant it cost him 'the greatest labour' and he warns us that the 'enquiry ... is somewhat deeply grounded' (Axvi). From a purely literary point of view the whole section is rather unfortunate, for the material is badly organized, repetitive, and sometimes contradictory. It helps to confirm the substantial historical support[1] for the 'patchwork' theory, the theory that much of the *Critique* is a 'patchwork' of manuscripts written at different periods and stitched together in great haste before publication in 1781.

The first part of the Transcendental Deduction (A84–95/B116–29) contains various introductory observations, including an explanation of the term 'Transcendental Deduction', criticism of Locke and Hume, who attempted to derive the categories *a posteriori*, and a further insistence that knowledge requires both concepts and intuitions. The remaining part (A95–130, B129–69), which contains the main argument, was completely re-written for the second edition, though the differences between the two editions are more of emphasis than of basic content. The main argument appears four times in the first edition and twice in the second, though Kant worries away at particular details many more times than that. The six versions are as follows:

(a) A98–110 ('Whatever the origin of our representations ...' to 'Only thus can any knowledge become possible at all').

---

[1] Cf. letters to Garve 7 Aug. 1783 and Mendelssohn 16 Aug. 1783 (Zweig, pp. 98–108).

(b) A110–11 ('There is one single experience ...' to 'This is exactly what we desired to prove').

(c) A119–25 ('We will now, starting from below ...' to '... belong to knowledge or even to our consciousness, and so to ourselves').

(d) A128–30 ('If the objects with which our knowledge ...' to '... our deduction of the categories has been developed').

(e) B129–37, 141–3 ('The manifold of representations ...' to '... together in one self-consciousness'; and 'But if I investigate more precisely ...' to '... necessarily subject to the categories').

(f) B159–65 ('In the *metaphysical deduction* ...' to '... can be known as an object of experience').

The general object of the exercise is to examine the *a priori* contribution of understanding to experience, to isolate the pure concepts of understanding, the categories. But in examining the argument as Kant presents it, we soon see that there is something very special about those concepts, for they are concepts of objects, external things which we perceive but which exist independently of our perceiving them. If therefore Kant proves that we must apply pure concepts of understanding, he proves that scepticism about the existence of the external world is misplaced. He will fulfil at least one of his promises for he will have avoided Humean scepticism with regard to the senses.

Kant begins very unambitiously with the assumption that there is a series of experiences or states of consciousness or 'representations'. He wants to show that there could not be such a series unless it were the experience of a person who employs concepts of objects, who perceives objects independent of himself. The main steps of the argument are as follows.

1. There is a series of representations, ordered in time.

2. For such a series to be possible, the representations must be synthesized, i.e. taken up and connected in one consciousness, 'brought to the necessary unity of apperception'.

3. That is, they must be connected according to the various *a priori* forms of synthesis.

4. The forms in question are the *categories*, already listed in the Metaphysical Deduction.

∴ 5. The categories, pure concepts of understanding, concepts of objects, must have application in experience.

We shall examine the argument in stages, beginning with steps 1 and 2. Although Kant's language is somewhat forbidding it can be translated into something slightly more comprehensible. We already know that 'representations' are experiences, and the 'necessary unity of apperception' is the unity of self-consciousness. Hence the first two steps can be translated as follows.

1′. There is a series of experiences, ordered in time.

2′. For such a series to be possible, someone must be aware of them as his, i.e. they must be united in one consciousness.

The first step is uncontroversial. Kant is deliberately adopting the starting point of the great classical empiricists. He begins with a series of representations or ideas or experiences or states of consciousness. He has not yet argued that any of them are perceptions of an external world, nor even that any of the experiences belong to anyone. Of course such philosophical self-denial cannot be maintained for very long, for we want to ask a number of pressing questions. For example we are tempted to ask, Whose experiences are they? What is the principle of unity of the series? What makes it a series? What, in the Humean phrase, ties the bundle together? The opportunities for muddle are immense but Kant resists many of the worst temptations. Although grappling with problems already attacked by Descartes, Hume, and many others, he avoids many of their mistakes. He helps us to untangle some of the muddle implicit in Hume's attempt to tie the bundle of perceptions, and illuminates some of the obscurity of Descartes's 'cogito' argument. There are frequent clear echoes of Descartes: 'It must be possible for the "I think" to accompany all my representations' (B131); 'I am conscious of myself, not as I appear to myself, nor as I am in myself, but only that I am' (B157). Kant helps us to see what is peculiarly self-defeating about doubting one's own existence.

Those salutary rewards emerge from Kant's explanation of step 2 of his argument, the claim that the series of experiences must be brought to the necessary unity of apperception, that someone must be aware of the experiences as his. It is really a conjunction of several connected claims. One is the very general claim that there cannot be unowned experiences, that every experience must be identified as belonging to someone. Experiences are not genuine substances, are not capable of existing independently of a perceiver. They are logically secondary things in the sense that any reference to experiences must be cashed into an account of someone experiencing this or that. Another much stronger claim buried in step 2 is that a particular experience is necessarily owned by a particular person, that all my experiences are necessarily mine, Tom's are necessarily Tom's, Dick's necessarily Dick's. Formally the criteria of identity of experiences are wholly dependent on the criteria of identity of people. Although we can have the 'same' experience in the sense that we can have exactly similar pains or twinges or visual impressions, I cannot literally have your pains, and you cannot have mine. Experiences are not like books and gramophone records, which can be literally shared, literally exchanged. I cannot lend you my experiences, exchange spare or soiled experiences for new ones, grab delightful experiences before my hated rival gets his hands on them. It is a matter of logic, not of fact, that I have my experiences, for they could not have been anyone else's. It is a matter of fact, not of logic, that I have my books, for they could have been someone else's.

But what have we achieved? Surely it is not important that my experiences are necessarily mine, for there is an equally clear sense in which all my physical states are mine. Formally there is an equally clear sense in which the criteria of identity of physical states are dependent on the criteria of identity of people. You and I can have exactly similar gashes on the leg, but my gash is necessarily mine and yours is necessarily yours. As Hobbes pointed out to Descartes in the third set of Objections, experiences have no greater epistemological significance than physical states. 'I walk, therefore I exist' is just as necessary and just as trivial as 'I think, therefore I exist'. But Hobbes missed the point. There is another claim to be extracted from step 2 which is of crucial importance in the inquiry, and which was at the heart of Descartes's 'cogito' argument. It is not so much a point about ownership of experiences as about *awareness* of ownership. Briefly, if I have an experience I am necessarily aware of it as mine, but if I am in a physical state I am not necessarily aware of it as mine. 'The abiding and unchanging "I" ... forms the correlate of all our representations in so far as it is to be at all possible that we should become conscious of them' (A123).

Let us suppose that I have a pain. There are many questions I can ask perfectly sensibly. The sensation may be faint or unfamiliar, and I may not be sure how I should classify it. I may not be sure whether it is toothache or ear-ache. It may be so faint that I cannot decide whether or not it has completely subsided. But there is one thing I can never doubt: I can never wonder who is having the sensation. I can try to work out whether I am suffering from toothache or from ear-ache, from a dull continuous pain or a sharp throbbing pain, but I cannot work out who is suffering. If I am in pain, I know who is in pain. The occurrence of my experiences and my awareness of them as mine are necessarily connected. But the case is quite different with physical states. It is not at all absurd for a man to wonder whether one of his physical states is indeed his. I may be in a certain physical state, such as sitting cross-legged, without realizing it. In the middle of a rugby scrum I may fasten my gaze on a protruding and extremely vulnerable foot in an intelligible and urgent attempt to decide whether it is mine. 'I know there is a foot somewhere in the room, but I couldn't positively say that I have got it' makes perfect sense, but 'I think there's a pain somewhere in the room, but I couldn't positively say that I have got it' makes no sense at all.[1]

---

[1] Cf. Dickens, *Hard Times*, Ch. IX.

So of the several connected points buried in step 2, the most important for Kant's purposes is the claim that I am necessarily aware of my experiences as mine. 'It must be possible for the "I think" to accompany all my representations; for otherwise something would be represented in me which could not be thought at all, and that is equivalent to saying that the representation would be impossible, or at least would be nothing to me' (B131-2); 'it is only because I ascribe all perceptions to one consciousness ... that I can say of all perceptions that I am conscious of them' (A122). And this claim about awareness of ownership of one's experiences, 'the principle of the necessary unity of apperception', is a necessary truth. 'This principle of the necessary unity of apperception is itself, indeed, an identical, and therefore analytic, proposition' (B135).

But what is awareness of one's own experiences? What is the unity of self-consciousness, the necessary unity of apperception? Hume examined the suggestion that self-consciousness is literally the consciousness of a self, and complained ironically that the introspective search for a self proved perpetually frustrating, for perceptions constantly obscured the view. He insisted, at least in Book I of the *Treatise*, that there can be no 'impressions', no perceptions, of a self, of a Cartesian substance. Kant agrees. Of course it is true that experience entails self-consciousness in the sense that I am necessarily aware of my experiences as mine, and it follows that I am one and the same person throughout my various experiences. But it does not follow that all the experiences belong to or inhere in some kind of Cartesian soul-substance. Indeed Kant's basic claim that knowledge requires both concepts and intuitions makes nonsense of the Cartesian self: '... in order to *know* ourselves, there is required in addition to the act of thought ... a determinate mode of intuition ... The consciousness of self is thus very far from being a knowledge of the self' (B157-8).

But if self-consciousness is not literally consciousness of a self, what is it? Kant seems to suggest that it is merely the ability to tell what experiences one is having, and who is having them. If I see something or hurt myself or feel depressed, I know who is doing the seeing, who is hurt, who is depressed, without ever having to work it out. When I am self-conscious I am not doing two things, namely picking out my self and then discovering the right experiences to attach to my self. I am merely doing one much less elaborate thing, namely identifying my experiences as mine. I am in a position to say 'I have a pain', 'I see a table', 'I am tasting beer', etc., with a very slight emphasis on 'I'. 'I am conscious of the self as identical in respect of the manifold of representations that are given to me in an intuition, because I call them one and all *my* representations, and so apprehend them as constituting *one* intuition' (B135).

In several places Kant tries to make the point in terms of a distinction between form and matter. He insists that the unity of self-consciousness is not a material unity, not a unity of content. For example there is no recurrent object such as a Cartesian soul underlying all my experiences. Nor is there any property common to all my experiences clearly identifying them as mine, no stamp or label or laundry-mark clearly pinned to each of my experiences, distinguishing them from Tom's or Dick's or Harry's. There is only a 'formal' unity; the experiences form a series solely in so far as they are all experiences of one and the same person. To talk of the unity of Tom's self-consciousness is only a rather windy way of saying that all these experiences are Tom's; to talk of the unity of Dick's self-consciousness is only to say that all those experiences are Dick's; and so on. Tom's experiences have a unity of form, not of content; Dick's experiences have a unity of form, not of content; and so on. As Kant says much later on, 'This "I" is, however, as little an intuition as it is a concept of any object; it is the mere form of consciousness ...' (A382).

Let us pause to review progress. We are wrestling with the first two steps of the main argument of the Transcendental Deduction. The first step is the uncontroversial assumption that there is a series of experiences, temporally ordered. The second is the claim that all the experiences must be 'brought to the transcendental unity of apperception', the necessary unity of self-consciousness. I have suggested that there are several important claims buried in that rather formidable declaration, most notably the claim that I am necessarily aware of my experiences as mine, and the claim that self-consciousness is not literally a consciousness of a self, for example of a Cartesian self. Knowledge requires both intuitions and concepts, and no intuitions of oneself are to be discovered in introspection. Self-consciousness is more happily understood as the ability to identify one's own experiences as one's own. The unity of self-consciousness is not a material unity, a unity of content, but a formal unity consisting simply in the formal fact that my experiences are mine, Fred's are Fred's, Tom's are Tom's, etc.

Where does that leave us? We know that if I have certain experiences I must be aware of them as mine, and we have examined various interesting claims about the nature of such self-awareness. In a rather ponderous Kantian phrase we know that experiences must fulfil the conditions of the unity of self-consciousness. But we have still to examine Kant's account of those conditions. The Cartesian conditions have been rejected in favour of conditions mentioned in the rest of Kant's argument, which proceeded as follows.

3. The representations must be connected according to the various *a priori* forms of synthesis.

4. The forms in question are the *categories*, already listed in the Metaphysical Deduction.

∴5. The categories, pure concepts of understanding, concepts of objects, must have application in experience.

But the three final steps do not yield the interest and excitement of the first two steps. They need radical revision as they stand, for three reasons. First, I have complained and will continue to complain that Kant frequently expresses his argument in psychological terms, that his search for the logically *a priori* conditions of experience often degenerates into an account of its psychologically *a priori* conditions. The policy is deliberate, for he seems to regard the logical and psychological inquiries as merely two versions of the same inquiry. But it is an unfortunate policy, both from a philosopher's and from a psychologist's point of view. The philosopher will contemplate with gloom the conflation of logical and psychological necessity, while the psychologist will deplore the *a priori* armchair psychology in which Kant is engaged. The latest move in the psychological story is the theory of synthesis, which makes its appearance in the second and third steps of Kant's argument. Instead of saying that intuitions must be brought under concepts, that perceptions must be classified, connected, organized, Kant prefers to say that intuitions must be synthesized. Instead of talking of pure concepts of understanding, concepts essential to experience, he talks of *a priori* forms of synthesis. Although I shall return briefly to the theory of synthesis in section 5, it is more helpful at the moment to translate all references to synthesis into references to the use of concepts.

Second, Kant's argument in its original form rests squarely on the unattractive 'Metaphysical Deduction' which purported to derive the categories from the main concepts of logic. He introduces without further discussion the assumption that the *a priori* forms of synthesis are the categories, so his argument is infected with all the weaknesses of the Metaphysical Deduction.

Third, we should examine the rather sly reference to objects in the conclusion of the argument. The categories, it appears, are concepts of objects, external things such as tables and chairs. To show that we must use the categories is in effect to show that scepticism about external things is incoherent. When I was discussing the Aesthetic I pointed out that Kant seemed to introduce the assumption that there are external things, but without arguing for it. The assumption may be acceptable but it requires supporting argument. But Kant seems to have committed a similar sin of omission here, for he appears to assume without any supporting argument that the categories, the pure concepts of understanding, the *a priori* forms of synthesis, are concepts of objects, external things.

In other words he appears to be refuting scepticism about the external
world by means of a stipulative definition of categories as *a priori* concepts
of objects. And that will not do. If he is to refute scepticism he must
indeed refute it, not merely rule it out of order by means of a stipulative
definition.

3. A RECONSTRUCTED ARGUMENT

So although Kant's argument in the Transcendental Deduction starts
rather memorably by making important observations about self-consciousness, it suffers a rapid decline in its fortunes thereafter. The
references to synthesis, the dependence on the Metaphysical Deduction,
and the repudiation of scepticism by means of a stipulative definition
leave a great deal to be desired. But there is nothing to prevent our engag-
ging in sympathetic repair and reconstruction, as long as we remember
that we are indeed reconstructing and not expounding Kant's argument.
And if we follow Strawson's lead in *The Bounds of Sense* (pp. 97 ff.) we
can construct an argument very close to the original and of great philosophical interest. The reconstructed argument is as follows.

1. There is a series of experiences, ordered in time.
2. Someone must be aware of the experiences as his.
3. So he must be able to distinguish himself and his experiences from
other things.
4. That is, he must be able to apply concepts of objects, external things.
5. The grounds of such application must be in the experiences themselves.
6. So he must be able to apply concepts of objects to at least some
of his experiences.
7. In other words he must regard at least some of his experiences as
perceptions of an external world independent of himself and his perceptions.

Some of the argument is virtually the same as Kant's original. The
second step is meant to incorporate the views on self-consciousness that
we have already discussed. The conclusion is essentially the same as
Kant's, namely that the pure concepts of understanding, the categories,
must be applied to our experience. But the crucial middle section of the
reconstructed argument tries to prove that such concepts are concepts
of objects, that we must believe in an external world if experience is to
be at all possible.

Let us consider the argument in more detail by first returning to the
discussion of self-consciousness. We were trying to find a way of unifying
a given series of experiences, of tying the bundle of perceptions. We were
asking the question, What are the conditions of the unity of self-con-

sciousness? Kant rightly rejected any Cartesian answer to that question, for he insisted that there was no self in self-consciousness, no single thing in which all the experiences inhere. The unity of self-consciousness is a formal unity and consists only in the experiences being the experiences of one and the same person. And it is a necessary truth that he must be aware of his own experiences as his own. But these admirable observations seem to leave us with as many difficult problems as before. Despite Kant's and Hume's attacks on the search for a Cartesian self we still want to talk of selves or people in some sense. We do not want our anti-Cartesian economy to prevent our talking of people, of perceivers, of the man who is having the experiences. If we are to identify the necessary conditions of the unity of self-consciousness, we want them to yield a non-Cartesian way of referring to people. Moreover we still have to say what makes a given series of experiences a series, to isolate the principle of unity of the series. The only explicit information available so far is that the experiences in question occur in a temporal sequence. But temporal succession is not likely to yield a very significant principle of unity. Queen Victoria's perceptions of Gladstone and mine of this sheet of paper certainly form a temporal series, but hardly the sort of series in which we are interested. They do not look even remotely like the experiences of one and the same person.

Briefly then our problem is to state the necessary conditions of the unity of self-consciousness. We expect two connected sets of conditions, the necessary conditions of our talking of perceivers or people in an innocuous, non-Cartesian, way, and the necessary conditions of the unity of a series of experiences. The reconstructed argument is supposed to do the double trick. It begins with the simple assumption that there is a series of experiences, ordered in time. It makes the Kantian point that they must all be experiences of one and the same person, who is aware of them as his own. So provisionally we have a principle of unity of the series, namely that they are all experiences of one and the same person, one and the same 'self'. But if they are all experiences of one and the same self, then we must look for the criteria of identity of that 'self'. Now to look for the criteria of identity of a thing is to look for a way of distinguishing between it and other things. So we are looking for the necessary conditions of distinguishing between the person who has the experiences and other things. Moreover the distinction has to be drawn within the experiences themselves, has to be a distinction which can be drawn by the person himself. We have already in a sense discovered a way of drawing one half of the distinction because we have already talked of the person's being aware of experiences as his. He can tell immediately, without having to work it out, who is having the experiences he is having.

We now find a way of drawing the other half of the distinction by introducing concepts of objects. The person regards at least some of his experiences as perceptions of an external world.

That is, if experiences are to occur at all their owner must regard them from two points of view, must apply two kinds of concept to them. On the one hand he must regard them as his experiences, as successive states of one and the same person, and on the other he must regard them at least in part as perceptions of objects, external things. Moreover the two kinds of concepts, the two points of view, stand and fall together. He cannot have any experience at all, cannot be aware of his experiences as his, unless he also regards some of them as perceptions of an external world. 'The original and necessary consciousness of the identity of the self is thus at the same time a consciousness of an equally necessary unity of the synthesis of all appearances according to concepts' (A108); 'the *analytic* unity of apperception is possible only under the presupposition of a certain *synthetic* unity' (B133). I must be aware of and be able to use a continuing distinction between myself and the external world. To ignore the distinction, or to attempt to use one half of it without the other, is to descend immediately into nonsense.

There is an important historical moral to be drawn. Empiricists of the seventeenth, eighteenth, and twentieth centuries began their investigations with collections of experiences or ideas or impressions or sense-data. They then encountered enormous difficulties in trying to justify our common-sense belief in the existence of the external world. Some attempted to deduce statements about objects from statements about perceptions or sense-data; some regarded external objects as merely theoretical constructs, as providing a plausible theoretical model to explain the regular occurrence of groups of sense-data; some, like Locke, regarded sense-data as the observed effects of unobservable objects; and some, like Berkeley, insisted that so-called 'objects' are merely collections of sense-data, collections of perceptions. Many were justifiably embarrassed by their failure to guarantee the existence of the external world. Hume insisted feebly that the existence of tables and chairs is simply something 'we must take for granted in all our reasonings' (*Treatise*, I, IV, II; Selby-Bigge, p. 187), and Locke claimed that it 'cannot pass for an ill-grounded confidence' (*Essay*, IV, xi, 3).

The importance of Kant's argument is that it suggests that empiricists have turned everything upside down. They have started with the premiss that there are various series of experiences and have then tried to establish the existence of the external world. But if we accept the empiricist premiss there can be no problem of the existence of the external world. It is a necessary condition of my having experiences at all that I regard some of them as perceptions of objects outside me and independent of me. I cannot contemplate my experiences in an effort to discover whether there is an external world, for unless there is an external world there can be no experiences. Awareness of myself and awareness of objects are irretrievably connected.

4. TWO OBJECTIONS

Before moving to less central features of the Transcendental Deduction we must consider two objections to the Kantian argument I constructed in the previous section. The argument was built around two central philosophical problems, the problem of personal identity in its Humean form, the problem of tying the bundle of perceptions, and the problem of justifying our belief in the existence of the external world. The main moral to be drawn from the reconstructed argument is that those two problems are inseparable. The bundle of perceptions is tied by their all being experiences of one and the same person, by his being aware of them as his, and the vital working component of his self-awareness is his distinguishing between himself and external things. In allowing the possibility of self-awareness, in adopting the Kantian way of tying the bundle, we have thereby disposed of the problem of the existence of the external world. Self-awareness and awareness of external things stand and fall together.

But two objections arise, corresponding to the two philosophical problems in question. To make the first objection we must recall the two irretrievably connected features of a series of experiences. On the one hand I must regard my experiences as mine, and on the other I must regard at least some of them as perceptions of external things. But consider the word 'regard'. It may be true that I must *apply* concepts of objects, that I must *regard* some of my experiences as perceptions of external things, that I must *believe* in the existence of tables and chairs. But it does not follow that I *successfully* or *correctly* apply such concepts, that I am *right* to regard some experiences as perceptions of external things, that my belief in the existence of the external world is *true*. Clearly there is a difference between applying a concept and successfully applying it. The reconstructed argument shows at most that we must *suppose* that there is an external world, not that there *is* an external world.

There is one rather feeble way of interpreting the objection which makes it completely harmless. We might interpret it as a complaint that the reconstructed argument makes no provision for partial sensory illusion, occasional hallucination, or perceptual mistake. So interpreted the objection would be harmless, for the argument could easily be made to accommodate it. Indeed later in the *Critique* Kant makes a vague reference to ways of distinguishing between veridical and illusory perceptions: 'All that we have here sought to prove is that inner experience in general is possible only through outer experience in general. Whether this or that supposed experience be not purely imaginary, must be ascertained from its special determinations, and through its congruence with the criteria of all real experience' (B278–9).

But the objection is surely meant to be more penetrating. It is not a complaint that the reconstructed argument fails to provide for partial sensory illusion, but that it has not ruled out complete and total illusion. It shows that we must suppose that there is an external world, but gives us no grounds for thinking that we are ever correct in the supposition. In this extreme form, however, the objection fails for reasons that are essentially those later deployed by Kant in his attack on traditional speculative metaphysics in the Dialectic. The objector wants us to distinguish between applying concepts and successfully applying them, between applying concepts of objects and successfully applying them. And that is certainly a most welcome distinction if we are concerned with familiar cases of partial sensory illusion. In our everyday perceptual contact with the world we do distinguish between successful and unsuccessful applications of concepts, between true and false descriptions of what we perceive. There are various simple 'criteria of all real experience'. For example sometimes perceptual mistakes or illusions are identified as such because they are inconsistent with the rest of our perceptions. Sometimes they have been obtained under peculiar conditions—the light is bad, I'm under the influence of drugs, I'm tired or sick, etc. Sometimes they have been obtained by the unskilled eye—I am not familiar with these lighting conditions, or with the secondary sexual characteristics of chicks, and my interpretation of my experience is faulty.

But we cannot generalize from such cases. Although we can distinguish between applying concepts and successfully applying them in the case of partial or occasional perceptual mistake, it does not follow and it is not true that we can use the same distinction to talk of complete and perpetual illusion. To make any distinction we must have a way of drawing the distinction. If we are talking of partial perceptual mistake we can distinguish between failure and success fairly easily in the ways I outlined. Perceptions are to be mistrusted if they are inconsistent with many others, or obtained under peculiar circumstances, or by an unpractised eye, and so on. But if all perceptions were illusory we would not be able to say so, for we would have no way in experience of telling the difference between perceptual success and perceptual failure. For example we could not contrast our 'illusions' with a large number of veridical perceptions, for in the state of total illusion envisaged every perception would be illusory. We could not contrast them with perceptions obtained under normal circumstances, for in a state of total illusion the norm would be illusion. We could not appeal to the practised eye, for even the most experienced eyes would be deceived. In a state of complete perceptual illusion we would have no way of distinguishing between perceptual failure and perceptual success, or more generally between merely applying concepts of external things and successfully applying them. But to have no way of drawing a distinction is to have no distinction. To have no way of identifying complete sensory illusion is to make nonsense of any speculation about it. Thus, once we have proved that we must apply concepts of objects, external things, and have made some provision for partial sensory illusion, we have in effect proved the existence of the external world. The question, Is there *really* an external world?, and the question, Am I *successfully* applying concepts of objects?, collapse into the question, Must I apply concepts of objects to my experience?

The first objection fails and we must move to the second. In expounding Kant's remarks on self-consciousness, on the necessary unity of apperception, I have deliberately concentrated attention on the problem of personal identity in its Humean form. That is, I have concentrated on the problem of tying bundles of experiences, of stating criteria for distinguishing Fred's series of experiences from Tom's, and from Dick's, and from Harry's. And I may have given the impression that whereas Hume failed to find a satisfactory way of tying each bundle, Kant succeeded. For I have argued that, sympathetically understood, Kant is claiming that the principle of unity of a series of experiences is yielded by their owner's continuing sense of his own identity, which is yielded in turn by the continuing distinction between himself and the external world. But it might be objected that Kantian string is no more reliable than Humean for tying each bundle. Indeed since Kant insists that the string is formal and not material it is clear that no advance on Hume has been made.

Consider a simple example. Suppose I perceived a chair yesterday and perceive the same chair again today. Hume tried vainly to show how I can be sure that yesterday's perception and today's perception are connected, form a series, part of the series of my experiences. Kant sympathetically understood will claim that I can be sure that they form a series because I am aware of both of them as mine, that I am thereby aware of my identity over twenty-four hours or so, and that the sense of my own identity is yielded by the continuing distinction during that time between myself and the external world, or more specifically between myself and an external chair. But, it will be objected, that will not do as it stands. The obvious weakness of the Kantian suggestion is its reliance on memory. It is no good merely to say that I am aware in the example of my continuing identity over twenty-four hours, for that is wilfully to ignore the role in such awareness of memory. My memory may well be faulty and I may not have seen the chair at all. I may have been fast asleep all day yesterday and my apparent awareness of my identity during the last twenty-four hours may be the result of the ingenious manipulation of my brain this morning by a brain surgeon.

More generally we must be very wary of such Kantian incantations as 'all my representations are known by me to be mine'. That is no doubt a necessary truth but only if certain temporal references are made explicit. It is necessarily true that my present representations are known by me now to be mine, and it is also necessarily true that my representations at 11 a.m. yesterday were known by me at 11 a.m. yesterday to be mine. But it is at best contingently true and may even be false that my representations at 11 a.m. yesterday are known by me now to be mine. George IV for example had an extremely peculiar impression in later years of his representations in 1815. He sincerely claimed to remember experiences at Waterloo which could not have been his at all. Hence as long as memory is fallible, there is no foolproof way of tying a bundle of perceptions if those perceptions occur at different times. Indeed one might argue that Kant was bound to fail as Hume was bound to fail, for like Hume he concentrated too much on the contents of consciousness, on representations or experiences. No rigorous criteria of personal identity can be established if we pay too much attention to purely psychological criteria and too little to physical criteria.

Although that objection is substantially correct, it is not true that Kant has made no advance on Hume. He has advanced in at least two respects. The first advance concerns the relation between experiences and people. Hume seemed to think of experiences as discrete bits of stuff which tend to congregate in groups or bundles but which are technically substances, capable of logically independent existence. One of the doctrines buried in Kant's 'principle of the necessary unity of apperception' is that experiences cannot have a logically independent existence, that they are necessarily the experiences of a person, that all references to experiences have to be cashed in terms of someone seeing, tasting, smelling, etc. The second advance is that despite their limitations Kant uses his remarks on personal identity to attack scepticism about the external world. He may not have a complete set of conditions sufficient to tie the bundle of perceptions securely, but he has isolated an important necessary condition which Hume overlooked, namely the belief in the existence of the external world. According to Kant the belief in external objects is not merely an accidental and logically dispensable feature of our experience but a necessary feature of any coherent experience. Experience logically requires a sense of one's own identity, and that in turn logically requires a belief in the existence of the external world. Kant may not have tied the bundle securely, but if my bundle is to exist at all I must use the distinction between myself and the external world.

5. THE THEORY OF SYNTHESIS

It is now time to consider one or two of the more peripheral features of the Transcendental Deduction, or at least features which are of peripheral interest to a modern philosopher. One of them is the theory of synthesis, which occupies a great deal of space in the first *Critique* but quickly exhausts one's patience. I have already argued that Kant tends to discuss philosophical problems both in a psychological and in a logical idiom, and seems to regard the search for the psychologically *a priori* conditions of experience as merely another version of the search for logically *a priori* conditions. The theory of synthesis is one of the more elaborate products of the psychological inquiry. It is first mentioned in introductory comments on the Transcendental Deduction in the Preface to the first edition: 'This enquiry, which is somewhat deeply grounded, has two sides. The one refers to the objects of pure understanding, and is intended to expound and render intelligible the objective validity of its *a priori* concepts. It is therefore essential to my purposes. The other seeks to investigate the pure understanding itself, its possibility and the cognitive faculties upon which it rests; and so deals with it in its subjective aspect. Although this latter exposition is of great importance for my chief purpose, it does not form an essential part of it' (Axvi–xvii). The theory of synthesis is an account of the workings of the mind, particularly of the faculty of understanding, in organizing, connecting, and classifying our experiences. Sensibility produces a disorganized jumble of experiences, a 'manifold of intuitions', and it is the job of understanding with the considerable assistance of imagination (A120–1) to sort them into a fairly coherent picture of the world, to connect them as experiences of one person. In the preferred Kantian shorthand it is the job of understanding and imagination to synthesize the manifold of intuitions. Although Kant claims that this psychological story does not form an essential part of his purpose, he devotes a great deal of space and effort to it. It is mentioned in the Metaphysical Deduction (A77/B103 ff.) and examined in great detail in the first-edition version of the Transcendental Deduction, where Kant divides the synthetic endeavours of the understanding into three, the syntheses of apprehension, of reproduction in imagination, and of recognition—that is, paying attention to a perception, recalling past perceptions, and recognizing something (A98–104). Mercifully the trinity is hardly mentioned in the second-edition version, but there are none the less regular references to synthesis.

There is little philosophical profit to be gained from a detailed examination of the theory of synthesis but it cannot be ignored, and there are four points that must be made if its role in the first *Critique* is to be understood. If we are to ignore it, we must be sure to ignore it for the right reasons. The first point is that although the theory of synthesis brings in its train a formidable battery of inflated technical terms, they can usually be translated into something less forbidding and more comprehensible. For example whenever Kant talks generally of the *a priori* synthesis of the understanding, we can take him to be talking about the necessary application of certain concepts. When he talks of rules of synthesis or forms of synthesis he is referring to concepts, and the *a priori* forms of synthesis are the pure concepts of understanding. Indeed it is only by 'synthesizing' or connecting various experiences that the understanding sustains the crucial distinction between perceiver and external world. For the perceiver 'synthesizes' all his representations, connects them together as a series of experiences of one and the same person. And he also 'synthesizes' certain perceptions, connects them as perceptions of a single object. For example I may have a perception of something hot, another of something hard, another of something heavy: I synthesize or connect my three perceptions as perceptions of a domestic iron. Or I have a perception of something liquid and brown during the summer, and a perception of something solid and white during the winter: I synthesize or connect these many perceptions as perceptions of the garden pond. 'This knowledge consists in the determinate relation of given representations to an object; and an *object* is that in the concept of which the manifold of a given intuition is *united*' (B137).

The second point is historical. In the first *Critique* Kant deliberately steers a middle course between rationalism and empiricism. He argues that knowledge requires both concepts and intuitions, that rationalists have attempted mistakenly to obtain knowledge from concepts alone, while empiricists have attempted mistakenly to obtain knowledge from intuitions alone. It is fairly easy to understand Kant's attack on rationalism, for we can interpret it as a demand that we can only make substantive knowledge claims about objects of experience, objects that we could in principle perceive. But it is more difficult to see what Kant meant when he accused empiricists of trying to obtain knowledge from intuitions alone. The theory of synthesis might help to clarify matters, for Kant is essentially arguing against the empiricists that the acquisition of knowledge is to some extent an activity. Empiricists regarded perception merely as the passive reception of sense-impressions, but Kant is insisting that the sense-impressions must be actively connected, classified, organized, if we are to gain knowledge of the external world. As he would say, the *passive* faculty of sensibility can only yield knowledge in conjunction with the *active* faculty of understanding; the passively received intuitions must be brought under concepts. As we might say, we are not merely passive receivers of information about the world. Our minds must actively digest the information if it is indeed to inform us of what is going on around us.

Third, the theory of synthesis is closely connected with the doctrines of transcendental idealism, which rear their dismal heads regularly throughout the Transcendental Deduction. Kant again uses the distinction between things in themselves or noumena, and things as they appear or phenomena, insists that we can only have knowledge of things as they appear, and claims that things as they appear do not exist independently of perceivers: 'appearances, as such, cannot exist outside us—they exist only in our sensibility' (A127); 'appearances do not exist in themselves but only relatively to the subject in which, so far as it has senses, they inhere' (B164). The theory of synthesis is connected with transcendental idealism because the theory is concerned with the atemporal activities of certain faculties, with the activities of the self in itself. It serves in part to explain how the self in itself, influenced by other things in themselves, constructs a picture of the external world in the form of a series of perceptions. At one point Kant finds himself embroiled in an exceedingly opaque problem about the relation between the self as it appears and the self as it is in itself, a problem which he introduces with disarming courtesy as 'the paradox which must have been obvious to everyone' (B152-6).

The fourth and most important point is that the theory of synthesis gives a special sense to the expression 'synthetic *a priori*'. The Transcendental Analytic is supposed to tell us about the pure concepts of understanding, the categories, synthetic *a priori* principles such as the principle that every event has a cause. In the previous chapters I attributed to Kant the following rough definition of a synthetic *a priori* proposition: a synthetic *a priori* proposition is logically synthetic, not reducible to a logical truth by appropriate definitional substitution, but is established independently of experience. Now in the light of the theory of synthesis that definition has a very special meaning for Kant. For he would say that a principle such as 'Every event has a cause' is logically synthetic precisely because the concept of causality is an *a priori* rule of synthesis, one of the essential rules of organization and classification obeyed by the understanding and imagination in connecting experiences together. For Kant the expression 'synthetic *a priori* principle' has two irretrievably connected senses, namely 'a logically synthetic principle established independently of experience' and 'a rule which governs the necessary synthesizing work of the understanding'.

Again, it would seem, logic and psychology are being conflated. But the conflation brings its rewards in the form of a clearer appreciation of Kant's rather crude formulation of the analytic/synthetic distinction (A6/B10 ff.). He claims that a proposition is synthetic if and only if its predicate is not contained in its subject, or, as we might say, if and only if subject and predicate are two logically independent terms. He thinks of a synthetic proposition as combining two separate terms in one judgement. Against the background of the theory of synthesis we can see why he offers that definition of 'synthetic', for the synthetic work of the understanding consists precisely in combining logically independent things, 'diverse representations', into one, into a connected whole. 'By *synthesis* ... I understand the act of putting different representations together, and of grasping what is manifold in them in one [act of] knowledge' (A77/ B103). For example I may connect a visual impression of red and a tactual impression of softness as impressions of one tomato. Or I may connect a perception of a lighted match and a perception of a burning paper as perceptions of a causal transaction. In short, for Kant a synthetic proposition is logically synthetic because it combines distinct subject with distinct predicate, and it is psychologically synthetic in the sense that it expresses the work of the understanding and imagination in connecting 'diverse representations' in a single judgement. He would make a corresponding point about analytic propositions: a proposition is analytic when the predicate is contained in or part of the subject, and analysis is the psychological operation of dividing a whole into its parts (cf. B130).

6. THE TRANSCENDENTAL UNITY OF APPERCEPTION

I want finally to return to the transcendental unity of apperception in an attempt to synthesize the manifold of philosophically interesting remarks. Although much of what I shall say has already been said, I think it is helpful to bring together all Kant's views on the transcendental unity of apperception. Characteristically he uses a bewildering array of expressions to refer to the same thing, such as 'the transcendental unity of apperception', 'the necessary unity of apperception', 'the original synthetic unity of apperception'. Sometimes he refers to the unity of apperception, sometimes to the principle of the unity of apperception, and even on one occasion to the 'faculty' of apperception, 'the understanding itself' (B133a).

However, five main points emerge fairly clearly, some sensible, some not. The first, to which we devoted considerable attention earlier, is that all my representations are necessarily mine in the sense that (a) there can be no unowned experiences, (b) particular experiences are identified as the experiences of particular people, and (c) most importantly, I am necessarily aware of my experiences as mine. It would be absurd for me to attempt to work out whose experiences I am having, for if I were not aware of them as mine they would simply not occur at all. 'It must be possible for the "I think" to accompany all my representations; for otherwise something would be represented in me which could not be thought at all, and that is equivalent to saying that the representation would be impossible' (B131–2). And Kant is concerned to emphasize that this 'principle of the necessary unity of apperception is itself, indeed, an identical, and therefore analytic, proposition' (B135).

Second, because the principle of the necessary unity of apperception or necessary unity of self-consciousness is analytic and not synthetic, it is not a knowledge-claim about a self distinct from one's experiences. Self-consciousness is not literally consciousness of a self, for there is nothing that could count as perceiving oneself in introspection. 'I am conscious of myself, not as I appear to myself, nor as I am in myself, but only that I am. This *representation* is a *thought*, not an *intuition* ... The consciousness of self is thus very far from being a knowledge of the self' (B157–8). In other words the unity of self-consciousness is not a material unity, afforded by some constant or recurrent feature of my experience. 'No fixed and abiding self can present itself in this flux of inner appearances' (A107). The unity is merely formal: my experiences form a series solely in so far as they are my experiences, in so far as I am aware of them, can tell what I am thinking, feeling, sensing, and so on. 'I am conscious of the self as identical in respect of the manifold of representations that are given to me in an intuition, because I call them one and all *my* representations, and so apprehend them as constituting *one* intuition' (B135).

Hence the third point is that the crucial work in maintaining self-awareness is done by one's using concepts of objects, external things. There is a logical relation between the necessary unity of self-consciousness and the application of concepts of external things. I am aware of myself by being aware of certain experiences as mine, and I am aware of them as mine only in so far as I use a distinction between myself and the external world. The series of experiences must be regarded by me both as a series of my experiences and as including perceptions of an external world. The 'subjective' and 'objective' aspects of the series stand and fall together. 'The transcendental unity of apperception is that unity through which all the manifold given in an intuition is united in a concept of the object' (B139). We can see why Kant sometimes refers to the 'original synthetic unity of apperception' (B131), for it is only by applying concepts of objects or forms of synthesis to my experiences that I give any content to the self-consciousness that is necessary for experience. 'This principle of the necessary unity of apperception is itself, indeed, an identical, and therefore analytic, proposition; nevertheless it reveals the necessity of a synthesis of the manifold given in intuition, without which the thoroughgoing identity of self-consciousness cannot be thought' (B135).

Fourth, when the theory of synthesis is being worked too hard and the spectre of transcendental idealism begins to lurch into view, Kant appears to suggest that self-consciousness, the necessary unity of apperception, consists in an awareness of the mysterious noumenal synthesizing work of the mind which is prior to and responsible for our experience. In the first edition the point is expressed at some length: 'the mind could never think its identity in the manifoldness of its representations ... if it did not have before its eyes the identity of its act, whereby it subordinates all synthesis of apprehension ... to a transcendental unity, thereby rendering possible their interconnection according to *a priori* rules' (A108). In the second edition the point is more crisply stated: 'This thoroughgoing identity of the apperception of a manifold which is given in intuition contàins a synthesis of representations, and is possible only through the consciousness of this synthesis' (B133). Kant appears to be toying with the idea that the unity of apperception, the unity of self-consciousness, involves or consists in access to the self in itself, whose faculties engage in the complicated work of synthesis which finally yields experience. If he is indeed entertaining that possibility then he is contradicting his central Critical claim that knowledge requires both intuitions and concepts. Even if there are various synthetic operations responsible for and preceding our experience, we have no way of knowing. If we knew anything at all about them, they would be part of our experience and not prior to it.

Fifth, Kant occasionally distinguishes between empirical and transcendental apperception (e.g. A107, B140). Although the distinction looks rather forbidding, it is quite manageable, and helps to make an important point which we discussed earlier. One way to approach the distinction is to consider yet again the problem of personal identity in its Humean form, the problem of tying the bundle of perceptions or experiences, of guaranteeing that my bundle is indeed one bundle, yours a second, Fred's a third, and so on. Hume realized that nothing is gained by reflection on the discernible features of the perceptions or experiences themselves, even if one includes the relations of resemblance and causality. None of those features will yield much of a principle of unity. Our experience consists of a ragbag of all sorts of different items, such as sense-impressions, bodily sensations, thoughts about this and that, memories, after-images, etc. There are no recurrent discernible features shared by and peculiar to my experiences which determine that they are indeed mine.

Kant repeats Hume's observation. 'Consciousness of self according to the determinations of our state in inner perception is merely empirical, and always changing. No fixed and abiding self can present itself in this flux of inner appearances' (A107). But he also explains why nothing is to be gained by reflecting on the discernible features of our experiences. Nothing is to be gained because the discernible features of experiences are wholly contingent, 'merely empirical, and always changing'. For example my experiences include tickling sensations, thoughts about the Mad Hatter and perceptions of my fountain-pen. But that is a wholly contingent matter. My experience might logically include no ticklings, no thoughts about the Mad Hatter, no perceptions of my fountain-pen. And it is because the content or matter of my experience is contingent rather than necessary, that it yields no principle of unity. No fixed and abiding self presents itself in the contingent content of my experience. If we are to find a principle of unity we must ignore the contingent content and concentrate on the necessary form of our experience. As we have seen, according to Kant the most important necessary or formal feature of experience is that all experiences must be 'brought to the necessary unity of apperception'. All my experiences are experiences of one and the same person, and I must be aware of them as mine. My self-awareness is then unpacked in terms of a continuing distinction between myself and the external world, yielded in turn by my using the categories, the concepts of external objects.

Thus Kant's distinction between empirical and transcendental apperception is best understood as a distinction between the contingent and discernible content or matter of our experiences and their necessary form. When he talks of empirical apperception he is referring to their contingent or empirical or discernible features. When he talks of transcendental apperception he is reminding us that a series of experiences must belong to a self-conscious person, and he is leading us into a discussion of the distinction between perceiver and external world. 'Consciousness of self according to the determinations of our state in inner perception is merely empirical, and always changing. No fixed and abiding self can present itself in this flux of inner appearances. Such consciousness is usually named *inner sense*, or *empirical apperception*. What has *necessarily* to be represented as numerically identical cannot be thought as such through empirical data. To render such a transcendental presupposition valid, there must be a condition which precedes all experience, and which makes experience itself possible' [i.e. transcendental apperception] (A107).

7. RETROSPECT

Kant's official plan is that the Transcendental Deduction should serve as the first main part of an investigation of the faculty of understanding in the Transcendental Analytic. Knowledge requires both intuitions and concepts, the Aesthetic is devoted to the pure forms of sensibility, the faculty of intuitions, and the Analytic is devoted to the pure concepts of understanding, the faculty of concepts. But that rather unexciting programme conceals a number of striking and important moves in the Transcendental Deduction. We find a general attempt to refute scepticism about the external world: Kant argues that experience is possible only if we can use concepts of external things, that the belief in the existence of an external world is irretrievably connected with one's self-awareness. Admittedly Kant's own version of the argument leaves a little to be desired, but we found it possible to do a certain amount of repair and reconstruction without departing far from the spirit or the letter of the original. Furthermore Kant offers important observations on self-awareness. He insists against Descartes that self-consciousness is not literally consciousness of a self. He is obviously aware of the defects of a Humean alternative, and attempts to tie the bundle of perceptions by linking together Hume's problems of personal identity and of scepticism with regard to the senses. The core of one's self-consciousness is the distinction between oneself and the external world. Hume overlooked the interdependence of self-awareness and awareness of objects.

Intertwined with those admirable observations is the theory of synthesis, the *a priori* psychology of experience, the account of the pre-conscious endeavours of understanding and imagination in classifying, organizing, and unifying experiences. As an appropriate counterpoint there are the doctrines of transcendental idealism, the distinction between things as they appear or phenomena, and things in themselves or noumena, and there is the Berkeleian claim that objects of experience or phenomena are merely collections of perceptions, entirely dependent on perceivers. Thus the final results of the Transcendental Deduction are incoherent in two respects. First, Kant claims that we can know nothing about things in themselves and yet provides detailed information about the synthetic work of the self in itself. Second, his Berkeleian tendencies undermine the central and admirable conclusion of the Transcendental Deduction. The central conclusion is that any form of phenomenalism is misguided, that we must preserve at all costs a clear distinction between perceiver and external world, between perceptions and objects of perception. It is extremely odd and disappointing that Kant should then carefully dismantle the distinction by insisting that external objects are 'only representations' (A109, B164), 'so many representations of the mind' (A114). He has reasons for maintaining such a peculiar position but they cannot mitigate its peculiarity.

Transcendental idealism will be discussed in detail in Chapter 9, and until then I will merely indicate when it plays an important part in Kant's argument. If we ignore it for the moment the present state of play is as follows. According to Kant a series of experiences is possible only if someone is aware of them as his own, and that in turn requires him to use concepts of external things. He must regard at least some of his experiences as perceptions of an external world independent of himself and his perceptions. That is an extremely general conclusion, and except for the occasional example Kant does not tell us which concepts are concepts of external things, categories. Unless we are satisfied by the optimistic attempt in the Metaphysical Deduction to conjure twelve categories from twelve concepts of logic, we are entitled to ask Kant to argue for specific categories such as substance or causality. He turns to that task in the second main section of the Analytic, the Analytic of Principles, and we shall peer over his shoulder in a new chapter.

4

THE ANALYTIC OF PRINCIPLES

1. INTRODUCTION

The Metaphysical Deduction supposedly produced twelve categories arranged in four sets of three, the Transcendental Deduction offered a general argument to prove that the categories must be applied in experience, and the Analytic of Principles is intended to argue for each of the twelve categories in turn. But the superficial impression of careful planning is misleading, for Kant finds it impossible to fulfil his own very optimistic demands. The first six categories are never mentioned in the Analytic of Principles. The first three are represented only by a general Axiom of Intuition and the next three by a general Anticipation of Perception. Nor are the Axioms and Anticipations of any great interest to us here. The Axioms are concerned with geometry and arithmetic, and are best left to the discussion of Kant's account of mathematics in Chapter 8, while the Anticipations raise obscure questions about degrees of intensity of sensations. The last three categories, the Postulates of Empirical Thought, are concerned with modal concepts, with the possible, the actual, and the necessary, and belong more to logic than to epistemology.

There might seem to be very little left but there is in fact a great deal. There is the chapter on Phenomena and Noumena to which I shall return in my discussion of transcendental idealism in Chapter 9. There is the Refutation of Idealism, inserted rather improbably in the middle of the discussion of the Postulates of Empirical Thought. And most important of all, there are the three Analogies of Experience, which are really the only three of Kant's twelve categories that are serious candidates for categorial status. Even then his passion for systematic presentation of the argument leads him astray, for the third Analogy has a very shadowy existence. In part it reproduces material from the second Analogy and in part makes nonsense of it. So most of my attention in this chapter will be focused on three vitally important passages, the first Analogy, the second Analogy, and the Refutation of Idealism, for they provide a fitting sequel to the argument of the Transcendental Deduction.

It is important to note the increasing prominence in this part of the *Critique* of the concept of time. It achieves that prominence both for reputable and for disreputable reasons. The disreputable reasons are celebrated in the first chapter of the Analytic of Principles, which is devoted to the problem of Schematism. Kant seems to think that, as things stand, we cannot apply the categories to experience, for they are so general, so abstract: 'pure concepts of understanding being quite heterogeneous from empirical intuitions, and indeed from all sensible intuitions, can never be met with in any intuition' (A137/B176). If they are to apply to ordinary objects, tables and chairs, they must be re-interpreted in more concrete terms, so that they have something in common with the objects to which they apply. He solves this fatuous problem by re-interpreting all the categories in temporal terms. With the aid of the schema of time we are able to derive schematized *principles* of the understanding from unschematized *categories* of the understanding. I see no point in paying attention to the Schematism here, save to record its existence and the existence of an associated distinction between schematized principles and unschematized categories. I will have something more to say of an equally uncomplimentary kind in section 8.

But there are very reputable reasons for the prominence of the concept of time in the Analytic of Principles, for time has already played a role in the argument of the *Critique*. One of the main claims of the Aesthetic was that objects of experience must be temporal, though Kant's supporting arguments were extremely sketchy. Time has already played a part in the argument of the Analytic, since Kant is discussing the necessary conditions of there being a temporally ordered series of experiences. Clearly before long we must ask important questions about time. We must ask for a definite proof that objects are temporal; we must ask questions about how we measure time, how we can measure the duration of experiences; we must ask how we can tell that one objective event follows or precedes another; we must ask whether the temporal order of our perceptions is an accurate guide to the temporal order of events perceived; and so on. Questions like those are woven into the sections of the Analytic of Principles that we are going to discuss.

One other preliminary observation. When sketching the background of Kant's enterprise in Chapter 1, I said that one of the problems worrying him is the problem of the status of mathematics and physics. The official programme of the Aesthetic was to investigate mathematics, that of the Analytic to investigate physics. So far in the Analytic there has been very little apparent concern with physics, but in several places in the Analytic of Principles there is a striking change of emphasis. It is no accident that the topics of the three Analogies are closely connected with the Newtonian concepts of matter, force, and reaction, nor that Kant attempts to draw conclusions that are basic assumptions of Newtonian physics. Whether Kant's philosophical infatuation with Newton is important or desirable is a matter for discussion in section 7, but it is beyond doubt that the infatuation exists.

2. THE FIRST ANALOGY

The three passages to be considered, then, are the first Analogy, which is concerned with the concept of substance and with a Newtonian conservation principle, the second Analogy, which consists mainly in an attempt to refute Hume's account of causality, and the Refutation of Idealism, which attempts to earn its title. As always it is vital to distinguish exposition from criticism, and each in turn from sympathetic reconstruction. I shall expound and criticize each passage in turn and then construct an argument that will, I hope, yield the more interesting and more important of the conclusions that Kant required.

Kant prefaces his discussion of the three Analogies with a general principle of the Analogies, the second edition version of which could easily be mistaken for a passage from the Transcendental Deduction: 'Experience is possible only through the representation of a necessary connection of perceptions' (B218). And the proof of the principle repeats many moves made in the Transcendental Deduction. But Kant is not merely interested in knowledge of an external world independent of our perceptions; in the Analogies he is more keenly interested in knowledge of the external world so far 'as it exists objectively in time' (B219). He wants to show how we can and must apply temporal concepts to our experience of objects, and the three Analogies are concerned with the concepts of temporal duration, temporal succession, and temporal coexistence respectively. There is no need for us to examine the proof of the general principle of the Analogies in detail, for its main themes are repeated in the separate proofs of the three Analogies.

So to the first Analogy, which illustrates among other things Kant's tendency to offer several consecutive versions of the same argument in the same paragraph. The main argument appears three or four times in succession in the first paragraph of the first edition (A182–4), and for good and clearer measure he adds a further version in the second edition right at the beginning (B224–5). The Analogy is entitled the 'Principle of Permanence of Substance' and the argument goes as follows.

1. All appearances (objects of experience) are in time, and in it alone can coexistence or succession be represented.

2. Time cannot by itself be perceived.

3. So there must be in the objects of perception the substratum which represents time in general.

4. That is, all change must be perceived in this substratum.

5. But the substratum of all that is real is substance, and all that

belongs to existence can be thought only as a determination of substance.

6. This permanent as the substrate of all change remains ever the same.

7. As it is unchangeable in its existence, its quantity in nature is neither increased nor diminished.

Thus Kant is both claiming that we must use a concept of substance and attempting to justify a Newtonian conservation principle, the principle that the total quantity of matter is constant whatever physical and chemical changes occur.

But his argument is both confusing and confused. The reference to succession and coexistence is a trifle confusing, for they are supposedly the topics of the other two Analogies. Moreover the assumption that objects of experience are in time has still to be justified. But Kant has none the less located at least one important problem about time. How can we use temporal concepts? What grounds do we have for identifying the temporal properties of things? After all, as Kant points out, 'time cannot by itself be perceived'. The temporal properties of things do not reveal themselves in the way in which colour does, or texture, size, shape. We cannot literally see or hear the passing of time. Kant seems to imply that time can only be understood in terms of the regular changes of persisting things, for example the regular changes of a persisting solar system, or the regular seasonal variations in the objects around us. We might say more dangerously that we must understand time in terms of the regular changes of a substance or substances (cf. A184/B227).

And that is where the rot sets in, for Kant seems unable to decide what he means by 'substance'. His original account of the (unschematized) concept of substance was quite promising, namely 'simply a something which can be thought only as subject, never as a predicate of something else' (A147/B186). That would seem clearly to suggest that a substance is logically independent of other things and cannot be analysed in terms of other things and their properties. Although such a suggestion might not help us to decide definitely which things are substances, it would help us to decide which things are not. For example experiences are not substances, because they are logically dependent on people. They have to be unpacked in terms of people thinking, seeing, tasting, imagining, etc. A nation is not a substance, for it can only be analysed in terms of the properties of various people, including their relational properties. A cricket match is not a substance, for it is logically dependent on there being people, bits of willow, and patches of grass related in certain ways.

If a substance is an object logically independent of other things, logically capable of an independent existence, then the Transcendental Deduction has already provided candidates for the status of substances, namely the external objects of experience. For it is a necessary condition of experience that we perceive external things, independent of ourselves and our perceptions. And Chapter 1 of Strawson's *Individuals* might give us grounds for thinking that those objects, those basic substances, are familiar material objects, tables and chairs. That is, we may reasonably be inclined to treat 'substance' and 'material object' as equivalent terms. But Kant wants the expression 'substance' to do much more work than that, and in the course of the first Analogy he uses at least five different notions of substance.

A *substance₁* is an ordinary material object, a table or a chair, which lasts for some time, a few months or a few years. Kant refers for instance to 'substances' in this sense at A188/B231.

A *substance₂* is a substance in the Aristotelian sense in which there is a supposed distinction between a substance and its 'accidents', between the vital and persisting essence of a thing and its various changing properties (cf. A184/B227, A186/B229).

Substance₃ does not have a plural. That is, instead of talking of a substance or several substances, whether in an ordinary or an Aristotelian tone of voice, Kant talks of 'substance', of the essential unchanging substratum of the whole world, 'the permanent' which underlies all the events that happen in the world. We might say that substance₃ is substance₂ writ large, that instead of contrasting the essential substance₂ of a chair with the 'accidents' or changing properties of the chair, Kant wants to contrast the essential substance₃ of the whole world with all the world's accidents. It is this elevated and mysterious substance₃ that in the main argument of the first Analogy is 'the substratum which represents time in general' (B225, A183/B226).

Substance₄ again has no plural, for it is Newtonian matter, the fundamental stuff of the Newtonian universe. According to Newton the total quantity of matter, of substance₄, remains constant whatever physical or chemical changes occur (cf. B225, A185/B228).

A *substance₅* is a strange hybrid of substance₁, substance₃, and substance₄. Kant muddles a concern with ordinary material objects (substances₁) an interest in 'the substratum which represents time in general' (substance₃) and a desire to prove the conservation of matter (substance₄), and finds himself arguing that ordinary things, ordinary 'substances', cannot be created or annihilated. There must be substances₅ which exist *in perpetuis* whatever changes they may undergo (cf. A185–6/B228–9, A188/B231).

The confusion of different senses of 'substance' causes havoc in the argument and blank incomprehension in the reader. Indeed it is only by sliding cheerfully from one sense of 'substance' to another that Kant is able to reach the astonishing conclusion that the total quantity of matter is necessarily constant. Consider the main argument again. Kant begins by suggesting that we must find some general grounds for our using temporal concepts. Time cannot literally be perceived, so we must explain how our experience can yield a concept of time, can give us a way of measuring the passage of time. As I observed earlier, an obvious solution is that we must perceive certain fairly permanent objects, which change regularly and systematically, such as the parts of the solar system, or plants affected by seasonal changes. We would understand time in terms of the regular and systematic changes of substances$_1$, of ordinary material things. The regular movements of sun and planets, or the regular seasonal changes of plants and climate, would give us primitive 'clocks', instruments for measuring the passage of time. We would not have to demand that such primitive 'clocks' should last for ever. As long as we were able to replace a useless clock with another, such as one set of perennial plants with another, we could maintain a grasp of the concept of time.

But Kant leaps to the much more ambitious conclusion that we must understand time in terms of the regular changes of a single all-embracing world-substance, a single absolutely permanent 'clock', 'the permanent', substance$_3$. Instead of merely populating the world with a few comparatively permanent objects or substances$_1$, such as the planets and the sun, or various plants affected by seasonal changes, he insists on an absolutely permanent substance$_3$ which underlies all change, all events in the world. To put it kindly, it is difficult to see what such a thing could be. To put it unkindly, Kant seems to ignore his central Critical thesis that knowledge requires both concepts and intuitions, since it is difficult to see what could count as perceiving the single substratum which represents time in general, or even what could count as perceiving the changes of such a thing.

Worse is to come. Kant seems to think that substance$_3$, 'the permanent', is identical with Newtonian matter, substance$_4$. Since he thinks that 'the permanent' or substance$_3$ neither increases nor diminishes, he thinks he can draw the final conclusion that Newtonian matter, substance$_4$, is conserved whatever physical and chemical changes take place. None of that will do at all. To begin with, the slide from substance$_3$ to substance$_4$ is unfortunate, for Kant's remarks on 'the permanent', 'the substratum which represents time in general', look even more foolish when applied to Newtonian matter. It is difficult enough to see why we should think of time in terms of the changes of a single all-embracing substance$_3$. But it is quite clear that we do not think of time at all in terms of the changes of the whole of Newtonian matter, of substance$_4$. Human beings understood the passage of time before they had any concept of matter, of a basic physical stuff of which all objects are composed. Even if they did not, even if we allowed the conflation of substance$_3$ with substance$_4$, the last step of Kant's argument, the claim that the quantity of matter must therefore be constant, is unacceptable. It is in no way necessary to our experience that we think of the quantity of matter as constant. Even if we thought of time in terms of the changes of Newtonian matter, we could easily imagine the quantity of matter as increasing, or as diminishing, or as constantly fluctuating.

Kant's application of the Newtonian conservation principle towards the end of the first Analogy is even more peculiar, for we find him arguing that we logically cannot allow new substances, new things, to come into existence, nor existing things to be annihilated. A substance (substance$_5$) is something that cannot be created, and must exist *in perpetuis*. 'We can therefore give an appearance the title "substance" just for the reason that we presuppose its existence throughout all time' (A185/B228). 'If some of these substances could come into being and others cease to be, the one condition of the empirical unity of time would be removed' (A188/B231). But it is impossible to see what could count as such a substance. Certainly our familiar material objects do not fill the bill, for my furniture was created comparatively recently and a judicious use of saw or bonfire would quickly guarantee its annihilation. Kant's remarks might, I suppose, be interpreted as a perverse re-statement of the Newtonian conservation principle but they would still be puzzling. My furniture is created from an equal quantity of matter and its 'annihilation' will leave an equal quantity of smoke and ashes, but that is a contingent truth, not a necessary truth. We could certainly make sense of a world in which certain things were spontaneously generated from nothing at all, or from an unequal quantity of matter, and were destroyed without any trace, or with traces of much smaller quantities of matter.

In short the main weakness of Kant's first Analogy is that the conclusions have a very tenuous connection with the premisses. Kant identifies a very important problem, that of explaining how we have a concept of time, how we grasp the passage of time. He sees that the problem can be solved by introducing some concept of substance. But his confusion of several quite different senses of 'substance' and his underlying wish to prove the necessity of a Newtonian conservation principle lead to several astonishing moves and unacceptable conclusions. But there may be important things to be salvaged from the debris, as we shall see in due course.

3. THE SECOND ANALOGY

The second Analogy deserves special attention, because it is concerned with the third of three important problems attacked by Hume and around which the Analytic is built, namely the problem of personal identity, the problem of the existence of the external world and the problem of causality. In effect Kant shows that the three problems are connected, by offering an argument that links them together. He tries to show that self-awareness, awareness of objects, and awareness of causality are intimately connected.

Characteristically Kant offers several different versions of his argument in the second Analogy, some of which are misleading. And apparently dissatisfied with his efforts in the first edition he adds two more paragraphs right at the beginning in the second edition. But examination of the first six paragraphs of the second edition yields the following argument, repeated for good measure at A197–9/B242–4 and at A201–2/B246–7.

1. I must be able to identify objects (cf. Transcendental Deduction).
2. In particular I must be able to identify objectively successive events.
3. The ground for such identification must be in my experience.
4. The ground in question is that successive perceptions of objectively successive events are necessarily connected, occur in a necessary order.
5. A concept that carries such necessity is a pure concept of the understanding, in this case the concept of causality.
6. Thus successive perceptions of objectively successive events are necessarily connected according to a rule, the rule of cause and effect.
7. Thus there must lie in that which precedes an event the condition of a rule according to which the event invariably and necessarily follows.
8. That is, all objective events occur in accordance with the Universal Law of Cause and Effect.

In the first edition Kant's conclusion is merely that 'Everything that happens ... presupposes something upon which it follows according to a rule' (A189) but it is reasonably clear from what follows that the 'rules' in question are causal laws.

This is a complicated and confused argument but the general drift of Kant's thinking is clear. He has established in the Transcendental Deduction that experience requires us to distinguish between ourselves and the external world, that we must use concepts of objects, external things. The proof of the general principle of the Analogies has prepared us for concentration on the temporal properties of objects, and the second Analogy is concerned with temporal succession. Kant wants to discover our grounds for identifying objectively successive events: the sun rises, the birds begin to sing; the clock strikes one, the mouse runs down; the referee blows a whistle, the spectators go home; and so on. We must find in our experience the clues that tell us we are perceiving successive objective events. According to Kant the main clue is very simple. When I say that I perceive the sunrise followed by the dawn chorus I am connecting two perceptions in time, for my perception of the sunrise is closely followed by my perception of the dawn chorus. But the vital point, he argues, is that those perceptions are connected in a *necessary* order, that perceptions of objectively successive events can occur in one and only one order. For example if I see a boat moving downstream my perceptions must occur in one order and only one. 'My perception of its lower position follows upon the perception of its position higher up in the stream, and it is impossible that in the apprehension of this appearance the ship should first be perceived lower down in the stream and afterwards higher up ... [I]n the perception of an event there is always a rule that makes the order in which the perceptions ... follow upon one another a *necessary* order' (A192–3/B237–8). Perceptions of objectively successive events occur in a necessary order according to a certain rule, and in this case, it appears, the rule in question is the concept of cause and effect. In other words, Kant concludes, all objective events must obey causal laws. I must apply the concept of causality to my experience: 'I render my subjective synthesis of apprehension objective only by reference to a rule in accordance with which the appearances in their succession, that is, as they happen, are determined by the preceding state' (A195/B240).

I have tried to expound the argument as sympathetically as possible but have none the less had to paper over many cracks. It is now our melancholy task to uncover them again. One very striking difficulty is that Kant discusses several different problems in the second Analogy without apparently realizing that they are different. Sometimes he is concerned with the notion of an objective event, sometimes with that of a sequence of objective events, and sometimes with that of a causal sequence of objective events. At least two versions of the argument seem to be addressed initially to the first, to the 'question for deeper enquiry what the word "object" ought to signify' (A189–90/B235), to 'an order of successive synthesis that determines an object' (A201/B246). To be fair to him, however, it is clear that he wants to concentrate on objective succession rather than mere objectivity. For example he contrasts perceptions of a house with perceptions of a boat moving downstream (A190–3/B235–8). Although both house and boat are objects the boat generates a special problem, because its movement downstream constitutes a *sequence* of objective events. The contrast between house and boat is reflected in features of the corresponding perceptions, for whereas perceptions of the parts of the house could occur in absolutely any order, perceptions of the movement of the boat must occur in a particular order. 'The order in which the perceptions succeed one another in apprehension is in this instance determined' (A192/B237).

So his main concern is with sequences of objective events, with 'objective succession' such as the progress of the boat downstream. But the conclusion of the second Analogy is that we must apply causal concepts to our experience of objects. There are obvious references to Hume, and Kant discusses the connection between causality and substance (A204/B249 f.). In other words Kant seems to be guilty of a serious confusion between objective *temporal* succession and objective *causal* succession. Not even Hume would argue that causality consists in mere temporal succession. Notoriously, as his critics have insisted, the sound of the hooter in London and the departure of workers in Glasgow are temporally but not causally successive. Even Kant's example of a boat moving downstream is not as it stands an example of causal succession. The boat's being upstream is not the cause of its being downstream, although it obviously precedes it. Similarly the earth's progress around the sun is a temporal succession of events, but not as it stands a causal succession. Causal succession involves more than temporal succession. Even if Kant is entitled to claim that we must have a concept of objective *temporal* succession, revealed in the necessary ordering of our perceptions, he is not thereby entitled to conclude that we must have a concept of objective *causal* succession.

Kant would draw my attention to steps 5 and 6 of his argument, which make the move from temporal to causal succession. He would argue that perceptions of objectively successive events, such as a boat moving downstream, occur in a necessary order according to a certain rule, and that the rule in question is the concept of causality. Hence to isolate our grounds for talking of objective temporal succession is in effect to talk about the need to apply a concept of causality. But that really will not do, for two reasons. First, Kant does not justify and cannot justify his claim that the rule that determines the order of perceptions is the concept of causality. He cannot say that the concept of causality carries necessity upon its brow, for that is true of any pure concept of the understanding. 'Categories are concepts which prescribe laws *a priori* to appearances' (B163) and therefore every category will connect different and successive perceptions together as perceptions of objects. Nor can Kant insist that he is interested in a particular group of objective events, in objectively *successive* events, and that causality is the rule that connects perceptions of objectively successive events. For that would merely be to repeat the false claim that temporal succession and causal succession are the same thing.

The second reason for looking askance at the later stages of Kant's argument in the second Analogy is that there is something very odd about the notion of a necessary ordering of perceptions. I have examined some of the oddities in a paper called 'Time, Cause and Object' but I will be content to make one point here. According to Kant perceptions of objectively successive events must occur in one order and only one, have a necessary temporal sequence: 'there is an underlying rule which compels us to observe this order of perceptions rather than any other, ... this compulsion is really what first makes possible the representation of a succession in the object' (A196–7/B242). An obvious objection is that the claim is simply false. Of course I would normally see the boat upstream first, then a little lower down, and then still further down, and so on. But that is a matter of fact, not of logic, and there is no 'compulsion' about it. A cunning arrangement of mirrors, designed to reflect some of the light over large distances before it reached my eyes, might ensure that I saw the later events before the earlier. Even without any elaborate apparatus we can reverse the order of our perceptions very easily. We know for example that sound waves travel much more slowly than light waves and that we may see the mouse run down before we hear the clock strike one, or see the fielder catch the ball before we hear the batsman hitting it. Kant's ignorance of cricket is no excuse. It is simply not true that 'in the perception of an event there is always a rule that makes the order in which the perceptions ... follow upon one another a *necessary* order' (A193/B238). In a very clear sense the order of our perceptions is contingent upon all sorts of things, such as the sensory media (vibrating air molecules, electro-magnetic radiation), the presence or absence of certain obstacles or refracting materials (mirrors, pieces of glass), and so on.

I suspect that Kant's use of the notion of a necessary ordering of perceptions is the result of a simple but disastrous muddle. Remember that for him the expressions 'necessary', 'pure', and '*a priori*' are synonyms, and that the categories or pure concepts of understanding or *a priori* rules of synthesis are necessary to experience. If we did not use those concepts there would be no experience. Now suppose for the purposes of argument that one of those categories is the concept of causality, that experiences must be synthesized according to at least one *a priori* rule of synthesis, the concept of causality. I suggest that with all that in mind Kant made a simple logical error. He moved from thinking that temporally successive experiences must be brought under a certain *a priori* concept, namely causality, to thinking that the temporal order of perceptions of cause and effect is necessary. He used the following invalid argument:

(a) Two perceptions are brought under the same *a priori* concept and (b) They are temporally successive.
Therefore they have a necessary temporal order.

The scope of '*a priori*' or 'necessary' has shifted in the course of the argument. The premisses merely say that we must regard the temporally successive perceptions as perceptions of cause and effect. The conclusion says that the perceptions must occur in one order and one only. And that is not at all the same thing. The premisses merely say that my applying the concept of causality to temporally successive perceptions is necessary for experience, but the conclusion says that the temporal succession itself is necessary. Not necessary *for* anything, just necessary.

My diagnosis of Kant's mistake may be incorrect but I have little doubt that he is very careless in his use of the word 'necessary'. For example there is a spectacular shift in the scope of 'necessary' between step 6 and step 7 of the argument of the second Analogy. Step 6 is the claim that perceptions of objectively successive events are necessarily connected, that there is a rule which requires that the perceptions occur in one and only one sequence. Step 7, on the other hand, is the claim that effects are necessarily connected with their causes: 'if the state which precedes is posited, this determinate event follows inevitably and necessarily' (A198/B243-4). In other words Kant moves from a necessary ordering of perceptions to a necessary ordering of events perceived. Not merely is the move invalid, it commits Kant to a rationalist account of causality which is not in the least essential to his general Critical purposes. He may reasonably wish to argue against Hume that we must use a concept of cause and effect, but there is no need for him to insist that causes and effects are necessarily connected. I shall return to the point in section 6.

I seem to have given the second Analogy rather short and unsympathetic shrift. I objected, first, that Kant confuses temporal and causal succession and, second, that his argument hinges on a claim which is false, the claim that the temporal order of perceptions of objectively successive events is necessary. I also argued that Kant's use of 'necessary' is very careless and commits him for no very good reason to a rationalist account of causality, to a belief in a necessary connection between cause and effect. But the second Analogy, like the first, is none the less full of useful material which may be reconstructed. The argument may not do as it stands, but Kant's general enterprise is fruitful and stimulating.

4. THE REFUTATION OF IDEALISM

Before sampling the fruit and the stimulation we must briefly look at the third passage in which I expressed a keen interest, namely The Refutation of Idealism. Critical response to the first edition of the *Critique* was largely unsympathetic, and Kant was particularly offended by the understandable suggestion that his own idealism was in many relevant respects similar to Berkeley's. In several parts of the *Prolegomena* (e.g. pp. 288-94, 374-5) he attempted to refute the accusation but only succeeded in confirming it. In the second edition of the *Critique* he returned to the attack and inserted a completely new Refutation of Idealism at the end of his discussion of the second Postulate of Empirical Thought (B274-9). The main argument is as follows.

1. I am conscious of my existence in time.

2. All determination of time presupposes something permanent in perception.

3. This permanent cannot be in me, since it is only through the permanent that my own existence in time can be determined.

4. So the permanent must be outside me.

5. Thus the consciousness of my existence is at the same time an awareness of outer things in space.

It is rather difficult to criticize the argument because it is a mixture of the main themes of the Transcendental Deduction and the first Analogy. That is, the general claim that experience must be of external things is interwoven with a problem about the measurement of time. Kant suggests that I am aware of my existence in time only if I am aware of external objects in space. The suggestion reminds us of the distinction originally made in the Aesthetic between inner and outer sense: time is the form of inner sense, of all our experiences, while space is the form of outer sense, of our ostensible perceptions of external things. To be reminded of the distinction is not of course necessarily to understand it, and it is not clear why awareness of one's existence in time presupposes awareness of objects in space. An important part of the argument seems to be missing. Thus, like the first two Analogies the Refutation of Idealism makes interesting suggestions but needs to be improved and developed. Regarded literally as a refutation of idealism it is both redundant and disingenuous. It is redundant because Kant has already produced a plausible refutation of idealism in the Transcendental Deduction, and it is disingenuous because it is part of Kant's persistent and mistaken attempt to distinguish his own idealism from that of Berkeley.

5. RECONSTRUCTION

Despite my criticism our examination of three key passages in the Analytic of Principles has not been in vain. Kant's 'architectonic', his passion for systematic presentation of his views, confuses us and divides the argument in a very artificial way, but there is none the less a great deal of material to be extracted, repaired, and reconstructed. There are three main conclusions of a Kantian kind struggling to emerge, conclusions which stitch together the main themes of the Aesthetic and Analytic. The first is that objects must be spatial and temporal, must be at some place at some time. The second is that objects must be 'substances', must be logically independent of other things, logically capable of an independent existence. Furthermore, given Kant's obsession with 'the permanent', they must be comparatively permanent. That is, we can leave room for a few fleeting and insubstantial things, for odd flashes and bangs which only last for a split second, but the basic objects in the world must be more enduring, must last rather longer than our perceptions of them. And the third conclusion is that objects must obey causal laws, must change in ways that can in principle be generalized and predicted.

I propose to produce an argument that will yield those conclusions. I have to confess that the argument is further from Kant's letter than my sympathetic reconstruction of the argument of the Transcendental Deduction in Chapter 3, but it is Kantian in spirit and uses quite a lot of Kant's material. Kant indicates very clearly the main route to the three conclusions in question: we must dwell on the consequences of the conclusion of the Transcendental Deduction, the consequences of the distinction between perceiver and external world, subject and object, private perception and public object perceived. 'How, then, does it come about that we posit an object for these representations, and so, in addition to their subjective reality, as modifications, ascribe to them some mysterious kind of objective reality?' (A197/B242). We must give some content to the claim that objects of experience are distinct from us, are logically independent of our perceptions. The conclusion will be that we can only do so if we regard objects as persisting substances, as spatial and temporal, and as governed by laws of change.

So much for preliminary fanfare. I now offer the following argument, designed to yield those conclusions.

1. There is a series of experiences, temporally ordered.

2. Someone must be aware of them as his own.

3. He must regard at least some of them as perceptions of external objects (cf. Transc. Deduction).

4. That is, he must be able to identify and re-identify external objects.

5. If the objects are distinct both from the perceiver and from each other they must be spatial and temporal.

6. If objects are independent of the perceiver but re-identifiable they must last longer than perceptions of them.

7. If objects are to be re-identified their changes must be law-governed.

The connection between my reconstruction and the Kantian original should be fairly clear. Step 4 and part of step 5 together form the conclusion of the Refutation of Idealism, step 6 is a weak version of the conclusion of the first Analogy stripped of its Newtonian overtones, step 7 is a weaker version of the conclusion of the second Analogy, and step 5 repeats a central thesis of the Aesthetic. The whole of the reconstruction turns on the conclusion of the Transcendental Deduction, namely that the objects of experience are logically independent of ourselves and our perceptions, and that we must therefore have ways of identifying and re-identifying them.

Indeed the notion of re-identification is crucial. If we are to think of objects as independent of us and our perceptions, we must think of them as existing even when we are not perceiving them. We must think of ourselves as re-identifying objects which have existed and perhaps changed since we last identified them. In other words to talk of re-identifying objects that are independent of us and our perceptions is to arrive at step 6, to insist that the objects of experience, in most cases at least, must last longer than perceptions of them. It might be objected, however, that we should insist on nothing of the sort, that we can easily imagine an experience in which sadly we never experience the same object twice, in which there is never any re-identification of objects. Indeed, it might be said, we can easily imagine the limiting case where objects only last as long as perceptions, where things appear and disappear, exist and cease to exist, as frequently as we look at them, listen to them, touch them, taste them, smell them. We might well talk of objects distinct from ourselves and our perceptions, but we would have no use for the notion of re-identification, and no grounds whatever for believing that objects last longer than perceptions. In other words step 6 is unacceptable.

I would insist that step 6 is true and that the situation envisaged in the objection is not intelligible. It is true that if objects only lasted as long as our perceptions we would have no use for the notion of re-identification. But much more to the point, we would also lose the distinction between objects and perceptions. If objects lasted as long as perceptions of them there would be no significant difference between objects and perceptions. But if there were no significant difference between objects and perceptions the perceiver would lose the distinction between his perceptions and objects, and so in turn between himself and objects. He would therefore lose all sense of his own identity and he would have no experience of any kind. In short, experience requires a distinction between perceiver and external world, and that distinction cannot be maintained if perceptions and objects temporally coincide. We must think of objects as lasting longer than perceptions of them.

What of step 7, the claim that objects must obey some laws of change? The argument here is slightly more complicated, but still hinges on the need to re-identify objects which exist independently of perceivers. Suppose that the world changes wholly chaotically, that events occur for no apparent reason, entirely unpredictably. As far as one can tell there are simply no general laws governing the universe, and everything is random and chaotic. Moreover suppose that I am confronted with a chair and am tormented by doubts about its identity. I want to know whether it is identical with the chair I sat on yesterday, or with a pack of cards I used two days ago, or with the camel I rode last week, or with the newspaper I read a few minutes ago. In a completely chaotic world I have no way of solving the problem. Since events happen at random the chair may have sprung from nothing at all, or have sprouted from a camel, or appeared full-blown from a heap of newspaper. In other words it would be impossible to *re-identify* the chair at all. Even if I saw a chair here now, and a similar chair here five minutes hence, I would have no grounds for talking of re-identification. For in a completely chaotic world absolutely anything could happen in five minutes, and the present chair might have no connection with the chair I see in five minutes' time. But if it is impossible to re-identify an object, I can have no notion of its existing independently of my perceptions, existing unperceived between the first and second perception. In other words I cannot rule out the possibility that objects only last as long as my perceptions. But if objects only last as long as perceptions of them, the distinction between objects and perceptions collapses, taking with it the distinction between objects and perceiver, and so in turn the perceiver's sense of his own identity.

The only way of salvaging re-identification is to tie it to some general laws of change. To re-identify my chair I must know at the very least that chairs cannot sprout from camels or piles of newspaper, that they can turn into heaps of ash, that they can lose legs, become dirty and scratched. To re-identify a caterpillar I must know that caterpillars change into chrysalids and then into butterflies, but never into pillar-boxes or postage-stamps. I can say that this lovely flower is identical with the dismal twig I bought some months ago only if I know that certain dismal twigs grow into lovely flowers. In short, re-identification of objects is necessary if the distinction between perceiver and external objects is to be preserved, but re-identification is possible only if one knows in principle how an object might have changed between past and present acquaintance. That is, the objects of experience must obey certain general laws of change.

I think Strawson is right to argue in *The Bounds of Sense* (p. 146) that the laws in question need not be causal laws, laws which describe successive events which are invariably conjoined. One consideration is that the notion of causality is a very muddy one anyway, and it is sensible to follow standard scientific practice by formulating laws of change as functional equations which merely express the relation between one set of variables and another. Such functional relations are more clearly understood when relieved of the gratuitous mystery of causal language. But there is another consideration, namely that a series of statistical generalizations stating fairly high probabilities would give us all we need. I could identify caterpillar with butterfly even if caterpillars only turned into butterflies in ninety-five cases out of a hundred. We do not need complete determinacy, completely invariable constant conjunctions of events. All we need is a fairly high degree of regularity, a fairly high degree of determinacy.

Incidentally, by embracing the weaker conclusion that objects of experience must obey some laws of change we avoid any problems arising from Heisenberg's much misunderstood Principle of Uncertainty or Indeterminacy, the claim that it is impossible even in principle to measure both the position and the velocity of an elementary particle. The Principle has been invoked against Kant's claim that all events obey causal laws. For if we cannot measure both the position and the velocity of an elementary particle we cannot formulate causal laws governing its behaviour, and we have to admit that sub-atomic events do not obey causal laws. But, for two reasons, I do not think that Kant should be profoundly disturbed by such an objection. First, in 'The Second Analogy and the Principle of Indeterminacy' Beck argues that our ability to identify indeterminacy at a sub-atomic level is wholly parasitic on a high degree of determinacy at a macroscopic level. For example if the physicist is to explore the peculiarities of elementary particles he must have complete faith in his apparatus and measuring instruments, must assume that they perform consistently and invariably according to the causal laws of mechanics, electronics, etc. Second, my weaker version of Kant's conclusion avoids the objection entirely. Even if the behaviour of elementary particles is indeterminate in the sense explained, it is still law-governed, because we can formulate probability-statements about the behaviour of groups or aggregates of particles. All objects, including sub-atomic 'objects', must obey general laws of change, even if the laws are only statistical generalizations which describe the behaviour of groups or aggregates of 'objects'.

So far in this section I have argued that objects must last longer than our perceptions of them, must be relatively 'permanent', and that they must obey general laws of change. We can now move to the last main conclusion I wanted to draw, namely that objects must be spatial and temporal. When I was discussing the Transcendental Aesthetic I sketched an argument designed to prove that objects must be spatial and temporal. It turned on the important fact that two things can share all their non-spatial and non-temporal properties, but cannot be in exactly the same place at exactly the same time. For example we cannot successfully distinguish two chairs by means of their colour or their shape or composition, for they may have the same colour or shape or composition.

Whether I am concerned to distinguish this chair from another or to re-identify it as a chair I have seen before, I must refer to its spatio-temporal properties in order to guarantee success. To show that the chair is different from those around it I need only show that it is in a different place at a given time, and to re-identify it as the chair I sat on yesterday I need only show that today's chair is spatio-temporally continuous with yesterday's. Thus, since I must have criteria of identification and re-identification of objects, and since the only secure criteria are spatio-temporal, objects must be spatial and temporal.

The argument is open to an obvious objection. The argument turns on the claim that two things cannot share all their spatio-temporal properties, cannot be in exactly the same places at exactly the same times. But it could be objected that that is only true of fairly solid material objects, such as shoes and ships and sealing-wax, and cabbages and kings. It is not true of certain other familiar and public objects of experience, such as rainbows, sounds, and smells. Whereas two chairs cannot be in exactly the same place at exactly the same time, two smells or two sounds, or a sound and a smell, certainly can. The smell of lavender and the sound of the drum may both be in the market square at twelve o'clock. They are public objects of experience, accessible to all who have ears to hear and noses to smell, and they are substances in at least one important sense, for they may exist independently of any perception of them. But they are not solid material objects and they may share their spatio-temporal positions with other things. Spatial and temporal position are no more central to the identity of public sounds and smells than any of their other properties. Thus one cannot argue that successful identification of objects of experience requires them to be in space and time. It certainly requires them to have distinctive properties of some kind, but not necessarily spatio-temporal properties. Indeed the only properties central to the identity of a smell or a sound seem to be its smell and its sound respectively.

There are various ways of replying to that objection. One is to deny that the 'objects' in question are genuine objects, genuine substances, to insist that their existence is logically dependent on something else. For example the smell of lavender in the market square is logically dependent on there being a material object (e.g. some lavender) exuding a certain smell. The sound of a drum logically depends on there being something (e.g. a drum) making a certain sound. Smells and sounds are no more objects within the meaning of the Kantian act than are nations, football matches, the average taxpayer, or the grin of the Cheshire cat. We are only interested in genuine objects, genuine substances, and it is certainly true that two genuine objects, two genuine substances, cannot share exactly the same spatial and temporal properties.

That reply, I fear, will not do. It is not a matter of logic but a matter of fact that smells and sounds require something to generate them. It is perfectly conceivable that the market square might contain public smells of lavender and public sounds of a drum without any lavender or drum in the vicinity. In a world in which we often failed to discover the source of a smell or sound we might have to concede that some smells and sounds are genuine objects, genuine substances, logically capable of independent existence. A more useful reply to the objection is to consider how we might distinguish between the lavender-smell and the drum-sound, and to ask how many objects are in the market square. Are there two objects, each with a single sensory property, or is there one object with two sensory properties? It is no good saying that there must be two objects, because one object smells and the other object sounds, for a pig is certainly one object for our purposes but equally certainly both smells and sounds. A great deal depends on the life-histories of the lavender-smell and the drum-sound. For example if the lavender-smell entirely coincided spatially and temporally with the drum-sound, moved around the world locked firmly in its noisy embrace, it would be most reasonable to talk of one thing in the market square, smelling of lavender and sounding like a drum. If on the other hand the smell approached from the east and departed for the north, and the sound approached from the west and departed for the south, it would be reasonable to talk of two things in the market square.

And that is where the objection can be made to collapse. We would treat sound and smell as one object if they shared exactly the same spatial and temporal properties. We would treat them as two objects if they were in different places before their arrival in the square, and moved to different places afterwards. In other words, even when we consider such strange objects as sounds and smells there is an intimate connection between the identity of an object and its spatio-temporal properties. If A and B follow exactly the same spatio-temporal route in our experience we treat them as the same thing; if not, not. Thus whether we are talking of material objects or of somewhat immaterial objects such as smells and sounds, their identity is intimately connected with their spatial and temporal positions. Thus to talk of the identification and re-identification of objects is necessarily to talk of objects that are spatial and temporal.

While we are discussing time and the temporal properties of things I want to make one more observation about the measurement of time. When I examined the first Analogy and the Refutation of Idealism I said that Kant seemed to recognize an important problem about the measurement of time and to indicate a possible solution. If I am to be aware of my own existence in time I must have some method of measuring time.

THE ANALYTIC OF PRINCIPLES

But 'time cannot by itself be perceived' (B225), and the contents of consciousness do not seem to yield a very reliable clock: '*representations themselves require a permanent distinct from them, in relation to which their change,
and so my existence in the time wherein they change, may be determined*'
(Bxxxixa). Despite his rather unfortunate account of 'the permanent'
which is 'to represent time in general', Kant's argument deserves careful
consideration and can be reconstructed in a very Wittgensteinian spirit
as follows. I must have a concept of time if I am to be aware of my own
experiences as temporal, if I am to understand the duration of my experiences, the intervals between them, and so on. Moreover I must have a
notion of objective time, so that I can occasionally contrast my own estimate of the passage of time with a precise objective measurement. I must
be in a position to say, for example, 'The pain seemed to last for hours,
but in fact it stopped after twenty minutes.' Now my series of experiences
cannot give an objective measurement of time, for, as Kant says, their
duration can only be measured against something else. I cannot say that
my pain lasted twenty minutes if my only 'clock' consists in my series
of experiences. For 'twenty minutes' would mean 'the time taken by the
pain' and 'my pain lasted for twenty minutes' would merely mean 'my
pain lasted as long as it lasted'. To measure the duration of my experiences against the duration of my experiences is viciously circular. If I
am to succeed in saying anything about the duration of my experience,
about 'my own existence as determined in time' (B275), then I must have
some objective or external standard of measurement. For example I must
measure the duration of my experience against the successive and regular
changes of certain material objects such as the parts of the solar system.
I can then make a significant remark about my pain: 'it lasted for twenty
minutes, that is, as long as it took the earth to rotate 5° on its axis relative
to the sun.' Briefly:
  1. I require a concept of time.
  2. Thus I require some objective standard of measurement of time.
  3. The contents of consciousness can only yield a wholly trivial, wholly
circular standard.
  4. The objective standard can only be yielded by the successive and
regular changes of external objects (such as the heavenly bodies).
  In this section I have been concerned to sketch a number of arguments
which, if successful, yield Kantian conclusions. According to the Transcendental Deduction I must distinguish between myself and external
things, must be able in principle to identify and re-identify things that
exist independently of my perceptions. I have argued that the conclusion
in turn requires that the objects be spatial and temporal, that (at least
in most cases) they last longer than any perceptions of them, and that

they obey general laws of change. I have also sketched an argument very close to that of the Refutation of Idealism to show that I must have an objective way of measuring time, an objective 'clock' in the form of the successive and regular changes of external things. My arguments have no doubt been sketchy, but they yield conclusions very similar to those of the Transcendental Aesthetic, the first and second Analogies, and the Refutation of Idealism. We have in outline the necessary conditions of a possible experience, namely that experience must be of external objects which are spatial and temporal, which obey laws of change, and which are substances in at least two connected senses. On the one hand they must be logically independent things, and on the other they must last longer than our perceptions of them, for they must be re-identifiable.

Before closing this section there are two incidental points to be made. First, my sympathetic reconstruction has unfortunate consequences for Kant's grand architectonic plan. According to that plan space and time are pure intuitions, the forms of sensibility, and sensibility is discussed in the Aesthetic. The Analytic is concerned with the categories, the pure concepts of understanding, such as substance and causality. But my reconstructed argument shows the artificiality of that division. One of the conclusions I defended was that objects of experience must be spatial and temporal, that they must have spatio-temporal properties, that we must apply spatial and temporal concepts to our experience. In other words I have defended the claim that space and time are categories. It may be true that space and time are in some sense pure intuitions, logically basic individuals, but it is also true that we must apply spatial and temporal concepts, the categories of space and time, to our experience. Thus it is impossible to detach the discussion of space and time from the Analytic. Kant is no doubt right to insist that knowledge requires both intuitions and concepts, but it does not follow that he should attempt to isolate an intuitional component in the Aesthetic and a conceptual component in the Analytic. Both in this context and in the Critical philosophy in general, Kant's superficially systematic arrangement of Books, Sections, and Chapters bears little relation to the actual structure of his argument.

Second, it is worth noting Kant's belief that the Analogies confirm one main doctrine of the Aesthetic, namely that there must be one space and one time. 'Taken together, the analogies thus declare that all appearances lie, and must lie, in *one* nature, because without this *a priori* unity no unity of experience, and therefore no determination of objects in it, would be possible' (A216/B263). It is frankly difficult to see how precisely that conclusion emerges from the Analogies, but there is none the less a crucial philosophical point to be applauded. Whether or not Kant is right about the unity of space and time, he is right to concentrate our attention on what he calls 'the unity of experience'. For in searching for the necessary conditions of experience he is searching for the minimum conditions required to yield the experience of one and the same person. In constructing our philosophical fantasies we must be sure that they yield a unified experience, that they make sense as the experience of a single person. It is of little interest to inquire whether the world must be spatial or temporal or causal or whatever, but it is of enormous interest to ask whether someone could have *experience* of a non-spatial or non-temporal world, or of a world that obeyed no causal laws, or of two spaces or two times. For example consider my discussion in Chapter 2 of the unity of space and time. I argued that the two-spaces hypothesis made sense, for all the events could be fitted into a single coherent experience, the experience of a man who has systematically alternating access to two spaces. In contrast I rejected the two-times hypothesis because it demolished basic criteria of personal identity, basic criteria of 'the unity of experience'. If a man really did have access to two times, we would have no grounds for treating him as one and the same man throughout, for we would be unable to fit all his experiences into a single consistent series. Generally we are not interested in the necessary features of the world, but in the necessary features of a unified *experience* of the world.

6. KANT AND HUME

There are still a few loose ends to be tied, and one of them concerns the relation between Kant's and Hume's accounts of causality. Kant makes two main points against Hume in the second Analogy, though he does not seem to appreciate the difference between them. The first is that experience must be of objects that obey causal laws, that 'All alterations take place in conformity with the law of the connection of cause and effect' (B232). Causality is a necessary feature of our experience, not contingent upon it. We must no doubt derive specific causal laws *a posteriori*, from experience, but it is necessary that objects obey causal laws of some kind. I must discover from experience what happens when I throw a beaker to the floor, whether it breaks or bounces back or turns into a cabbage, but I can be confident that it obeys some causal laws. Hume appears to think that the world could in principle be completely chaotic, obey no causal laws of any kind.

Kant's second point is that causes are necessarily connected with their effects: 'if the state which precedes is posited, this determinate event follows inevitably and necessarily' (A198/B243–4). Our notion of causality 'makes strict demand that something, A, should be such that something else, B, follows from it *necessarily*' (A91/B124). In other words he appears to want to resurrect the rationalist account of causality that Hume attacked. He does not appear to realize that his second point is quite different from his first, nor that he does not need to defend the second point at all. The two points are clearly different, since the first insists that causality is necessary for experience, while the second claims that causes are necessarily connected with their effects. One could certainly argue that causality is necessary for experience without arguing for any particular account of the relation between cause and effect. Indeed in the previous section I argued in very much those terms, for although I argued that laws of change are a necessary feature of experience I did not attempt any very detailed account of the laws in question. And Kant has no need to resurrect a rationalist account of the relation between cause and effect. His main purpose is to prove that our notion of causality is necessary to experience, not contingent upon it. He could cheerfully have incorporated Hume's account of causal connections into his own view. He could have argued that causality is necessary for experience, and that causes and effects are merely temporally successive and constantly conjoined. As I suggested in section 3, the villain of the piece is probably his very careless use of the word 'necessary' in the second Analogy. By changing the scope of 'necessary' in the course of the argument he commits himself to an account of causal connections that is both unattractive and wholly irrelevant to the principal matter in hand.

7. KANT AND NEWTON

This section may seem rather foolishly placed, for I want to ask what the Analytic of Principles is actually about. One might think that the question should have been asked at the beginning rather than towards the end of this chapter. But I think it is most conveniently considered now, because we are in a position to review my interpretation of the first two sections of the *Critique*, the Aesthetic and the Analytic. According to Kant's official account of the *Critique* he is to show how synthetic *a priori* judgements are possible, and the Analytic is concerned with the synthetic *a priori* judgements of Newtonian physics. They are justified in general in the Analytic of Concepts, in the Metaphysical Deduction and Transcendental Deduction, and then they are 'schematized' and justified individually in the Analytic of Principles. I offered a slightly different interpretation of his enterprise. I suggested that Kant is searching for the necessary conditions of a possible experience, that the references to Newtonian physics are neither an essential nor a central part of the arguments presented in the Analytic.

Those two interpretations of Kant's programme will obviously yield different views of the Analytic of Principles. According to my interpretation the Analytic of Principles is extremely important, for it contains arguments or fragments of arguments that articulate the necessary conditions of experience. For example it contains arguments to show that the objects of experience must be causal substances. But those who accept the other interpretation will be less impressed by the Analytic of Principles. For example in his book on Kant (p. 79) Körner prefers to take Kant at his word, and sees the Analytic of Principles as a misguided attempt to justify *a priori* the basic assumptions of Newtonian physics, an attempt which is no more successful than the attempt in the Aesthetic to justify the postulates and theorems of Euclidean geometry.

Is it possible or desirable to choose between the two interpretations, to decide whether Kant is interested in the presuppositions of Newtonian physics, or rather in the necessary conditions of a possible experience? I think that there is no need to make a choice. To begin with it could be argued that Kant was never entirely sure what he wanted to do, that the first *Critique* is the result of a number of different and in some cases incompatible plans. Certainly he was very concerned to justify Newtonian physics, because he wanted to show that mathematics and physics yield *a priori* knowledge of the world, whereas metaphysics does not. To justify *a priori* certain Newtonian claims is to steer neatly between the radical scepticism of Hume and the absurdly ambitious rationalism of Leibniz, Descartes, *et al.*, 'the pretensions of dogmatic metaphysics'. Thus it is no accident that the general topics of the three Analogies, substance, causality, and 'reciprocity', are near cousins of the Newtonian concepts of matter, force, and reaction, nor that Kant forces a Newtonian conservation principle into the first Analogy. Indeed the corresponding sections of the *Prolegomena* are very much an extended *a priori* defence of Newtonian physics. But at the same time we cannot overlook the many references in the first *Critique* to the necessary conditions of a possible experience, and little effort is required to see the Transcendental Deduction, the Analogies, and the Refutation of Idealism as parts of a single continuous argument.

But there is another consideration. As I pointed out in Chapter 1, Kant would argue that the necessary conditions of a possible experience are precisely the basic presuppositions of Euclidean geometry, simple arithmetic and Newtonian physics. The question, What are the necessary conditions of a possible experience?, and the question, How are synthetic *a priori* judgements possible?, cannot be separated. Experience must be of a world that obeys the theorems of arithmetic, is Euclidean and Newtonian. For reasons which Körner and others have given, Kant is clearly wrong because Euclidean geometry and Newtonian physics have been superseded. I would argue that the approach I have adopted to the *Critique of Pure ·Reason* minimizes the effects of Kant's scientific and mathematical parochialism. None of the conclusions I defended in section 5 have much to do with Euclid and Newton, and the attempt to discover the necessary conditions of a possible experience is in no way vitiated by the development of non-Euclidean geometries or the theory of relativity or quantum physics. But we should remember that Kant's account of the necessary conditions of a possible experience will consist of an account of what he took to be the basic presuppositions of Euclidean geometry, simple arithmetic, and Newtonian physics.

8. APPENDIX: THE SCHEMATISM

Finally we must return to a passage which has mystified many commentators and which I left with indecent haste in section 1, the passage entitled 'The Schematism of the Pure Concepts of Understanding' (A137–47/ B176–87). I have called this section an 'appendix' because the Schematism serves no useful purpose and can in my opinion be ignored without loss. But Kant clearly thinks that it is extremely important, and for that reason alone we should attempt to understand it. It is addressed to a supposed problem about our using the categories, the pure concepts of understanding. The Metaphysical Deduction derived a list of twelve categories from twelve concepts of logic by reflecting on the connection between the general work of understanding in inference and its specific work in making judgements about objects. The Transcendental Deduction showed that those categories or pure concepts must be applied in experience if experience is to be possible. Then, says Kant, a problem arises. 'In all subsumptions of an object under a concept the representation of the object must be *homogeneous* with the concept; in other words, the concept must contain something which is represented in the object that is to be subsumed under it ... Thus the empirical concept of a *plate* is homogeneous with the pure geometrical concept of a *circle*. The roundness which is thought in the latter can be intuited in the former. But pure concepts of understanding being quite heterogeneous from empirical intuitions, and indeed from all sensible intuitions, can never be met with in any intuition. For no one will say that a category, such as that of causality, can be intuited through sense and is itself contained in appearance. How, then, is the *subsumption* of intuitions under pure concepts, the *application* of a category to appearances, possible?' (A137–8/ B176–7). Kant's solution is to introduce a 'transcendental schema', namely time, to mediate between category and object. It mediates because it is in one respect 'intellectual' and therefore similar to the categories, and in another 'sensible', similar to the intuitions to be conceptualized. By schematizing the categories, by giving them a temporal interpretation, we obtain concepts that can find application in experience (A138–9/

B177–8). Thus the unschematized categories of the Metaphysical Deduction are transformed into the schematized categories or *principles* of the Analytic of Principles.

Even assuming that the observations reported in the previous paragraph make sense, and making allowance for Kant's characteristic confusion between intuitions and objects of intuition, it is difficult to see how he could have spent so much time and effort on an entirely spurious problem. The opening comment, that object and concept must have something in common, is simply false. Or rather the only features common to objects and concepts are extremely trivial or extremely general, such as being a topic for philosophical discussion. The important and interesting features cannot be shared. For example tomatoes are red, round, soft, and wet inside, but the concept of a tomato has no colour or shape or texture, neither an inside nor an outside. Tomatoes are at certain places at certain times, but the concept of a tomato is not. Yet no problem arises from such obvious differences. We are not tempted to doubt the applicability of the concept of a tomato on the ground that we cannot find a similarity between concept and tomato. It is perhaps significant that Kant's own illustrative example is irrelevant. No one doubts that the concept of a plate is similar to the concept of a circle, for they are both concepts. What has to be shown is that problems arise about concepts and objects, not concepts and concepts.

So if we interpret the opening sentences literally the passage on Schematism is addressed to a spurious problem. However, there may be a genuine problem buried there somewhere and several philosophers have attempted to excavate it. I shall consider three suggestions in turn. The first is by W. H. Walsh, who argues in his paper on 'Schematism' that a problem arises because the categories are extremely general, extremely abstract concepts. Indeed they are so general, so abstract, that it is impossible to use them. For example contrast the category of causality with the empirical concept of blue. We can always explain the meaning of 'blue' in terms of sense-experience or possible sense-experience, can define it ostensively. More crudely, we can see the blueness of a thing. In contrast we cannot explain the meaning of 'cause' in terms of sense-experience or possible sense-experience, cannot define it ostensively. We cannot even crudely see the causality of a causal transaction. We can see the lighted match and we can see the exploding gas but we cannot see the causal relation between them. Thus Kant's complaint is that the categories must be made more specific, more concrete, if they are to find application. A schematized category will be a pure 'sensible concept' (A146/B186), a more specific version of the highly general unschematized category: 'the schema of a category is, in effect, a second concept which

has the advantage over the concept in its abstract form of being directly
cashable in terms of sense-experiences, and can yet be plausibly thought
to provide an interpretation of it' (op. cit., p. 102; Wolff, p. 82).

I think Walsh has probably interpreted Kant very well. He does justice
for example to Kant's observation that 'no-one will say that a category,
such as that of causality, can be intuited through sense' (A137/B176).
But I am not convinced that Kant so interpreted has located and solved
a genuine problem. One reason is that his schematized categories are just
as abstract as the unschematized. For example the schema of cause 'consists ... in the succession of the manifold, in so far as that succession
is subject to a rule' (A144/B183). It is very difficult to see how that can
be unpacked in terms of possible sense-experience, for we cannot point
to succession-according-to-a-rule. We cannot even crudely see succession-according-to-a-rule. I can see the match and I can see the exploding
gas but I cannot see the succession-according-to-a-rule. A second reason
is that Kant so interpreted will be condemned to a perfect orgy of schematism. For there are many non-categorial concepts that are abstract and
have no direct or simple empirical interpretation, that are not concepts
of the sensible features of things, features identifiable directly through
the senses. The concepts of courage, nationalism, even force and mass,
all have application in experience but are not concepts of the sensible
features of things. We cannot point to courage or nationalism or force
or mass in the way in which we can point to red or blue or yellow. Indeed
even our crucially Kantian temporal concepts have no direct or simple
empirical interpretation. We cannot even crudely see the passing of time,
point to five minutes; 'time cannot by itself be perceived' (B225). I can
see the moving sun or the sand shifting through the hour-glass, but I
cannot literally see the passing of time. If Walsh's interpretation of the
Schematism is correct then Kant is committed to schematizing any concept that cannot be defined ostensively, cashed directly in terms of actual
or possible sense-experience.

So although Walsh's interpretation may be a correct interpretation,
it does not absolve Kant from the charge that he is attacking a spurious
problem. Let us therefore move to a second attempt to infuse the Schematism with philosophical significance. Kant frequently mentions the role
of imagination in schematism. 'The schema is ... always a product of
imagination' (A140/B179). Schemata are not themselves images, but are
rather rules for producing images appropriate to a given concept. 'This
representation of a universal procedure of imagination in providing an
image for a concept, I entitle the schema of this concept' (A140/B179-
80). And 'image' refers not merely to mental images but also to drawings,
blueprints, models, exploded diagrams of this or that. Thus the schema

of the concept of a plate is a rule for producing images of plates, drawings of plates, designers' sketches of plates, even plasticine models of plates. We seem to need a threefold distinction between the concept of a plate, the schema of the concept of a plate, and images or drawings or models of plates.

One point of historical interest emerges. Kant makes the very Berkeleian point that concepts cannot consist in certain peculiar images, for images are particular things with specific properties: 'it is schemata, not images of objects, which underlie our pure sensible concepts. No image could ever be adequate to the concept of a triangle in general. It would never attain that universality of the concept which renders it valid of all triangles, whether right-angled, obtuse-angled, or acute-angled' (A140–1/B180). But that echo of Berkeley's *Principles* (Introduction, §XIII) seems to exhaust the interest of the proposal that schemata are rules for generating images appropriate to a given concept. For first, as Kant himself admits, the proposal can only apply to non-categorial concepts. There are no images appropriate to the categories: 'the schema of a *pure* concept of understanding can never be brought into any image whatsoever' (A142/B181). No amount of reflection on the connection between schemata and images will explain why Kant wants to schematize the categories. Second, even if we ignore the irrelevance of the proposal to the schematism of the categories, what difference would there be between concepts and schemata? It is no good saying that schemata are rules for generating images appropriate to a given concept, for that is also true of concepts. That is, part of what is meant by saying that I have the concept of a plate is that I can summon up an image of a plate, or make a rough sketch of a plate, or make a plasticine model of a plate. Of course concepts are not merely rules for generating images, and in the case of the categories are not even that, but that is part of what concepts are. Schemata serve no useful function not already served by concepts.

Since the second proposal fails to dispel our confusion let us turn to a third. I borrow it from §37 of Bennett's *Kant's Analytic*, where it is presented more as a reconstruction than as an interpretation of Kant. Bennett suggests that the 'modest point' that Kant might usefully have pursued is that the categories are so abstract that they can only be used *in conjunction* with other, more concrete, concepts. We cannot point to substance and causality in the way in which we can point to colour or feel texture. We can only use the concepts of substance and causality if substances and causes have other, ostensively definable, properties such as colour, shape, texture. For example we can only use the concepts of cause and effect if we can also use the concepts of a lighted match, of white paper turning black and burning. By identifying the colour, shape, texture, smell, of match and paper we are able to use the much more abstract concept of cause (the application of the lighted match) and effect (the combustion of the paper). So whereas Walsh interprets the Schematism as a move from more general to more specific versions of the categories, Bennett reconstructs it as a demand for certain concrete concepts to be used in conjunction with the categories. Walsh's Kant wants to give the categories a 'sensible' interpretation, whereas Bennett's Kant would insist that the categories can only be used if we also use other, more concrete or more 'sensible', concepts. Each Kant would justify his enterprise by arguing that the categories are extremely abstract, extremely general, and cannot be applied to experience as they stand. Bennett's Kant would of course write a shorter *Critique of Pure Reason*, since he would not have to distinguish between unschematized categories and schematized principles. He would only need a distinction between the categories and the sensible concepts used in conjunction with the categories.

I have briefly examined three interpretations of the Schematism. According to the first, the categories are so general that they cannot find application in experience. They must be given an empirical interpretation and transformed into pure sensible concepts which can be cashed directly in terms of actual or possible sense-experiences. According to the second, schemata are rules for generating images appropriate to given concepts. According to the third, the categories are so general that they cannot be applied without the simultaneous application of other, more concrete, sensible or ostensive, concepts. I would tentatively draw three conclusions. First, the first few sentences of the passage on Schematism present us with a wholly spurious problem. If the purpose of the Schematism is to make categories homogeneous with intuitions it is entirely foolish. Second, of the three interpretations we have discussed, Walsh's interpretation does most justice to Kant's remarks in the rest of the Schematism. But it is still difficult to see any philosophical point in the enterprise so interpreted. And third, the third 'interpretation' is not a proper interpretation of Kant but does make an important philosophical point, namely that the very abstract categories could not be applied unless other, more concrete or ostensive, concepts were also applied. I cannot apply the concept of causality unless I also have concepts of shape, colour, texture, etc. In Kantian language, we could not apply the *a priori* categories unless we had a large repertoire of *a posteriori* or empirical concepts. But that is perhaps a rather meagre reward for Kant's efforts in the Schematism. It is interesting and perhaps significant that although he continues to claim in the *Prolegomena* that the Schematism is 'indispensable, though very dry' (p. 315), he finds it possible to dismiss it in one cryptic sentence.

PART IV

TRANSCENDENTAL DIALECTIC

5

THE PARALOGISMS

1. THE DIALECTIC

Despite the superficial arrangement of material in the *Critique*, which makes the Analytic and Dialectic two parts of 'Transcendental Logic', there is very much a great divide between Aesthetic and Analytic on the one hand, and Dialectic on the other. As we saw in Chapter 1, the main inspiration of the whole work is a search for the general conditions of knowledge. Disturbed by apparent contradictions in rationalist metaphysics and impressed by certain Humean arguments, Kant hopes to draw a clear distinction between disciplines that can yield *a priori* knowledge, such as mathematics and physics, and those that cannot, such as much of traditional metaphysics. The distinction is to rest firmly on the general claim that knowledge requires both concepts and intuitions, that we can only make coherent knowledge-claims about objects that we can in principle perceive. More specifically we can only make coherent knowledge-claims about objects that are spatial and temporal, because space and time are the pure forms of human intuition. Thus mathematics and physics yield genuine knowledge, for they are concerned with objects of a possible experience. And the Aesthetic and the Analytic examine and defend a number of corresponding synthetic *a priori* knowledge-claims or judgements, such as the claim that objects of experience must be spatial, temporal, causal, substantial. Those synthetic *a priori* judgements express both the essential features of our knowledge of objects and the limits of such knowledge. To stray beyond the limits, to talk about objects that are non-spatial and non-temporal, objects that cannot yield possible intuitions, is to talk straightforward nonsense.

The Dialectic is devoted to an attack on those who attempt to infringe the limits, who talk such nonsense. Whereas the Aesthetic and Analytic are concerned with the genuine sciences of mathematics and physics, the Dialectic is concerned with the pseudo-science of speculative metaphysics. Kant hopes to expose the mistakes of such philosophers as Descartes and Leibniz, who attempted to make claims about objects that are not and could not be objects of a possible experience, objects such as the soul, the limits of the universe, and God. He wants to expose 'the *logic of illusion*' (A293/B349), which consists in using concepts to which no intuitions correspond, concepts of objects that are not spatial and temporal.

In his introductory remarks on the Dialectic Kant invokes a faculty model to explain why many metaphysicians are tempted to make vacuous claims, why their investigations take them beyond the limits of a possible experience. They are misled, it seems, by the faculty of reason. Kant's general remarks on the faculty of reason, and on the relation between reason and understanding, are puzzling and inconsistent. I do not want to clutter my own exposition with a lengthy discussion of the relation between reason and understanding, but will assume without further argument that Kant wants to distinguish between two *uses* of a single intellectual faculty rather than between two *faculties*. Apart from its very general use in logic in making inferences, in drawing conclusions from premisses, the intellectual faculty can be used to make judgements about objects. Sometimes it will be used to manipulate actual or possible intuitions and sometimes it will be used in the absence of actual or possible intuitions. The intellectual work involved in classifying and organizing intuitions or perceptions is called the work of understanding and is discussed in the Analytic, while the intellectual work of speculative metaphysicians in the absence of any intuitions is called the work of reason and is discussed in the Dialectic. There is fundamentally one intellectual faculty at work, used properly in the first case and improperly in the second.

According to Kant the impropriety is due to reason's having two remarkable features. First, reason is dissatisfied with partial or incomplete explanations of any event or state of affairs. It urges us constantly to search for complete or comprehensive or exhaustive explanations. Kant regards explanation as the examination of a series of interconnected 'conditions', and it is the natural urge of reason to search for more and more basic conditions until it reaches a condition that is 'unconditioned' and does not depend on any further condition: 'Reason concerns itself exclusively with absolute totality in the employment of the concepts of the understanding, and endeavours to carry the synthetic unity, which is thought in the category, up to the completely unconditioned' (A326/ B383). Kant seems to mean that reason urges us to seek more fundamental explanations of things. Suppose for example that we are trying to explain the evolution of human beings. We might first draw attention to certain primitive reptilian ancestors and to certain climatic conditions, and show how certain mutations were maintained. Reason will then demand an explanation of the climatic conditions or of the appearance of primitive reptiles, and will not be satisfied until we reach some explanatory condition or state of affairs that is basic or 'unconditioned', that explains everything else but is not itself in need of further explanation, such as a massive explosion in the universe or a week of intense divine creative effort. Or suppose we want to explain a specific event such as an explosion in a

factory. We might trace the explosion to a piece of crumbling and therefore volatile gelignite. Reason would then force us to some more general
explanation of the volatility of gelignite under certain circumstances, such
as an account of its chemical composition. And reason will continue to
pester us until we reach an explanatory condition that is basic or 'unconditioned', that supports the entire explanation but is not itself in need
of further explanation, such as an account of the structure of the atom
or of the wrath of a malign god.

So the first main feature of reason is that it searches constantly for
complete or exhaustive or comprehensive explanations. But that admirable first feature is irretrievably connected with a second which is much
less admirable. In seeking complete and comprehensive explanations
reason is inevitably led beyond the limits of a possible experience, because
it uses concepts to which no intuitions correspond. The concepts, known
henceforth as the ideas of pure reason, 'are not arbitrarily invented; they
are imposed by the very nature of reason itself, and therefore stand in
necessary relation to the whole employment of understanding' (A327/
B384). But unlike the concepts of understanding examined in the Analytic, they take us beyond the limits of experience, for there are no corresponding intuitions: 'they are transcendent and overstep the limits of
all experience; no object adequate to the transcendental idea can ever
be found within experience' (ibid.).

Thus reason plays a very paradoxical role in the search for genuine
knowledge already undertaken in the Aesthetic and Analytic. On the one
hand it seems positively to encourage and assist the search, for its concepts, its ideas, encourage us to seek a more and more complete account
of the world, to push our knowledge further and further. In that sense the
ideas are *transcendental* because they positively assist the acquisition of *a
priori* knowledge of objects. But on the other hand they thereby inevitably
lead us outside the limits set by the Aesthetic and Analytic. They are concepts to which no intuitions correspond, concepts of objects that are not
objects of a possible experience. In that sense the concepts or ideas of
pure reason are *transcendent* because they transcend the limits of experience. Thus the very paradoxical view defended in the Dialectic is that
reason may have an important function in enlarging our knowledge but
its deliverances do not themselves count as knowledge.

Kant's faculty model leads him to divide the Dialectic into three main
sections. Reason is very generally the faculty of inference, the faculty
which draws conclusions from premises, and according to Kant there
are three kinds of conclusion in a syllogism, namely categorical, hypothetical, and disjunctive (A323/B379, A340/B397–8). Hence there
will be three kinds of illusion of reason, three kinds of search for

an unconditioned, three kinds of 'pseudo-rational inference'. The first section, on the Paralogisms, is concerned with rational psychology, with the idea of a Cartesian soul; the second, on the Antinomies, is concerned with rational cosmology, with various ideas of the extent and structure of the universe; and the third, on the Ideal of Pure Reason, is concerned with rational theology, with the idea of God.

I would not attempt to justify the very neat division of metaphysical mistakes into three and it does not prove very illuminating when we turn to the arguments themselves. It is certainly true that Kant maintains throughout that reason leads us beyond the limits of experience, that the concepts of a soul, of the extent of the universe, of God, etc., are concepts to which no intuitions correspond. But the introductory examination of the faculty of reason and the talk of pseudo-rational inferences, of the search for the absolutely unconditioned, give a very misleading impression of the content of the Dialectic. Kant uses a number of other arguments against his opponents, arguments which are often much more prominent than his views about reason's inevitable search for the unconditioned. For example a very prominent theme in the Paralogisms and the Ideal of Pure Reason is that the rationalist arguments in question are simply bad arguments, that their conclusions do not follow from their premises. Another theme, prominent in the Paralogisms and the Antinomies, is transcendental idealism. One serious weakness of speculative metaphysics, it seems, is the lack of a distinction between noumena and phenomena, and a failure to reduce objects of experience to collections of perceptions. Finally there is a very clear and rather frantic attempt in the Dialectic to leave room for ethics and some form of theology. So far the results of the Aesthetic and Analytic bode ill for ethics and theology, because they seem to restrict our knowledge to knowledge of spatio-temporal objects. Taken literally they seem to demolish ethics and theology unless we embrace some form of ethical naturalism and a rather crude natural theology, that is, unless we reduce ethical and theological terms to the properties of people and other spatio-temporal objects. In the Dialectic Kant tries to mitigate the force of that threat, and tries to leave room for the unattractive ethics and heretical theology he was to develop in later works.

2. THE ATTACK ON DESCARTES

Thus the official programme of the Dialectic is to expose the illusions generated by reason's inevitable search for the absolutely unconditioned, and its equally inevitable use of concepts to which no intuitions correspond. But the official programme is sometimes rather muted and occasionally drowned by other arguments and more pressing concerns. This

complexity of purpose is very evident in the first main section of the Dialectic, which is devoted to the Paralogisms of Pure Reason and which
attacks the 'rational psychology' founded upon Descartes's account of
persons. Although Descartes is only occasionally mentioned by name
there can be no doubt that Kant has him very firmly in mind. There
are many references to the Cartesian 'cogito, ergo sum', and extensive
discussion of the significance of the proposition 'I think'.

Kant is mainly interested in two Cartesian doctrines. One, slightly less
important for our purposes, is Descartes's causal theory of perception,
the view that there are external things which cause certain perceptions
in us and whose existence is inferred from our perceptions. I shall return
to that doctrine in section 3. The second and more important doctrine
is that people are essentially non-physical minds or souls attached to
physical bodies. In an attempt to find firm foundations of knowledge
Descartes tried to doubt everything he believed, but found that there
was something peculiarly self-defeating in trying to doubt his own existence as a thinking thing. Whatever mental state he was in, it seemed to
follow that he existed. Indeed in the very process of doubting he seemed
to guarantee his existence as a thinking thing: 'this proposition: I am,
I exist, is necessarily true each time that I pronounce it, or that I mentally
conceive it' (Meditation II: Haldane and Ross I, p. 150). The crucial
fact about Descartes, according to Descartes, was that he was a thinking
substance (where 'thinking' referred to more or less any mental state).
But thinking substances, he argued, are different kinds of thing from
physical substances, for thinking substances are necessarily non-
extended, non-spatial, whereas physical substances are necessarily
extended. Hence a person, or more properly a Descartes, is a non-physical
substance. People may possess bodies, be attached to bodies, but are
themselves non-physical things: 'although ... I possess a body with
which I am very intimately conjoined, yet because, on the one side, I
have a clear and distinct idea of myself inasmuch as I am only a thinking
and unextended thing, and as, on the other, I possess a distinct idea of
body, inasmuch as it is only an extended and unthinking thing, it is certain
that this I [that is to say, my soul by which I am what I am], is entirely
and absolutely distinct from my body, and can exist without it' (Meditation VI; Haldane and Ross I, p. 190). I cannot doubt my own existence
as a thinking substance; thinking substances are logically quite different
from physical substances; so I exist as a non-physical substance.

Kant's attack on those views was the only passage apart from the
Transcendental Deduction and the Preface to be completely re-written
for the second edition. The second-edition version is crisper and less
repetitive. There are four Paralogisms corresponding to the four groups

of categories and they are supposed to prove that the soul is a substance, that it is simple, that it is unitary, and that it is in relation to possible objects in space (A344/B402). Those four conclusions are in turn supposed to prove that the soul is immaterial, that it is incorruptible, that it is a person, and that it is the principle of life in animals (A345/B403). A paralogism is simply a fallacious syllogism, and the fallacy to be examined consists in an improper use of certain concepts, most notably the concept of substance. According to the argument of the first Analogy the concept of substance has and must have a perfectly legitimate use in our perception of spatial and temporal objects. But Kant wants to show that the concept of substance is very seriously misused in the Cartesian psychology that generates the four Paralogisms, the first four examples of 'the logic of illusion'.

Kant works solemnly through each Paralogism in turn, slowly in the first edition and quickly in the second. But the fourfold division of the argument is just as contrived as the fourfold division of groups of categories on which it rests, and bears little relation to the Cartesian target. The main consequence for Kant's discussion is excessive repetition. So I propose to discuss the Paralogisms as a whole, first discussing Kant's specific objections to Descartes, and then his general diagnosis of the Cartesian disease. Kant seems to offer three main specific criticisms of Descartes' account of people. First, he objects that the Cartesian soul is not and could not be an object of a possible experience. Knowledge requires both concepts and intuitions, so the claim that there are Cartesian souls is not a proper knowledge-claim. We may think we have a clear concept of a simple, unitary, non-physical substance but there can be no corresponding intuitions or perceptions of such a thing. 'I do not know an object merely in that I think, but only in so far as I determine a given intuition with respect to the unity of consciousness in which all thought consists. Consequently, I do not know myself through being conscious of myself as thinking . . .' (B406). I can have knowledge of my experiences, my states of consciousness, but I cannot have knowledge of any soul-substance in which they supposedly inhere.

The second, very ingenious, criticism is only mentioned in the main text but is explained at greater length in a footnote with the aid of a characteristically Newtonian analogy. The criticism is that, even if we concede that the concept of a Cartesian soul-substance makes sense, it is difficult to see what philosophical work it could do. For example it is difficult to see how it could be made to yield any criteria of personal identity. Descartes offers no guarantee that each person consists of one and only one soul. Since he gives us no way of identifying or observing the souls, we have no way of telling whether each man has one soul or ten or twenty or a thousand. The very most that can be counted is the number of experiences, states of consciousness, and the difficulties of counting non-physical soul-substances are insuperable. Indeed there might be as many souls as experiences. 'An elastic ball which impinges on another similar ball in a straight line communicates to the latter its whole motion . . . If, then, in analogy with such bodies, we postulate substances such that the one communicates to the other representations together with the consciousness of them, we can conceive a whole series of substances of which the first transmits its state together with its consciousness to the second, the second its own state with that of the preceding substance to the third, and this in turn the states of all the preceding substances together with its own consciousness and with their consciousness to another' (A363a). In other words, if by 'same person' we mean 'same substance', we are reduced to admitting that there might be as many people as experiences. The notion of a person or a soul-substance would do no more philosophical work than the notion of an experience. Indeed, since such soul-substances are unobservable they would do very much less philosophical work than experiences, which are observable. The obvious moral to be drawn is that our criteria of personal identity should not be tied to the notion of a Cartesian substance.

The third criticism of Descartes is not particularly prominent in the Paralogisms and I include it only because it illustrates how much Kant was still influenced by rationalist assumptions. Descartes claimed that non-physical minds (or people) and physical bodies are of logically different kinds, but that there are causal relations between body and mind. For example our perceptions are the result of certain transactions in the physical world, and our sensations are dependent on the state of our bodies. But he found the causal relation in question extremely difficult to understand. Indeed some of his sensations, such as those of hunger and thirst, seemed so irreducibly physical that he was tempted to talk of the 'apparent intermingling' of non-physical mind and physical body, and to suggest that the picture of non-physical mind in physical body is very misleading: 'I am not only lodged in my body as a pilot in a vessel, but . . . I am very closely united to it, and so to speak so intermingled with it that I seem to compose with it one whole' (Meditation VI; Haldane and Ross I, p. 192). Sadly his anti-Cartesian scruples do not seem to have lasted for very long.

Kant discusses the causal relation between Cartesian mind and body at A384 ff. The most interesting sentences are at A386: 'as soon as we hypostatise outer appearances and come to regard them not as representations but *as things existing by themselves outside us, with the same quality as that with which they exist in us* . . . then the efficient causes outside us assume a character which is irreconcilable with their effects in us. For the cause relates only to outer sense, the effect to inner sense—senses which, although combined in one subject, are extremely unlike each other.' The idealist overtones I shall leave until later. The point of immediate interest is the suggestion that causes and effects must be very similar kinds of thing, that minds and bodies cannot interact in the Cartesian fashion because non-physical effects are so very different from physical causes. Kant's recollection of David Hume obviously did not convince him that anything can cause anything, that we cannot rule out any specific causal laws *a priori*. He will not allow that physical causes might in principle have the most bizarre non-physical effects. Thus although Kant is very much concerned in the Paralogisms to demolish Descartes's account of people, his views on causality are very near to Descartes's. For example they are close to Descartes's view 'that there must at least be as much reality in the efficient and total cause as in its effect. For, pray, whence can the effect derive its reality, if not from its cause? And in what way can this cause communicate this reality to it, unless it possessed it in itself?' (Meditation III; Haldane and Ross I, p. 162). Kant appears to believe that physical bodies do not have the right sort of 'reality' required to influence non-physical minds.

Those then are Kant's three principal criticisms of Descartes's account of people, namely that the Cartesian mind or person or soul is not an object of a possible experience, that we cannot guarantee a perfect correlation between the number of souls and the number of people, and that the causal relation between non-physical mind and physical body is unintelligible. But Kant is not merely concerned to point out specific weaknesses in 'rational psychology'. He wants to give a general diagnosis of the Cartesian disease, to expose the fundamental mistake which misled Descartes from the very beginning. The fundamental mistake, it appears, is that Descartes completely misunderstood the nature of self-consciousness. He thoroughly misunderstood the meaning and significance of 'I think'. Kant takes up again the main threads of the discussion of self-consciousness or apperception which he left in the Transcendental Deduction. Among several points yielded by that discussion two are very prominent in the discussion of the Paralogisms. The first is that my experiences or representations are necessarily mine in the sense that I am necessarily aware of my experiences as mine. It makes sense for me to ask whether a certain sensation is painful or not, or how long it lasts, or whether it has subsided, but not whether it is mine. I cannot work out whose sensations I am having, for if I have them I am aware that I am having them. Secondly, the unity of self-consciousness, which may be expressed in such sentences as 'I think' or 'cogito', is not literally consciousness of a self. It is a formal rather than a material unity. It does not consist in any special or recurrent property of experiences, in any material similarities between them, but rather in the entirely formal fact that my experiences are mine, Fred's are Fred's, Tom's are Tom's, etc. In a more elaborate but familiar Kantian phrase, the proposition 'I think' does not express the bringing of an intuition of the self under a concept. It is not a synthetic knowledge-claim at all, but an elliptical reminder of the analytic truth that I am aware of my experiences as mine.

Thus Descartes's fundamental mistake consists in mistaking a unity of self-consciousness for knowledge of a self, in mistaking a purely formal unity for a material unity, in mistaking the purely analytic principle of the unity of self-consciousness for a synthetic knowledge-claim about a soul-substance. He has committed the cardinal error of claiming knowledge from concepts alone, in the absence of any appropriate intuitions or perceptions. We may think we have the concept of a simple, unitary, substantial mind or soul or person, and may attempt to express it in Cartesian terms, but we can never succeed in making a coherent knowledge-claim because there are no appropriate intuitions or perceptions of such a self. 'The unity of consciousness ... is here mistaken for an intuition of the subject as object, and the category of substance is then applied to it. But this unity is only unity in *thought*, by which alone no object is given, and to which, therefore, the category of substance, which always presupposes a given *intuition*, cannot be applied. Consequently, this subject cannot be known' (B421–2).

Despite its superficial simplicity and directness, Kant's diagnosis of Descartes's fundamental mistake is obscure in many respects. He may be right to insist that 'I think' and 'I exist' could not count as synthetic knowledge-claims expressing knowledge of a Cartesian self, that they are at best elliptical reminders of the purely analytic truth that I am aware of my experiences as mine. But surely there is more to be said. Surely there is a sense in which 'I think' and 'I exist' can and do express synthetic knowledge-claims. After all, it is only contingent that Descartes exists or that he thinks, and it is perfectly in order for him to remind us that he does contingently exist or contingently think, by using those sentences or some French or Latin equivalent. Sadly nothing but confusion results from Kant's attempt to deal with that very obvious point and to explain in more detail the function of 'I think' or 'I exist': 'the representation "I" ... [is] ... a mere thought'; 'in attaching "I" to our thoughts we designate the subject of inherence only transcendentally, without noting in it any quality whatsoever'; ' "I think" expresses an indeterminate empirical intuition' (A364, A355, B422a).

Moreover Kant's diagnosis of Descartes's mistake is very oblique, and it would be difficult to find anything in Descartes's work that could count as mistaking 'the unity in the synthesis of thoughts as a perceived unity in the subject of these thoughts' (A402). Descartes does not talk of perceiving himself at all. As I indicated earlier, his route in the *Meditations* to the traditionally Cartesian position is briefly as follows: I can doubt everything except that I am a thinking thing, that I feel, want, hope, doubt, understand, etc.; hence thinking is essential to me; but thinking substances are different kinds of thing from physical substances, for thinking substances are non-extended; therefore I am essentially a non-physical thinking substance. The crucial mistake in the argument is not a confusion between the unity of consciousness and the consciousness of a unitary thing. It is rather the dangerously ambiguous assumption that thinking things and physical things are different kinds of thing. The most Descartes shows is that psychological and physical *properties* are different kinds of *property*, because physical properties are logically connected with the property of having extension, while psychological properties are not. But it does not follow that one thing, such as a person, cannot have both kinds of property, that things that are essentially thinking things cannot also be physical things. One might as well argue that roses cannot have a smell, as follows: roses are essentially coloured; colour properties are different kinds of property from smell properties; i.e. coloured things and smelling things are different kinds of thing; therefore roses are coloured, non-smelling things.

However, although Kant's account of self-consciousness is obscure in some respects and although his attack on Descartes is rather oblique, he can always return to the first of the three specific criticisms I mentioned, for it is sufficent to undermine 'rational psychology'. That is, however Descartes actually reaches his conclusion the conclusion is vacuous, because it purports to make a claim about an object that is not an object of a possible experience. Knowledge requires both concepts and intuitions, and nothing could count as perceiving or intuiting a Cartesian soul. Perhaps that is a small reward for Kant's labour in the chapter on the Paralogisms. After all, Hume had already made very much the same point more eloquently in the *Treatise* (I, IV, VI; Selby-Bigge, p. 252): 'when I enter most intimately into what I call *myself*, I always stumble on some particular perception or other, of heat or cold, light or shade, love or hatred, pain or pleasure. I never can catch *myself* at any time without a perception, and never can observe any thing but the perception.' But no one, least of all Kant, should be embarrassed by having to borrow from Hume.

3. TRANSCENDENTAL IDEALISM

We must now complicate matters a little. I have so far over-simplified Kant's rejection of Cartesian psychology by ignoring his prominent and extended defence of transcendental idealism in the discussion of the fourth Paralogism, particularly in the first edition. The discussion is concentrated on Descartes's causal theory of perception, the theory that our perceptions are the effects of certain events in the external world, and that we infer the existence and properties of external objects from the properties of our perceptions: 'from the fact that I am sensible of different sorts of colours, sounds, scents, tastes, heat, hardness, etc., I very easily conclude that there are in the bodies from which all these diverse sense-perceptions proceed certain variations which answer to them' (Meditation VI; Haldane and Ross I, p. 192). Kant argues that the inference from perceived effects to unperceivable causes is extremely shaky. There is in principle no way of checking the inference since further observation will only yield further perceptions and will not bring us any nearer the objects themselves. Thus we can have no guarantee that our perceptions are caused by external objects, nor that they give an accurate impression of the objects' properties: 'all our sensuous representations are inadequate to establish their reality' (A369).

If that were Kant's only objection to Descartes's theory of perception we could dismiss it as grossly unfair. It is true that causal theories of perception have serious weaknesses, including the weakness to which Kant is pointing. But the Transcendental Deduction offers a possible escape route for the causal theorist. The main conclusion of the Transcendental Deduction is that we must regard some at least of our experiences as perceptions of external things: if I am to have any experience at all, I must be able to use a distinction between myself and external things. Now there is nothing to prevent a causal theorist from embracing that conclusion and going on to argue that in distinguishing between myself and the external world I must regard my perceptions as the effects of certain objective events. Indeed if Kant could be persuaded to abandon his transcendental idealism, which serves no useful philosophical purpose in the first *Critique*, that would be the most natural position for him to adopt. That is, it would be natural for him to argue that experience is possible only if the perceiver can distinguish between himself and external things, only if he regards some of his experiences as perceptions of external things, and to argue that the relation between external objects and perceptions is that of cause and effect. Kant's anti-sceptical argument in the Transcendental Deduction can be enlisted just as much in support of Descartes as in support of Kant.

But Kant has an idealist axe to grind, namely 'the doctrine that appearances are to be regarded as being, one and all, representations only' (A369). Thus in his discussion of the fourth Paralogism there are clear traces of the distinction between things in themselves or noumena and things as they appear or phenomena. Things in themselves or noumena are non-spatial and non-temporal, and are not therefore possible objects of human experience. Things as they appear or phenomena are the ordinary spatial and temporal objects of our experience. More important for our immediate purposes and more frequently expressed is the Berkeleian claim that strictly objects of experience or phenomena or things as they appear are and are only collections of perceptions: 'External objects ... are mere appearances, and are therefore nothing but a species of my representations, the objects of which are something only through these representations. Apart from them they are nothing' (A370). So it seems that Descartes's mistake consists not so much in making a shaky inference from perceptions to objects, but in neglecting to notice that objects are collections of perceptions. His doubts about the existence of objects would have disappeared had he only observed that simple fact. 'In order to arrive at the reality of outer objects I have just as little need to resort to inference as I have in regard to the reality of the object of my inner sense, that is, in regard to the reality of my thoughts. For in both cases alike the objects are nothing but representations, the immediate perception (consciousness) of which is at the same time a sufficient proof of their reality' (A371).

The defence of transcendental idealism is regrettable for a number of reasons, some of which I shall examine in Chapter 9. But it is particularly unfortunate in the discussion of the Paralogisms, for it undermines the attack on Descartes very severely. Kant's principal weapon against Descartes's account of people can be turned against himself with equally devastating results. Kant claims that Descartes attempted to talk about objects that are not and could not be objects of experience. Knowledge requires both an appropriate concept and an appropriate intuition, but there can be no intuitions of a non-physical soul-substance, no perceptions of a Cartesian person. But one of the main doctrines of transcendental idealism, slightly muted in the discussion of the Paralogisms but certainly present, is that there are two kinds of object, noumena or things in themselves and phenomena or things as they appear. In particular, Kant would argue, we must distinguish between people in themselves and people as they appear. Indeed Kant's ethical plans commit him to talking of noumenal people, of selves in themselves. But it is just as absurd for him to talk of a self in itself as it is for Descartes to talk of a non-physical soul-substance, for neither is an object of a possible experience.

Selves in themselves are non-spatial and non-temporal and are not proper objects of human knowledge. Kant has no right to talk cheerfully of 'the being which thinks in us' (A401) or of 'the *being itself*' (B429), even in an attempt to expose the Cartesian illusions to which the being is subject. Neither Descartes's soul nor Kant's self in itself is a possible object of experience, a possible object of human knowledge.

4. KANT'S CONCEPT OF A PERSON

Having examined the attack on Descartes and having reminded ourselves of the earlier discussion of self-consciousness or apperception in the Transcendental Deduction, we might try to formulate the main outlines of Kant's account of persons. Sadly his views are wholly destructive and only give us reasons for rejecting certain traditional views. For example he has given us reasons for rejecting any Humean way of tying the bundle of perceptions. Hume concentrates too much on the contingent observable features of our experience, and 'No fixed and abiding self can present itself in this flux of inner appearances' (A107). Indeed to postulate a bundle of experiences and then to search for a way of tying the bundle is to turn things upside down. There could be no such bundle unless the owner of the bundle regarded some of his experiences as perceptions of the external world. That is, we can only begin to articulate a notion of personal identity in terms of the perceiver's distinguishing between himself and the external world. Moreover we should resist any Cartesian account of people. The proposition 'I think' or 'I exist' is not a genuine synthetic knowledge-claim, does not express a literal awareness of a Cartesian self distinct from various experiences. The transcendental unity of apperception is a formal, not a material, unity.

Many of those observations are unexceptionable. People are not Cartesian people and they are not Humean people. But Kant does not really offer us a positive alternative and many of his remarks are very unsatisfying. For example one hesitates about accepting his claim that 'I think' is not a genuine synthetic knowledge-claim, that it merely expresses the analytic unity of self-consciousness, the analytic truth that I am aware of my experiences as mine. Surely there is a clear sense in which 'I think' can be used to make synthetic knowledge-claims in which 'I' clearly refers to something or someone. It may not refer to a Cartesian soul-substance, nor to a Humean bundle of perceptions, but it seems to refer to something. After all, our Kantian perceiver is supposed to distinguish between himself and external things, and must therefore be able to refer to himself. In the light of Kant's later ethical writings it is reasonable to suppose that he wanted personal pronouns to refer fundamentally to noumena, to selves in themselves. But if we refuse to take that unfortunate step it is difficult to extract any plausible account of the reference of personal pronouns from Kant's remarks, either in his discussion of the Paralogisms or elsewhere. He has ruled out several accounts but does not rule in any clear alternative.

It is very striking that Kant pays no attention to the very obvious physical criteria of personal identity. He does not even discuss them in an effort to display their limitations. The omission is unfortunate because if we could treat people as material objects we could give our personal pronouns a reference. The distinction between myself and the external world would be a distinction between one physical object, occupying a special position in my experience, and other physical objects. But as far as I can tell, Kant only refers to men as material objects twice in the chapter on the Paralogisms. The first reference is at A342/B400, where Kant refers to the human body as an object of outer sense. But that is only part of an exposition of Cartesian psychology, and so it is in a sense Descartes who is speaking, not Kant. The second reference is at A359–60, and contains more than a hint of the main thesis of Chapter III of Strawson's *Individuals*: '. . . we should have to fall back on the common expression that men think, that is, that the very same being which, as outer appearance, is extended, is (in itself) internally a subject, and is not composite, but is simple and thinks.' But the passage is only part of a brief discussion of some of the consequences of abandoning transcendental idealism, of assuming that matter is 'a thing in itself', and Kant soon moves on to something else 'without committing ourselves in regard to such hypotheses' (A360). And that, as Austin might have said, is an infernal shame. As an account of persons the section on the Paralogisms is disappointing. It offers a comparatively neat criticism of Descartes but makes no real advance on the remarks on the necessary unity of apperception in the Transcendental Deduction.

One final comment on Kant's discussion of the Paralogisms. In section I I said that Kant's strategy in the Dialectic is quite complicated, that although he wants in general to expose the natural urges and pretensions of speculative reason, he uses many different weapons in his attack. In the discussion of the Paralogisms his original programme is only fulfilled in part. Kant returns constantly to the theme that reason leads us inevitably beyond the limits of experience, that it manipulates concepts to which no intuitions correspond, such as the concept of a non-physical soul-substance. But the other half of the programme, the claim that reason inevitably seeks more basic and remote explanatory conditions right up to the 'absolutely unconditioned', is not woven into the discussion with any confidence. And there are several claims that are much more prominent than any claim about the function of speculative reason.

There are the doctrines of transcendental idealism. There is the simple and devastating claim that the rationalist arguments under discussion are bad arguments, formally invalid syllogisms or 'paralogisms'. Most important of all are two doctrines or hints of two doctrines that become increasingly obtrusive as the Dialectic proceeds. First, there is a hint of an attempt to allow some useful role to the ideas of pure reason, which are the topic of the Dialectic and which are incapable of yielding knowledge. For example, as we have seen, the concept of a soul-substance yields no knowledge because it is a concept to which no intuitions or perceptions correspond. But according to Kant it may none the less play an important epistemological role. Although the concept of a soul-substance is not 'constitutive', cannot help to constitute our knowledge of any object, it may have an important 'regulative' or methodological function: 'It sets impassable limits to speculative reason in this field, and thus keeps us, on the one hand, from throwing ourselves into the arms of a soulless materialism, or, on the other hand, from losing ourselves in a spiritualism which must be quite unfounded so long as we remain in this present life' (B421). And that first doctrine, that the concept of a Cartesian soul may have 'regulative utility', is connected with a second which is vitally important in Kant's later works, namely that the belief in a soul is of great ethical significance. It is 'necessary for practical employment' and is crucial for our 'consciousness of the moral law' (A365, B431). For the moment I will refrain from explaining those doctrines and will merely record them for future consideration.

6

THE ANTINOMIES

I. INTRODUCTION

If Kant is to be believed, the Antinomies played a special part in the composition of the *Critique of Pure Reason*, for his general dissatisfaction with rationalist metaphysics concentrated on a number of apparent contradictions, apparent 'conflicts of reason with itself'. 'It was not the investigation of the existence of God, immortality, and so on, but rather the antinomy of pure reason—"the world has a beginning; it has no beginning, and so on", right up to the 4th: "There is freedom in man, versus there is no freedom, only the necessity of nature"—that is what first aroused me from my dogmatic slumber and drove me to the critique of reason itself, in order to resolve the scandal of ostensible contradiction of reason with itself' (Letter to Garve, 21 Sept. 1798; Zweig, p. 252). Presumably Kant's advanced age explains the confusion between the third and fourth antinomies, and the implication that it was not after all the recollection of David Hume that first aroused Kant from his dogmatic slumber.

It is in the discussion of the Antinomies that Kant does justice to his general claim that reason investigates various series of conditions in an attempt to discover the absolutely unconditioned. It is here that he examines our systematic scientific investigation of the world, our attempts to discover complete series of explanatory conditions. We explain any given event or state of affairs A in terms of its relation to another, B, and that in turn in terms of its relation to another, C, until the series is 'complete', until reason's explanatory desires are satisfied. When all the searches have been completed, reason will have explained everything there is to explain, 'the absolute *totality* of all existing things' (A419/B447). Since there are four groups of categories there will be four kinds of absolute totality and four kinds of search for a complete series of explanatory conditions, right up to the absolutely unconditioned. First, there is the search for a complete series of objects in space and a complete series of events in time. Second, there is the search for a complete series of parts of matter. That is, we begin with some material object and attempt to divide and sub-divide it into its constituent parts, so obtaining a series of tinier and tinier parts of matter. The third and fourth searches are for two kinds of complete causal series, consisting of a given event, the cause of that event, the cause of that cause, and so on. In every case reason urges us to pursue the search until the series of conditions is completed, until we reach the absolutely unconditioned, the explanatory condition that requires no further explanation. But it seems that in every case reason runs into difficulties, and despite arguing rigorously from apparently true premises it arrives in every case at an antinomy, an apparent contradiction. The general explanation of reason's embarrassment is not hard to find, because reason is attempting to use categories completely divorced from experience. It is using concepts to which in this context no intuitions correspond.

I confess I find the grandiose language of 'conditions' rather obscure but Kant's discussion of the four Antinomies is more manageable. In each case he states a 'thesis', with supporting argument, and an 'antithesis', with supporting argument. By conjoining thesis and antithesis we obtain an antinomy, an apparent contradiction. The four theses are supposed to represent 'the side of *dogmatism*' (A466/B494) or the natural views of a rationalist, and the four antitheses are supposed to represent 'the side of *empiricism*' (A468/B496) or the natural views of an empiricist. But that distinction is grossly misleading, and S. J. Al-Azm has argued convincingly in his *Origins of Kant's Arguments in the Antinomies* that the theses represent the views of Newton's disciple, Clarke, and the antitheses the views of Leibniz. A much more important distinction than that between theses and antitheses, however, is the distinction between the first two Antinomies, the Mathematical, and the last two, the Dynamical. The labels themselves are unhelpful, for the first two Antinomies are not very closely connected with mathematics, nor the last two with dynamics. But there are vitally important differences between them. In particular Kant's solution of the Mathematical Antinomies is quite different from his solution of the Dynamical. I shall therefore examine the two sets of Antinomies separately and shall be concerned to summarize the arguments, examine Kant's solution, and discuss some of the general philosophical issues arising.

2. THE MATHEMATICAL ANTINOMIES: ARGUMENTS

The Mathematical Antinomies are to be found at A426/B454 ff. In the original editions each thesis and antithesis were printed on opposite pages, and Kemp-Smith retains roughly the same arrangement in his translation, printing thesis and antithesis on opposite sides of the same page. The arguments in outline are as follows.

First Antinomy: Thesis: The world has a beginning in time and limits in space.
Antithesis: The world has no beginning in time and no limits in space.
Argument for Thesis: (a) Suppose the world has no beginning in time. Then up to the present moment an infinite series of events has been completed. But an infinite series cannot be completed through successive synthesis, so the world has a beginning in time.

(b) Suppose the world has no limits in space. The thought of such a totality involves successively synthesizing every part of it. But it is impossible successively to synthesize every part of an infinite world, for the synthesis could never be completed. So the world has limits in space.

Argument for Antithesis: (a) Suppose the world has a beginning in time. Then the beginning is preceded by empty time. But in empty time there is nothing to give rise to a beginning of the world. So the world has no beginning in time.

(b) Suppose the world is finite in space. Then it is bounded by and related to empty space. But it is absurd to talk of being related to empty space, for that is to be related to nothing. So the world is infinite in space.

Second Antinomy: Thesis: Nothing exists save what is simple or composed of simples.
Antithesis: There is nothing simple.
Argument for Thesis: Suppose composite substances are made up of composite parts, not simple parts. If all composition be removed in thought, no composite part remains; but *ex hypothesi* no simple part remains; so nothing remains. Therefore composite substances are made up of simple parts.

(This argument is very muddy, but the gist seems to be this. Suppose composite things are made of composite parts. We could theoretically carry on dividing and sub-dividing the parts until we reach parts which cannot be divided any further. Those parts are not composite, but from our original premiss they are not simple either. That is, they are nothing at all! So our original premiss is false, and everything is simple or composed of simples.)

Argument for Antithesis: (a) Suppose that composite things are made up of simple parts. Each simple part occupies a space. But since space is composite, anything occupying a space is composite. Therefore composite things are not made up of simple parts.

(b) An absolutely simple object is not an object of a possible experience, and so no simple object can be found in the world.

Whatever else might be said about these Antinomies they do deal with recognizable problems which both in eighteenth-century and modern philosophy occupy an important area where science and philosophy overlap. The first Antinomy is concerned with the extent of the world in space and time. Notice that that is not quite the same thing as the extent of space and time. It is tempting to follow Kant's remarks at A411/B438 f. and to talk loosely of the extent of space and time, but there is a good reason for treating the first Antinomy as a discussion of the extent of the *world* in space and time. Kant would be aware of a special

objection to Leibniz's relational account of space and time, an objection
which is reflected in the curious references to 'empty space' and 'empty
time' in the proof of the antithesis of the first Antinomy. The objection
fails but must none the less be recorded to show that the first Antinomy
is concerned with the extent of the world in space and time rather than
with the extent of space and time. As stated in Clarke's fifth letter to
Leibniz the objection is only concerned with space, but it can be applied
to both space and time as follows. According to Leibniz space and time
are fundamentally sets of relations between objects, and in the absence
of objects there can be no space and no time. But, the objection goes
on, it follows that for Leibniz space and time must be wholly occupied,
because every point of space and every instant of time must be defined
by a spatial and temporal object. That is, Leibniz must abhor a vacuum.
More specifically Leibniz cannot make sense of the quite reasonable
suggestion that there might be empty space beyond the furthest objects
and empty time before the earliest events.

I would not wish to defend the objection. As I have already explained,
I merely mention it in order to make the important point that the first
Antinomy is concerned in general with a problem about the extent of
the world in space and time, and more specifically with the notion of
empty space beyond the furthest objects and empty time before the
earliest events. The second Antinomy must also be set within its historical
context. In the eighteenth century there appeared to be a contradiction
between a prevailing atomistic physics and the mathematics of infinitesimals. Atomism demanded that matter has simple parts, that it can only
be divided and sub-divided to a finite degree, that we eventually reach
parts of objects or 'atoms' which cannot be further divided. The mathematics of infinitesimals, however, demanded that space is infinitely divisible, that space has no basic, irreducible, simple parts. A contradiction
seems to arise if we introduce an assumption which Kant seems to have
held, namely that any object or part of an object that occupies a space
occupies the whole of that space (cf. A435/B463). Atomistic physics
demanded that an object is only finitely divisible, but the mathematics
of infinitesimals demanded that the space wholly occupied by the object
is infinitely divisible. Surely, it was said, if the space wholly occupied
by the object is infinitely divisible, the object itself must be infinitely
divisible.

Modern developments in physics should make us dissatisfied with
Kant's formulation of the Mathematical Antinomies. For example in the
first Antinomy he makes the naïve assumption that a world finite in space
is a world that quite literally has limits or bounds. He assumes that if
the world were finite in space we would literally be able to travel to the

edge or the limits of the world. The *reductio* proof of the second half of the antithesis of the first Antinomy begins by assuming that 'the world in space is finite and limited' (A427/B455), and throughout the discussion of the Mathematical Antinomies Kant takes 'finite' to mean 'limited', and 'infinite' to mean 'unlimited'. But Einstein's account of space distinguishes clearly between the finite and the limited or bounded. According to Einstein space is finite in the sense that anything travelling in a straight line in any direction from a given point will eventually arrive back at that point; but space is unbounded or unlimited. Nothing would count as literally finding the edge or the bounds or the limits of space.

Similarly modern atomic physics should make us dissatisfied with Kant's formulation of the second Antinomy. He asks us to decide whether matter is finitely or infinitely divisible, whether it has simple or composite parts, but the question is now seen to be rather misleading. We could, somewhat dangerously, regard elementary particles as simple or basic or irreducible things but it does not follow that my table is composed of billions of particles in the sense of 'composed' that Kant has in mind. He discusses divisibility rather as though dividing an object into its parts is like dividing a wall into the constituent bricks. He talks as though the problem is to discover whether there are any very tiny bricks of which things are composed, as though the 'parts' of an object are like the object but very much smaller. He is not alone in talking in that way. Locke explicitly claims that the 'minute and insensible parts' of matter will have the same primary qualities, including extension and impenetrability, as the larger objects of which they are the parts: 'take a grain of wheat, divide it into two parts, each part has still solidity, extension, figure, and mobility; divide it again, and it retains still the same qualities; and so divide it on, till the parts become insensible: they must retain still each of them all those qualities' (*Essay*, II, viii, 9). But the relation between particles and tables is not like that between bricks and wall. Although my table consists of billions of interacting particles, it is quite wrong to think of particles as like the table but very much smaller. For example, although they have the primary qualities of position and velocity, they do not have extension, 'figure', or impenetrability. Notoriously we cannot attribute to them the sort of causal properties that we cheerfully attribute to tables and grains of wheat. And we allow that there is a sense in which a particle can occupy a space without occupying the whole of the space. Indeed it is still quite common for popularizers of science to explain that material objects consist of billions of interacting particles separated by vast spaces, rather like the stitches of an extremely loosely knitted sweater. However dangerous their metaphors may be, we can see what they mean. There is a sense in which we can argue both that my table occupies the whole of the space it occupies, and that the 'parts' or elementary particles of the table do not occupy the whole of the spaces they occupy.

So our appreciation of the Mathematical Antinomies is a little dulled by advances in modern physics. We think we can distinguish between a finite space and a bounded or limited space, we are not so ready to assume that the 'parts' of an object are very much like the object but smaller, nor that something that occupies a space must occupy the whole of it. But I think it also has to be admitted that even by eighteenth-century standards the arguments for thesis and antithesis in each case are really not very good, and belie Kant's bland assurance that in 'stating these conflicting arguments I have not sought to elaborate sophisms' (A430/ B458). For example the argument for the first half of the thesis of the first Antinomy rests on the superficially attractive but fundamentally silly assumption that an infinite series can never be completed. The argument goes like this: assume an infinite series of events has elapsed up to a given moment; that means the series is completed by the given moment; but an infinite series cannot be completed; so an infinite series of events cannot have elapsed; the series must have been finite, must have had a beginning. Kant overlooks the obvious objection that an infinite series need only be open *at one end*. It cannot be completed at both ends but can certainly be completed at one end. Thus even though the series of events has been completed at this end by the present moment, it may well stretch infinitely remotely in the other direction, into the past.

To take another example, consider Kant's use of the notion of empty space in the antithesis of the first Antinomy. The argument goes as follows. Suppose the world is finite in space; it is then bounded by and related to empty space; but that is absurd, for to be related to empty space is to be related to nothing; so the world is infinite in space. This attempted *reductio* of the assumption that the world is finite in space tries to have things both ways. It begins by allowing empty space to figure as a term in a relation, by allowing us to talk of empty space beyond the world. But Kant then claims precisely the contrary, that being related to empty space is being related to nothing at all, that empty space is not after all a possible term in a relation. He has certainly arrived at a contradiction, and he must certainly resolve it by rejecting at least one of the following three claims: (i) that the world is finite in space, (ii) that empty space can figure as a term in a relation, and (iii) that empty space cannot so figure. He gives us no reason for rushing to reject the first rather than the second or the third.

3. MATHEMATICAL ANTINOMIES: SOLUTION

It would be tedious to examine the arguments of the Mathematical Antinomies in any further detail and would divert us from our main purpose,
which is to examine Kant's solution. For the solution is of enormous importance in the general strategy of the first *Critique*. So although the Antinomies are derived by feeble argument from dubious premisses, I propose for the purposes of argument to assume otherwise. I shall assume
that Kant has presented us with two genuine antinomies, two genuine
'conflicts of reason with itself', and examine his proposed solution, which
is to be found initially in sections 6 and 7 of the Antinomy of Pure Reason
(A490–507/B518–535).

We have assumed that in each case we have a pair of incompatible
propositions derived by rigorous argument from apparently true
premisses. Kant does not attempt to impugn the logic of the arguments
but suggests that they all rest on a false premiss, namely that the world
exists as a whole, as an absolute totality, in itself, independent of any
perceptions. It is that assumption that has generated the contradiction
between thesis and antithesis in each case. If we make the implicit
assumption explicit, the Mathematical Antinomies are in outline as
follows.

First Antinomy: If the world exists as a whole, independent of our
perceptions, then it is both finite in space and time (thesis) and infinite
in space and time (antithesis).

Second Antinomy: If the world exists as a whole, independent of our
perceptions, then it is both finitely divisible (thesis) and infinitely
divisible (antithesis).

The consequent in each case is false, because it is self-contradictory.
As a matter of logic the antecedent is therefore false, for
$((p{\rightarrow}q)\,\&\sim q){\rightarrow}\sim p$. That is, the world does not exist as a whole, as an
absolute totality, as a thing in itself, independent of our perceptions.

In other words the Mathematical Antinomies have provided an in-
direct proof of transcendental idealism. The Antinomies arise from a misguided realism, an attempt to make claims about a world quite independent of our perceptions, about the 'world as a whole', as Kant opaquely
expresses it. The attempt inevitably issues in contradiction, demonstrat-
ing that the world does not exist as a whole, that it only exists as a collection of actual and possible perceptions. 'If the world is a whole existing
in itself, it is either finite or infinite. But both alternatives are false (as
shown in the proofs of the antithesis and thesis respectively). It is therefore also false that the world (the sum of all appearances) is a whole existing in itself. From this it then follows that appearances in general are

nothing outside our representations—which is just what is meant by their transcendental ideality' (A506–7/B534–5). So the solution of the Mathematical Antinomies is very straightforward. The theses and anti-theses purport to make claims about the world as a whole independent of our perceptions. But there is no such thing, and thesis and antithesis are in each case false. Since there is no such world, it is neither finite nor infinite in space and time, neither finitely nor infinitely divisible. 'Since the world does not exist in itself, independently of the regressive series of my representations, it exists *in itself* neither as an *infinite* whole nor as a *finite* whole' (A505/B533).

It might be said that Kant is absurdly simple-minded in assuming that anything we say about a non-existent thing is false, for it would probably be more sensible to say that such claims were vacuous rather than false. But I do not wish to press the point. The most interesting part of Kant's solution of the Mathematical Antinomies is the crucial suggestion that they indirectly confirm transcendental idealism. For the suggestion has important consequences for Kant's philosophy of science, consequences which are examined in the section beginning at A508/B536. Two con-sequences are of great importance. The first is that if we are to be con-sistent idealists we must stop talking about the world and its properties, and talk instead about our perceptions or observations and their proper-ties. We may only refer to the world or bits of the world if we regard the references as shorthand for more complicated references to actual and possible observations. For example we must be prepared to translate all references to the extent of the world in space and time or to the parts of objects into references to observations of things in space and time or observations of the parts of objects.

Thus the superficially realist search for more and more remote condi-tions becomes a search for more and more observations. I argued earlier that it is only in the discussion of the Antinomies that Kant uses the language of serial 'conditions' with any confidence. Although the Dialec-tic is heralded as an examination of reason's inevitable search for the un-conditioned, for the complete and exhaustive series of explanatory condi-tions of the world around us, only the Antinomies really fit the bill. The Mathematical Antinomies are expounded as though science consisted of a systematic examination of objects progressively more remote in space and time, or of progressively tinier parts of objects. The systematic ex-amination is supposed to yield a series of 'conditions' in each case, a series of objects progressively more remote in space and time, and a series of progressively tinier parts of objects. But the intrusion of idealism yields instead a series of *observations* in each case, a 'successive synthesis of representations' in the familiar Kantian phrase. Instead of the realist interest in the series of objects in space and time, or in the series of divided and sub-divided parts of objects, we have an idealist interest in the successive observations of objects in space and time, or in observations of the parts of objects. Instead of asking whether the world is finite or infinite in space and time, and whether objects are finitely or infinitely divisible, we must ask whether a given series of *observations* is finite or infinite. 'The question, therefore, is no longer how great this series of conditions may be in itself, whether it be finite or infinite, for it is nothing in itself; but how we are to carry out the empirical regress, and how far we should continue it' (A514/B542).

The second consequence of Kant's idealist solution of the Mathematical Antinomies concerns his distinction between regulative and constitutive uses of concepts. As we have seen, according to Kant we must avoid references to the world and its properties except as shorthand for the more correct references to observations and their properties. It seems that we should in turn realize that the concepts handled to such contradictory effect in the Mathematical Antinomies have no constitutive function at all, that they do not yield any genuine knowledge-claims about the world, because there are no appropriate intuitions of the world as a whole. For example 'the existence of the absolutely simple cannot be established by any experience or perception' (A437/B465). So the concepts in question, the concepts of extent and division, have at best a regulative use. Although they yield no knowledge of the world they have a methodological function in spurring us to further scientific work. We can never intelligibly claim to know that the world is finite or infinite in space and time, or that objects are finitely or infinitely divisible. But the ideas of reason constantly urge us to further observation of objects in space and time, observation of more and more microscopic bits of matter. 'The principle of reason is thus properly only a *rule*, prescribing a regress in the series of the conditions of given appearances, and forbidding it to bring the regress to a close by treating anything at which it may arrive as absolutely unconditioned' (A508-9/B536-7). The ideas of reason are, as it were, specific variations on the general instruction 'Extend your observations even further!'

There is one slight complication, for Kant distinguishes (A512/B540 f.) between an infinite series, one which has no last member, and an indefinite series, one whose last member is not specified. To embark on an *infinite* regress of observations is to embark on a series that has no last member, however far we extend it, whereas to embark on an *indefinite* regress of observations is to embark on a series whose last member is not specified. According to Kant it is appropriate to talk of an indefinite regress of observations when discussing the topic of the first Antinomy, but when we are discussing the topic of the second Antinomy it is appropriate to talk of an infinite regress of observations. The reason is that in the first case we begin with an observation of one object in space or one event, and then move to an observation of another object in space or another event. Crudely, we begin with only a small part of what is to be observed and do not know how much or how little remains to be observed. But in the second case we begin with everything to be observed and gradually concentrate on tinier and tinier parts of it. We begin with an observation of a complete object, then move to an observation of a part of it, and so on. So 'when the whole is given in empirical intuition, the regress in the series of its inner conditions proceeds *in infinitum*; but when a member only of the series is given, starting from which the regress has to proceed to absolute totality, the regress is only of indeterminate character (*in indefinitum*)' (A512/B540). Thus we might say that Kant's idealist solution of the Mathematical Antinomies yields two rules of method: 'Extend your observations of objects in space and time *in indefinitum*' and 'Extend your observations of the parts of things *in infinitum*'.

4. KANT'S PHILOSOPHY OF SCIENCE

So we are to substitute idealist expressions about observations for realist expressions about the world, and we are to remember that the various concepts of extent and division are at best regulative, not constitutive. They purport to yield claims about a world independent of our perceptions, but can only have a methodological function. To the distinction between constitutive and regulative uses of a concept I shall return at the end of the next chapter. Before leaving the Mathematical Antinomies, however, I want to develop two objections to Kant's philosophy of science. One is a general objection to his whole conception of scientific investigation, the other is a more specific objection to his idealist science, to the reduction of statements about objects to statements about sets of observations or perceptions or intuitions.

The first and general objection is that Kant's conception of science is extremely naïve. And the *naïveté* is obvious, whether we concentrate on the superficially realist remarks he makes in introducing the Mathematical Antinomies or on the idealist remarks he makes in solving them. One might think that there is nothing particularly ominous in his realist remarks about serial conditions, in his reference to a series of events or a series of objects in space or a series of progressively tinier parts of matter. But even there he talks as though the scientist is anxious successively to synthesize or successively to observe the members of each series. 'What reason prescribes is therefore an absolutely ... complete synthesis, whereby the appearance may be exhibited in accordance with the laws of understanding' (A416/B443). He unfolds the first Antinomy as though the scientist must first observe one object in space or one event, and must then move to a more remote object or event, then to another even more remote, and so on. If the 'regressive synthesis' of objects or events comes to an end, then the world is finite in space or time; if not, not. He expresses the second Antinomy as though the scientist observes a given object, then a part of the object, then a part of that part, and so on. If the successive observation of progressively tinier parts comes to an end, the object is finitely divisible; if not, not.

Kant lacks any appreciation of the importance of inductive techniques in enlarging our scientific knowledge. Only a very crude positivism could persuade a scientist solemnly to peruse successive events in an effort to discover the extent of the world in time, or successive objects in an effort to discover the extent of the world in space. He is much more likely to examine one region of time and space in some detail, and arrive inductively at a generalization about the temporal or spatial extent of the whole world. For example a careful examination of the properties of objects in our own universe, especially the properties of light and matter, has yielded answers to some of the questions asked in the first Antinomy. It has yielded the conclusion that there could be empty space, space that contains no matter; and it has yielded Einstein's conclusion that space is finite and of constant curvature. There was no need for Einstein to engage in a successive synthesis of all the parts of space, or all the objects of space, in order to arrive at his conclusion. Similarly consider the topic of the second Antinomy, the divisibility of matter. Kant insists in the proof of the antithesis that scientists could not know that objects are finitely divisible, because the simple parts of an object are not possible objects of experience: 'the existence of the absolutely simple cannot be established by any experience or perception' (A437/B465). A modern scientist would regard that remark as beside the point, and would not be at all distressed by the knowledge that the tiny 'parts' of objects cannot literally be perceived. He will develop an account of the 'parts' of things, their basic atomic structure, with the aid of comparatively few observations of macroscopic things such as cloud-chambers and electron microscopes, and a great deal of mathematics.

Hence my general objection to Kant's philosophy of science is that it is very naïve and leaves no room for important, notably modern, scientific activity. He is right to insist that answers to the questions discussed in the Mathematical Antinomies must be established or refuted in experience by direct observation of something or other. But he is wrong to insist that the scientist must 'successively synthesize' large numbers of observations, must attempt to observe every part of space, every event, every tiny part of matter. He realizes that such demands cannot be fulfilled, and draws the conclusion that the questions asked in the Antinomies are incoherent as they stand and must be replaced by less ambitious idealist analogues. I would draw a quite different conclusion, namely that the demands are ridiculous, that we can understand the scientific questions in roughly their original form, and that we can in principle answer them. But we must first cast off the shackles of a naïve Kantian science.

I said that Kant's general conception of science is naïve, whether we concentrate on the realist remarks he makes in introducing the Mathematical Antinomies or on the idealist remarks he makes in solving them. It might be argued that he has such a concept of science precisely because he is an idealist, that he allows his destination to influence the course of the argument from the start. Certainly if one wants to reduce statements about objects to statements about observations, it is natural (but not inevitable) to think of science as the successive synthesis of the parts of space, or of series of events, or of progressively tinier parts of matter. And even when he is on his best realist behaviour and is struggling to construct the first Antinomy, Kant uses the language of successive synthesis or successive observation of objects, rather than the language of successive objects. 'Now the infinity of a series consists in the fact that it can never be completed through successive synthesis' (A426/B454). 'In order ... to think, as a whole, the world which fills all spaces, the successive synthesis of the parts of an infinite world must be viewed as completed' (A428/B456).

Whether or not Kant's troubles can all be traced to the doctrines of transcendental idealism, there is certainly a very specific objection to his idealist reduction of statements about objects to statements about sets of observations. It is worth noting at the outset that the reduction flies in the face of our normal assumptions about the natural sciences. We assume that the scientist wants to describe the world as it is, independent of any perceivers, that science is a public activity designed to establish certain publicly verifiable claims, that scientific generalizations describe the properties and changes of objects rather than the properties and changes of our observations (unless of course the observations are themselves objects of further scientific investigation). By reducing the world to observations or perceptions Kant engages the scientist in an entirely different enterprise. The Kantian scientist confronts a world that is wholly perceiver-dependent. He and his scientific colleagues produce various private accounts of the world, various sets of observations, but they have no way of incorporating all the accounts into a common and publicly verifiable account. The generalizations that they make do not describe the properties and changes of the world but only describe the properties and changes of their observations of the world. The generalizations are not of the form 'Hydrogen is readily combustible in oxygen' but are rather of the form 'Hydrogen-like observations accompanied by oxygen-like observations tend to be followed by explosion-like observations.'

Kant might of course face such consequences with equanimity. But he lays himself open to the specific objection that he cannot give an adequate analysis of certain crucial mathematical and scientific notions. Consider the notion of infinity, which is in a sense the general topic of the Mathematical Antinomies, and concentrate on such expressions as 'a world infinite in space', 'a world infinite in time', 'an infinitely divisible object'. As long as we know what 'space', 'time', and 'divisible' mean, and as long as we are free of the burden of Kantian idealism, we can analyse the expressions very easily. One way, which has a deceptively Kantian air to it, is to think of various kinds of series, a series of objects in space, a series of events, a series of parts. For example we might think of the following spatial series. We take any given spatial object A; the next member of the series is another spatial object, B, which is outside A; the next member is another spatial object, C, which is outside B and further than B from A; the next member is another spatial object, D, which is outside C and further than C from A and B; and so on. We can then explain the notion of a world infinite in space very easily: the world is infinite in space if the series A, B, C, D ... etc. has no last member. We can similarly construct a temporal series. The first member is any given event, A, such as the battle of Hastings; the next member, B, will be an event immediately preceding A, such as William's arrival on the beach; the next, C, will be an event immediately preceding B; and so on. The world is infinite in time if the series A, B, C ... etc. has no last member. And finally consider the notion of infinite divisibility. We construct a series in which A is any given object, B is a part of A, C a part of B, D a part of C, and so on. The object A is infinitely divisible if the series A, B, C, etc., has no last member.

I would not pretend that my informal account of infinity is watertight. For example I would have to qualify my account of a finite spatial series to accommodate Einstein's view of space, for a series of objects in Einsteinian space technically would have no last member. But of course since Einsteinian space is finite the members of the series would reappear at regular intervals in the series, as we returned to our starting point. So I think my informal account of infinity could be tightened fairly easily and does give a fairly clear indication of what we mean by infinity. An infinite series is one that has no last member. Now the question at issue is whether Kant can give an account of infinity, hampered as he is by a crude idealist reduction of objects to observations. As I hinted in the previous paragraph, we should not be misled by the apparent similarity between my account of infinity in terms of various kinds of series and Kant's own constant references to various kinds of series. For I was constructing series of objects, of objective events, of objects and parts of objects. Kant would reject such construction on the ground that it involves talking about the world as a whole, about objects independent of our perceptions. The only series he is interested in are series of observations. He wants to reduce all object expressions to expressions referring to a successive synthesis of observations.

In the cases under consideration he is bound to fail. For example the nearest he can get to an analysis of 'a world infinite in space' or 'a world infinite in time' is 'infinite series of observations of spatial things' or 'infinite series of observations of events'. But as he so rightly points out in the argument for the thesis of the first Antinomy, the expression 'infinite series of observations' is nonsensical, because it is not clear that it is even in principle possible to synthesize an infinite number of observations. In short, since the expression 'a world infinite in space and time' makes sense in the way I explained, whereas the expression 'infinite series of observations' does not make sense, the Kantian reduction of 'a world infinite in space and time' to 'infinite series of observations of spatial objects and events' is misguided.

Of course Kant avoids the objection by refusing to allow us to talk of infinite series of observations in the discussion of the first Antinomy. He tells us we are to talk only of a successive synthesis of observations *in indefinitum*, of an indefinite series. He avoids any problem about infinity by writing it out of his philosophical dictionary. But he allows us to talk of a successive synthesis *in infinitum* in the discussion of divisibility, the topic of the second Antinomy. So I shall use the same objection again, this time with reference to the notion of infinite divisibility. According to Kant space is infinitely divisible. 'Every space intuited as within limits is such a whole, the parts of which, as obtained by decomposition, are always themselves spaces. Every limited space is therefore infinitely divisible' (A524/B552). Thus it is possible to talk of infinitely small spaces, of infinitely small parts of a space. I can perceive the space between my table and the wall, and talk perfectly intelligibly of its being infinitely divisible. But if we are to embrace Kant's particular brand of idealism we must be able to translate all expressions into the language of a successive synthesis of representations, of successive observations. Presumably the strict idealist analogue of 'infinitely divisible space' will be 'infinite series of perceptions of parts of a given space'. For example 'I perceive the space between table and wall' is equivalent to 'I have successively synthesized an infinite series of perceptions of the parts of the space between table and wall'. And that looks nonsensical to me. I would never succeed in perceiving any space if I had first to gather together an infinite number of perceptions of the parts of the space. I suppose it might be argued that Kant only has to allow that I must be able *in principle* to synthesize an infinite number of observations of the parts of a given space, that objects need only be reduced to possible observations, possible successive syntheses. But I confess I cannot make sense of successively synthesizing an infinite series of perceptions of the parts of a given space, even in principle, even *in possibile*. For such a synthesis would in principle take infinitely long, and again I would never succeed in perceiving any space, because the synthesis of the parts would take too long! In short, it is possible to perceive a given space and to think of it as infinitely divisible, but it is impossible to have an infinite series of perceptions of all the parts of a given space. Therefore 'infinitely divisible space' cannot be replaced by an expression such as 'infinite series of perceptions of all the parts of the space'. Indeed it would be difficult to attach any sense to such an expression.

In this section I have been concerned to make two main points. First, Kant's general view of science is very naïve. Both in his superficially realist formulation of the Mathematical Antinomies and in his idealist solution of them, he talks as though the scientist solemnly examines each member of the series in turn, successively synthesizes all the members of the series in an attempt to give a complete account of the world. Second, his idealist solution makes an even greater nonsense of science. He is forced to reduce all scientific terms to the restricted terms of transcendental idealism, to the language of successive observations. I have argued that at least one term, the notion of infinity, resists such treatment.

5. THE DYNAMICAL ANTINOMIES: ARGUMENTS

The Dynamical Antinomies are initially presented in precisely the same way as the Mathematical. Each consists of a pair of incompatible propositions derived by rigorous argument from apparently true premises. They are the inevitable result of reason's constant search for the absolutely unconditioned, for the most basic explanatory conditions of certain events or states of affairs. It is vital to resolve such scandalous contradictions and to expose the main illness of speculative metaphysics of which they are symptoms, namely the failure to confine speculation within the bounds of a possible experience. Each thesis is supposed to represent the interest of 'dogmatism' or rationalism, and each antithesis the interest of empiricism. The arguments in outline are as follows (A444/B472 ff.).

Third Antinomy: Thesis: There is both ordinary natural causality and free causality.

Antithesis: There is only ordinary natural causality.

Argument for Thesis: Suppose there is only ordinary natural causality. Then every event is caused by a preceding event, and that in turn by a preceding event, and so on. Thus there will never be a first beginning, never a complete series. But nothing takes place without a cause sufficiently determined *a priori.* So the claim that there is only ordinary natural causality is self-contradictory, and we must assume a first, absolutely spontaneous cause, that of transcendental freedom.

Argument for Antithesis: Suppose there are both free and natural causes. There could be no laws governing the occurrence of a free cause, and so it would render all unity of experience impossible. A free cause is not an object of a possible experience, and is an empty thought-entity.

Fourth Antinomy: Thesis: There belongs to the world, either as its part or its cause, an absolutely necessary being.

Antithesis: No absolutely necessary being exists, either in the world or outside it.

Argument for Thesis: The world contains successive events, each of which occurs under certain preceding conditions. Anything so conditioned presupposes a complete series of conditions up to an absolutely unconditioned, something absolutely necessary. And if it is to generate the series of conditions, the absolutely necessary being must belong to the sensible world, either as the whole series of events or as part of the series.

Argument for Antithesis: (a) If we assume a necessary being exists in the world, there are two alternatives: either the beginning of the series of events is necessary, or the series of contingent events is necessary as a whole. But the first conflicts with the dynamical law of the determination of all appearances in time, and the second is self-contradictory, for a series cannot be necessary if no part of it is necessary.

(b) Suppose instead that an absolutely necessary being exists outside the world and generates the series. But to generate the series it must be in time and so part of the world, which would contradict the hypothesis. Therefore there is no absolutely necessary being, in the world or outside it.

The arguments are not very good, though the overall standard is higher than in the Mathematical Antinomies. For example the argument for the antithesis of the third Antinomy hinges on the salutary claim that a free cause is not an object of a possible experience. A free cause is non-spatial and non-temporal and is therefore an 'empty thought-entity' (A447/B475). But the other arguments are unimpressive. The argument for the thesis of the third Antinomy rests on a thinly disguised version of the principle of sufficient reason, in the form of the claim that we cannot give an adequate explanation of an event by locating its place in an infinite series of causes and effects. Every event requires 'a cause *sufficiently* determined *a priori*' (A446/B474) and an infinite series of causes and effects cannot yield the sufficient reason required. This is a further indication of Kant's failure to rid himself of rationalist prejudices about explanation. Without those prejudices he could not take the argument seriously. An equally bizarre argument is that for the thesis of the fourth Antinomy, where Kant makes the assumption that a conditioned event presupposes an unconditioned event, that a contingent event must be contingent on a necessary event or thing. Again the assumption seems to be a version of the principle of sufficient reason, for it insists that an account of the dependence of contingent events upon contingent events can never be adequately explanatory. Incidentally the argument for the thesis of the fourth Antinomy is not strictly addressed to the thesis. The argument reaches the conclusion that there must be an absolutely necessary being which is contained in the world, either as the whole world or as part of it. That is, the argument specifically excludes the possibility that there is an absolutely necessary being outside the world. Yet the thesis claims that there is an absolutely necessary being, either as part of the world or as the cause of the world, and Kant's remarks in the solution of the Antinomy specifically leave open the possibility that the necessary being is entirely outside the world.

As with the Mathematical Antinomies there is little profit in examining the argument in detail. We can only assume for exegetical purposes that Kant has generated *prima facie* Antinomies and press on to his solution. But first we should pause to wonder which philosophical problems are being discussed in the Dynamical Antinomies. Our wonder cannot be dispelled without anticipating a great deal of Kant's later work, for the third Antinomy introduces the ethical doctrines to be developed in the *Groundwork* and second *Critique*. At A532/B560 ff. we see the first sketchy outlines of Kant's moral psychology, of the basic distinction between noumenal reason and phenomenal sensibility, and of the claim that it is pure practical reason that yields our moral imperatives. In the third Antinomy Kant is particularly preoccupied with the traditional problem of free will. We might well think that in the Aesthetic and Analytic Kant undermines our notion of free will very considerably. For he argues that we can only have experience of objects that are spatial and temporal and obey causal laws; every event in the world accessible to human experience must have a complete causal explanation. But if every event has a complete causal explanation and is completely determined by antecedent events, and those in turn by antecedent events, it is difficult to see how we can continue to treat human beings as free agents. They are just as much objects of experience as tables and chairs, just as much governed by causal laws, and their behaviour is just as much determined by antecedent events. Just as we can in principle give complete causal explanations of the activities of inanimate things and are never tempted to treat them as free agents, so we can in principle give complete causal explanations of human behaviour and should not be tempted to treat humans as free agents.

So the topic for discussion in the third Antinomy is the problem of free will, but what of the fourth? What on earth, or indeed outside earth, is the 'absolutely necessary being'? There is some truth in the cynical view that the fourth Antinomy is only there to complete the quartet, that Kant felt obliged to manufacture an Antinomy to correspond to the last group of categories. But it is eventually made clear that the absolutely necessary being is more familiarly known as God. The fourth Antinomy helps to introduce the next part of the Dialectic, the Ideal of Pure Reason or Critique of All Theology, which I shall discuss in the next chapter.

6. THE DYNAMICAL ANTINOMIES: SOLUTION

But first we must attend to Kant's proposed solution of the Dynamical Antinomies. If he is to follow the example of the Mathematical Antinomies it is absolutely clear what he ought to say. He ought to insist that we have a genuine antinomy or contradiction in each case; that the arguments are rigorous, the explicit premisses are true, and that therefore there must be a false implicit premiss; that the implicit premiss in question is the assumption that the world exists as a whole, in itself, independent of our perceptions. That is, he ought to argue that the Dynamical Antinomies, like the Mathematical, furnish a further proof of transcendental idealism. The world does not exist in itself, independent of our perceptions, for objects are only collections of perceptions. We cannot ask whether or not the world contains a free cause or a necessary being. The theses and antitheses are all false, because they purport to make claims about the world in itself independent of our perceptions, and there is no such thing. We can only ask how our successive observations, our successive syntheses of representations, are to be continued, whether for example we should seek further observations of more remote causal conditions. The concepts of free causality and necessary being have no constitutive function, yield no genuine knowledge-claims, but they may have an important regulative function. For they may urge us to extend our observations further and further.

That is what Kant ought to say. Indeed his preliminary outline of the solution to the Antinomies promises precisely the same solution throughout. 'What we have here said of the first cosmological idea ... applies also to all the others' (A505/B533). But his later more detailed remarks offer an entirely different solution. Instead of using the Dynamical

Antinomies to prove one thesis of transcendental idealism he invokes another thesis of transcendental idealism in an attempt to show that the alleged Antinomies are not antinomies after all. He does not search for any hidden premiss responsible for the contradictions but insists that there were no contradictions. The third and fourth Antinomies were not antinomies.

First we must distinguish two theses of transcendental idealism. So far in this book I have tended to treat them together, but they are quite distinct and each could be maintained without the other. I shall borrow two very convenient labels from previous commentators and call the two theses 'noumenalism' and 'phenomenalism'. Noumenalism is the thesis that there are two kinds of object, things in themselves or noumena or the intelligible world, and things as they appear or phenomena or the sensible world. Noumena are non-spatial and non-temporal and are not objects of human experience, whereas phenomena are the ordinary spatio-temporal objects of experience. Phenomenalism is the thesis that objects of experience are and are only collections of representations, groups of perceptions. It is phenomenalism that featured prominently in the Mathematical Antinomies. Those Antinomies rested on the false premiss that the world exists in itself independent of our perceptions, and to deny the premiss is in effect to assert that the world is wholly perceiver-dependent, that objects are collections of perceptions.

In the Dynamical Antinomies it is noumenalism that does all the work and enables Kant to offer an entirely different solution from that of the Mathematical Antinomies. He argues that if we allow a distinction between noumena and phenomena, between intelligible objects and sensible objects, the thesis and antithesis in each case may after all be true, because they have a slightly different scope. The thesis refers to both intelligible and sensible worlds, the antithesis only to the sensible world. The thesis of the third Antinomy, that there are two kinds of causality, natural causality and free causality, is true when interpreted as a statement about both intelligible and sensible worlds. The antithesis, that there is only natural causality, is true when interpreted as a statement solely about the sensible world. Similarly the thesis of the fourth Antinomy, that there is a necessary being, and the antithesis, that there is not, both turn out to be true because the thesis refers to both intelligible and sensible worlds, the antithesis only to the sensible. Thus 'we arrive at a conclusion altogether different from any that was possible in the case of the mathematical antinomy. In it we were obliged to denounce both the opposed dialectical assertions as false. In the dynamical series, on the other hand, the completely conditioned ... is bound up with a condition which, while indeed empirically unconditioned, is also *non-sensible*

... and the propositions of reason, when thus given this more correct interpretation, may *both* alike be *true*' (A531–2/B559–60).

Thus *inter alia* Kant is confident that he can solve the problem of free will. I said that the arguments of the Aesthetic and Analytic seem seriously to undermine our notion of free will. If objects of experience must obey causal laws, if every event is completely determined by antecedent events and those in turn by antecedent events, then it would seem absurd to treat human beings as free agents responsible for their actions. For they are just as much objects and just as subject to causal generalizations as tables and chairs. Just as we are satisfied with complete causal explanations of the activities of tables and chairs and are not tempted to treat them as free agents, so we should be satisfied with complete causal explanations of human behaviour and should not treat humans as free agents. Kant would agree. If we are talking about objects of experience and if we are talking about phenomenal or natural causality, i.e. causal relations between phenomenal or spatio-temporal objects, then there is no room for freedom. Regarded as a phenomenal or spatio-temporal object man is no more a free agent than a table or a tree, and his behaviour can be completely explained in causal terms, in terms of the occurrence of antecedent causal conditions. Indeed Kant argues in the second *Critique* that it does not matter whether a man's behaviour is determined by 'internal' or psychological causes, or whether it is determined by 'external' causes. No phenomenal explanation of his behaviour, no explanation in terms of antecedent events, will yield an interesting notion of free will: 'it would at bottom be nothing better than the freedom of a turnspit, which, when once it is wound up, accomplishes its motions of itself' (op. cit., Ak., p. 97; Abbott, p. 191).

But, he insists, we can preserve a notion of free will if we step outside and beyond the world of phenomenal objects and phenomenal causality. That is, we must explore the possibility that the spatio-temporal series of phenomenal causes and effects rests on and is generated by non-spatial and non-temporal causes, noumenal or spontaneous or free causes. We must regard human beings not merely as phenomenal or sensible or spatio-temporal objects of experience, but also as noumenal or intelligible objects. In particular we should reflect that human beings have a faculty which is intelligible or noumenal, but which influences their behaviour profoundly, which generates effects in the phenomenal world. It is the faculty of pure practical reason, the faculty that freely or spontaneously generates our behaviour. 'That our reason has causality, or that we at least represent it to ourselves as having causality, is evident from the *imperatives* which in all matters of conduct we impose as rules upon our active powers. "*Ought*" expresses a kind of necessity and of connection with grounds which is found nowhere else in the whole of nature' (A547/ B575). So according to Kant the problem of free will is easily solved. We must concede to the determinist that regarded as phenomenal objects humans have no freedom, because they are just as much subject to rigid causal laws as any other phenomenal objects. But regarded as noumenal or intelligible objects with the noumenal faculty of pure practical reason, they are free agents and their behaviour can be explained only by referring to noumenal, non-spatial and non-temporal, causes, the noumenal prod- dings of practical reason. For example consider the case of 'a malicious lie by which a certain confusion has been caused in society' (A554–5/ B582–3). We could no doubt find a complete phenomenal explanation of the action 'in defective education, bad company, in part also in the viciousness of a natural disposition insensitive to shame, in levity and thoughtlessness', and so on. And as far as that explanation goes, it is absurd to treat the liar as a free agent, for his behaviour is completely determined by antecedent causal conditions. But as soon as we regard him as an intelligible or noumenal object, as a man with a faculty of pure practical reason which is capable in principle of influencing his pheno- menal behaviour, we can treat him as a free agent and can blame him. For 'we regard reason as a cause that irrespective of all the above- mentioned empirical conditions could have determined, and ought to have determined, the agent to act otherwise.'

Kant's analysis of that example is a grim foretaste of the severe moral views later expressed in Part II of the *Metaphysics of Morals*. And the general account of free will which underlies it has some very odd con- sequences. For example Kant eventually finds himself committed to the view that the only actions that we can properly call 'free' are those that are morally admirable. Free actions and morally admirable actions are those spontaneously generated by the noumenal faculty of reason, inde- pendent of the phenomenal faculty of sensibility. That is, it makes perfect sense to say that I freely kept a promise, or gave my money to charity, or helped others less fortunate than myself, but it makes no sense to say that I freely went for a drink or bought a gramophone record or painted my house my favourite colour. Such actions are prompted by phenomenal sensibility, are the phenomenal effects of phenomenal causes.

Even if we ignore the ethical trimmings Kant's account of free will in the third Antinomy is unsatisfactory. A determinist will see no more scope for freedom in noumenal causes than he sees in phenomenal causes. Of course, he might concede, there are differences between noumenal or 'free' causes and phenomenal causes. Noumenal causes are non-spatial, non-temporal, and spontaneous, and do not depend on any further causal conditions. Phenomenal causes are spatial and temporal and are entirely dependent on further antecedent causal conditions. Every phenomenal cause is the effect of a previous cause and the cause of a succeeding effect, but noumenal causes are not themselves caused. But the determinist will argue that such differences hardly yield a notion of free will. The most Kant has proved is that human behaviour is open to two kinds of causal explanation, phenomenal and noumenal. That is, he has proved that from one point of view an action has a complete phenomenal explanation, and that from another it has a complete noumenal explanation. But it does not follow that the agent is free in any interesting sense. Indeed it follows that he is not merely a victim of his phenomenal circumstances but is also a victim of his noumenal circumstances.

Before closing this section I would offer two general comments on Kant's solution of the Dynamical Antinomies. First, the inconsistency between the solution of the Mathematical and the solution of the Dynamical Antinomies is wholly indefensible. No doubt Kant appreciates that his general epistemological views in the first *Critique* may have a devastating effect on ethics and theology, but his rather tawdry attempt to mitigate it really will not do. He should either have used all the Antinomies to confirm the truth of phenomenalism or have invoked noumenalism to show that the appearance of contradiction is in every case deceptive. On the whole the first course is more attractive since at least it involves some serious attempt to prove some of the doctrines of transcendental idealism. Apart from the 'proof' offered in the solution of the Mathematical Antinomies it is very difficult to find any proper arguments for transcendental idealism in the first *Critique*. Kant refers constantly to the results of the Aesthetic but, as we saw in Chapter 2, those results prove on inspection to consist of assertion rather than argument.

The second and much more important comment is that Kant's invocation of noumenalism sits very awkwardly with one of the main doctrines of the Dialectic and indeed of the whole *Critique of Pure Reason*, that metaphysics must confine its attention to objects of a possible experience, that knowledge claims can only be made about objects that could in principle yield intuitions or perceptions. It is odd to castigate traditional rationalism for bringing news from nowhere and then blithely to introduce noumena, which are not and could not be objects of human experience. Admittedly Kant does hedge a little about the existence of noumena and tries to avoid producing a positive claim that there are such non-spatial and non-temporal things. He tends to take refuge in references to two points of view or two 'characters' or two 'aspects', rather than to two sets of objects. Instead of claiming that there are noumena he talks rather of allowing the *possibility* that there are. At one point he claims that he is trying to establish neither the reality nor the possibility of noumenal freedom. He is not trying to show that thesis and antithesis in the third Antinomy are true, but that they could be true. 'What we have alone been able to show ... is that this antinomy rests on a sheer illusion, and that causality through freedom is at least *not incompatible with* nature' (A558/B586). But methinks the gentleman doth protest too much. Kant cannot claim that freedom is compatible with nature unless he can understand what 'freedom', 'noumenon', and their cognates mean. For admirable Kantian reasons it is difficult to see how he can understand them, since they purport to refer to objects that are not objects of a possible experience. He is depriving rationalism of its preferred mysterious metaphysical objects while enjoying his own.

7. GENERAL REVIEW OF THE ANTINOMIES

So there is a very considerable contrast between Kant's treatment of the Mathematical Antinomies and his treatment of the Dynamical Antinomies. In one case he insists that there are genuine contradictions in need of resolution and uses them to prove the phenomenalist part of transcendental idealism. In the other he invokes the noumenalist part of transcendental idealism to prove to his own satisfaction that the appearance of antinomy is deceptive, that the 'opposed dialectical assertions' can be so interpreted as to live in decent and cheerful philosophical wedlock.

The contrast between the two sets of Antinomies necessarily affects their role in the general strategy of the Dialectic, the general attack on speculative metaphysics. According to Kant's official programme the mistakes of metaphysicians can be traced to two connected features of the faculty of reason, namely first, its constant search for more complete and exhaustive explanatory conditions, its attempt to follow every series of conditions back to an absolutely unconditioned, and second, its inevitable tendency thereby to stray beyond the limits of a possible experience. As I have observed already, that account of the faculty of reason makes much more sense in the discussion of the Antinomies than in the rest of the Dialectic. The Antinomies are expressed as problems about various kinds of series, a series of objects in space, a series of events, a series of tinier and tinier parts of matter, a series of causes and effects, a series of interdependent contingent conditions. We are able to translate the rather extravagant metaphor of reason's search for remoter conditions, since the 'conditions' are members of the various series under discussion. We can also understand Kant's claim that reason takes us outside the limits of experience, for according to him the four concepts that yield the four Antinomies are not constitutive. There can be no intuitions of the limits of the Universe, or of a simple object, or of a free cause, or of a necessary being. The concepts may have a regulative function but that is all.

I would continue to argue that the Mathematical Antinomies reflect the picture of reason's inevitable search for the absolutely unconditioned and its equally inevitable straying beyond the limits of experience. But the picture is grossly misleading when we turn to the Dynamical Antinomies. Superficially no doubt all is well. There is an obvious concern with serial conditions, with a series of causes and effects and with a series of interdependent contingent conditions. There is an apparent search for the absolutely unconditioned, for a free cause and for a necessary being. And reason strays beyond the limits of experience, since free causes and a necessary being are not objects of a possible experience. But the superficial impression is misleading in two connected respects. First, in his discussion of the Dynamical Antinomies Kant cannot afford to press the claim that reason leads us beyond the limits of experience, for his own noumenalism yields a decided surfeit of objects beyond the limits of experience. Although he tries to avoid committing himself to a belief in non-spatial and non-temporal objects his later ethical views force him to leave room for them. Second, we should treat with scepticism his claim that the ideas of free causality and of a necessary being are only regulative. The claim is made strongly and frequently (e.g. at A554/B582 and A561/B589) but the concession to the central doctrines of the Aesthetic and Analytic is misleading. It is quite clear from Kant's later work that the concept of free causality and all its ethical trimmings are not merely to be relegated to the status of methodological directives. They are eventually to be given a much more obviously constitutive role, a role which will raise serious doubts about Kant's sincerity in claiming that knowledge requires both intuitions and concepts. He will attempt to argue that they do not constitute 'theoretical' knowledge but that they do constitute knowledge 'from a practical point of view', that they do not help to constitute knowledge of tables and chairs but that they do constitute knowledge of right and wrong. Even the idea of God, the absolutely necessary being of the fourth Antinomy, is to be resurrected as a postulate of pure practical reason, a necessary feature of our awareness of right and wrong. I shall return to the ethical issues in Chapter 9, but we can turn now to the theological issues and examine in a new chapter the illusions of rational theology.

7

GOD

Like all intellectual disciplines philosophy has acquired its own legends, a set of popularly held assumptions about the great landmarks in the history of the subject. One legend is that Plato planned a Utopian state, another that Descartes revolutionized scientific method, and another that Hume demolished the belief in miracles. The legends are firmly grounded in historical fact, as every self-respecting legend should be, but they tend to give an excessively rosy and complimentary picture of what actually happened. Another legend of the same kind is that Kant disposed for ever of all the arguments for the existence of God. It is based on the historical fact that in Chapter III of the Dialectic we can find a number of incisive criticisms of philosophical theology, but it overlooks the equally important fact that the chapter also contains a great deal of obscurity and muddle. Kant gets the right answers on the whole, but sometimes for the wrong reasons.

His introductory comments at A567–91/B595–619 examine in more detail the rather obscure doctrines expressed in the thesis of the fourth Antinomy. It seems that it is an inevitable and natural urge of reason to attempt to explain the contingent events of experience by reference to an original event or being that is 'necessary'. Moreover it is apparently natural that reason should attribute a large number of striking and elevating properties to the absolutely necessary being, thereby transforming it into a genuine 'Ideal of Pure Reason': 'they supply reason with a standard which is indispensable to it, providing it, as they do, with a concept of that which is entirely complete in its kind, and thereby enabling it to estimate and to measure the degree and the defects of the incomplete' (A569–70/B597–8). That is, having located the absolutely necessary being, reason attributes to it properties of great moral and theological significance. We are encouraged to regard the absolutely necessary being as God, as omnipotent, omniscient, morally perfect, and so on.

Of course such theological illusions do not simply overtake us like measles or whooping cough, but are nourished by a number of tempting arguments, arguments for the existence of God. We could be forgiven for supposing that Kant is primarily interested in the first-cause argument, for that argument was invoked to support the thesis of the fourth Antinomy and is repeated on several occasions in the introductory comments on the Ideal of Pure Reason (especially at A584/B612). That is, we could be forgiven for supposing that Kant argues mainly that reason inevitably misleads us into explaining the occurrence of events in the world around us as the eventual effects of the creative and sustaining efforts of a divine first cause. But it soon becomes clear that Kant also has other theological arguments in view. With his usual bland and desperately misguided assurance he claims at A590/B618 that there are three and only three arguments for God's existence, namely the ontological, the cosmological (or first-cause argument), and physico-theological (or argument from design). That is certainly not a promising beginning, for many arguments for God's existence could not be interpreted very comfortably as versions of any of the three arguments he mentions. For example the argument from revelation and the argument from miracles do not belong to Kant's holy trinity.

2. THE ONTOLOGICAL ARGUMENT

So with our enthusiasm a trifle diminished let us pass to the first and most important of the three arguments, the ontological argument. The version Kant has in mind is Descartes's and is to be found in the fifth Meditation. It consists essentially in the claim that the notion of a non-existent God is self-contradictory. God by definition has every perfection, including existence: 'I clearly see that existence can no more be separated from the essence of God than can its having its three angles equal to two right angles be separated from the essence of a [rectilinear] triangle' (Haldane and Ross I, p. 181). God is perfect and existence is a perfection, so God exists.

Kant offers two main objections to the ontological argument in that form. One is an objection used later by G. E. Moore in 'Is Existence a Predicate?', namely that existence is not a property, that 'exists' is not a genuine predicate. Although grammatically 'exists' is a predicate, it functions differently from such predicates as 'is round', 'is red', 'is square', 'is divine', 'is a tame tiger'. I can quite intelligibly inform you that something is red or round, tame and a tiger, for those are all important facts about it. But if I say that it exists, I am not adding to your information or offering a further description of the thing. It would be odd for me to say for example, 'The three crucial facts about these animals are (i) that they are tigers, (ii) that they are tame, and (iii) that they exist.' ' "Being" is obviously not a real predicate; that is, it is not a concept of something which could be added to the concept of a thing' (A598/B626). In other words, when I say that something exists I am not referring to a further property of the thing. I am rather indicating that there is in fact something that has the properties already mentioned. Hence one premiss in the ontological argument is ill-formed. Since existence is not a genuine property it cannot be a perfection.

That objection is splendid as far as it goes but it has a very definite drawback. For if we are to deny that existence is a genuine property, that 'exists' is a genuine logical predicate, then we must be prepared to articulate the defining features of a property or a predicate. We must be able to say what criteria distinguish genuine from spurious properties or predicates. And Kant does not do that very well. He talks rather vaguely of the amount of information afforded in each case. He argues that learning of the properties of a thing is learning more about it, but that learning about its existence is not learning something more about it. 'By whatever and by however many predicates we may think a thing . . . we do not make the least addition to the thing when we further declare that this thing *is*' (A600/B628). But surely taken literally that claim is straightforwardly false. We do make the most important addition to a thing when we say that it exists. For example existing chairs differ from non-existent chairs in at least one vital respect, because they can be sat on. Similarly existing motorways are much more offensive than non-existent motorways, and it is much easier to score against a non-existent football team than against an existing football team. Even Kant concedes that my financial position is affected much more by 100 real thalers than by 100 conceived thalers (A599/B627).

So although the first objection, that existence is not a genuine property, may be true, it requires a great deal of extra polish before it can be allowed to stand. Kant's other objection is much more promising, though it is very clumsily expressed and fails to yield a complete account of the notion of existence. But sympathetically understood it demolishes the ontological argument. The main point of the objection is that whether or not we treat existence as a genuine property, the ontological argument cannot prove that God exists. The crucial passages are to be found at A594–8/B622–6. Kant argues that the proposition 'God exists' is either analytic or synthetic. According to Descartes it is analytic, of the same logical form as 'a triangle has three angles'. But, says Kant, if it is analytic, it is a 'miserable tautology'. We have merely posited or assumed the existence of God and then made his existence explicit. Just as Descartes's proposition about the triangle merely says that *if* there is a triangle it will have three angles, so his proposition about God merely says that *if* there is a God he exists. We have shown that existence is part of our notion of God, just as having three angles is part of our notion of a triangle. But that is far from showing that there is anything answering to our notion of God, just as we are very far from showing that there are in fact any triangles. 'To posit a triangle, and yet to reject its three angles, is self-contradictory; but there is no contradiction in rejecting the triangle together with its three angles. The same holds true of the concept of an absolutely necessary being' (A594/B622). As for the other alternative, that 'God exists' is synthetic, Kant needs only to point out that synthetic propositions can be denied without self-contradiction and are not of the same kind as 'triangles have three angles'.

Descartes clearly intended 'God exists' to be an analytic truth, and it is the earlier part of Kant's objection that is to the point. But some of his remarks need clarification, and I shall try to clarify them with the aid of modern predicate logic. For example it might be said that the onto-logical argument is of the following form:

1. $\exists x(Gx \ \& \ Px)$ God is perfect
$ \underline{(x)(Px \rightarrow Ex)}$ $\underline{\text{Existence is a perfection}}$
$ \therefore \exists x(Gx \ \& \ Ex)$ $\therefore$ God exists

The argument in this form treats 'exists' as a genuine predicate and is formally valid. But it is useless for Descartes's purposes, because if the first premiss is of the form '$\exists x(Gx \ \& \ Px)$' it assumes what is to be proved. It assumes that there is something answering to the descriptions 'God' and 'perfect'. And Descartes could not avoid the difficulty by treating 'God' as a proper name, by regarding the first premiss as of the form 'Pg'. For again the argument would assume what is to be proved, since it would assume that 'g' has a reference.

Descartes insists that there is a logical relation between the notions of God, perfection and existence, so perhaps the ontological argument is really of the following form:

2. $(x)(Gx \rightarrow Px)$ Anything God-like is perfect
$ \underline{(x)(Px \rightarrow Ex)}$ $\underline{\text{Anything perfect exists}}$
$ \therefore \exists x(Gx \ \& \ Ex)$ $\therefore$ God exists

Again 'exists' is being treated as a genuine predicate, and the premisses now reflect the *a priori* analysis of the concept of God that is supposed to be the characteristic feature of the ontological argument. Although '$\rightarrow$' is techically only the connective of material implication, we would in context regard the two premisses as analytic hypotheticals which reveal the intimate logical connection between divinity, perfection, and existence. Unfortunately in that form the argument is invalid because the existential conclusion does not follow from the two analytic hypothetical premisses. Although there may be a deductive link between the expressions 'God', 'perfect', and 'exists', it does not follow that there is anything answering to such descriptions.

We might regard the conclusion of the argument in another way:

3. $(x)(Gx \rightarrow Px)$ Anything God-like is perfect
$(x)(Px \rightarrow Ex)$ Anything perfect exists

$\therefore (x)(Gx \rightarrow Ex)$ $\therefore$ Anything God-like exists

'Exists' is still being treated as a genuine predicate, the argument is now valid, and it looks very much like a rigorous analysis of certain concepts, a series of systematic analytic moves from divinity to perfection and to existence, as rigorous as the move from the notion of a triangle to the notion of a plane figure with three angles. But of course it will not do the work that Descartes requires of it, because it still does not entail that there is actually anything that is divine or perfect or existing. It is wholly hypothetical in form and, as Kant would say, we can without contradiction reject divinity together with perfection and existence. Even in its logically purest form the ontological argument fails miserably.

I would make two final comments about Kant's discussion of the ontological argument. First, it could be argued that my account of Kant's second objection in the language of the predicate calculus is much too generous, that the Kantian original is clumsy and confused. And one source of the clumsiness and confusion is Kant's limited understanding of the notion of existence. He is rightly satisfied that existence is not a genuine property and that even if it were, the ontological argument would still fail. But his few positive remarks on existence leave a great deal to be desired, and hardly justify Bennett's references to the 'Kant-Frege' view of existence in §21 and §72 of *Kant's Dialectic*. Consider for example the remarks at A598–9/B626–7. ' "*Being*" is obviously not a real predicate ... Logically, it is merely the copula of a judgment. The proposition, "God is omnipotent", contains two concepts, each of which has its object—God and omnipotence. The small word "is" adds no new predicate, but only serves to posit the predicate *in its relation* to the subject. If, now, we take the subject (God) with all its predicates (among which is omnipotence), and say "God is", or "There is a God", we attach no new predicate to the concept of God, but only posit the subject in itself with all its predicates, and indeed posit it as being an *object* that stands in relation to my *concept*.'

The first sentence of that quotation rightly repeats the point that 'exists' or 'is' is not a genuine predicate. The last sentence points rather inconclusively in the direction of the Fregean view that 'exists' is logically

a quantifier, a device for indicating whether there is anything answering
to a certain description, or how many things have a certain property. But
the rest of the quoted passage is a horrible muddle, for it confuses a copula
with a quantifier. I am not very concerned to discuss whether Kant failed
to understand the distinction or whether he merely expressed himself
rather badly. But it is important that the distinction between copula and
quantifier is understood, so that the weaknesses of the ontological argument are properly understood. A *copula* is a grammatical device for linking a grammatical subject, such as 'God' or 'Fred', to a grammatical
predicate, such as 'omnipotent' or 'bald'. In English and *mutatis mutandis*
many other languages we cannot say 'God omnipotent' or 'Fred bald'.
We have to insert a part of the verb 'to be' to link subject and predicate,
and the link is the copula. It is of little philosophical interest and in some
languages is occasionally omitted. Indeed there is no separate copula in
the predicate calculus, no separate device for linking the subject expressions 'a', 'b', etc., to the predicate expressions 'F', 'G', etc. We do not
say 'a is F' but simply 'Fa'. A *quantifier* on the other hand is a device
for indicating whether a certain property has instances or how many
things have that property. The existential quantifier is a device for indicating whether a certain property has instances, whether there is anything
answering to a given description. In English 'there is . . .', 'there are . . .',
'. . . is', and '. . . exists' are common existential quantifiers.

It is easy to confuse copula and existential quantifier because in many
languages the verb 'to be' and its cognates can be used for both purposes
(and indeed for many other purposes as well). Obviously there are differences of idiom, and in German for example a very common existential
quantifier is 'es gibt', literally 'it gives'. But at the same time the verb
'sein' can be used as an existential quantifier, as is shown in the passage
whose translation I quoted above. The important point arising is this.
In the ontological argument it is the role of 'is' or 'exists' as a quantifier
that has been misunderstood. Descartes's mistakes stem from treating
'exists' or 'is' as a predicate rather than as a quantifier. He treats the proposition 'God exists' as a subject–predicate proposition of the same logical form as 'A triangle has three sides', and tries to exploit a logical relation
between divinity and existence, just as one might exploit a logical relation
between the notion of a triangle and the notion of a three-sided plane
figure. So although Kant is in a sense correct to observe that 'Being' or
'Sein' is a copula, the observation is irrelevant because it is the role of
'Being' as a quantifier that Descartes has misunderstood.

The second comment on Kant's treatment of the ontological argument
is that he overlooks one interesting criticism entirely. The criticism is
that the argument in its Cartesian form refers constantly to perfection,

as though 'perfect' is a complete predicate in its own right. But it is not a complete predicate. Something cannot simply be perfect but must be perfect in a certain respect. And the perfection of a thing will vary depending on the respect under discussion. A man may be an imperfect carpenter, a moderately perfect driver, and a perfect boor. A car may be a perfect death trap, an imperfect means of transport, and an extremely imperfect cooking utensil. Of course when we talk of God's perfection we usually have a set of standards in view, for God is perfectly moral, perfectly intelligent, perfectly powerful, and so on. But in treating existence as a perfection the ontological argument does rather tax one's ingenuity, since it is not obvious that an existing God is more perfect than a non-existent God.

To sum up, Kant's discussion of the ontological argument has certain weaknesses, for his positive account of existence is a muddle and he seems to tolerate the references to perfection. But those are minor blemishes in an otherwise lively and penetrating attack and his main objections to the argument are admirable: the ontological argument either assumes what is to be proved or attempts invalidly to draw a synthetic existential conclusion from entirely hypothetical analytic premises. Moreover it uses 'exists' as a predicate, and 'exists' is nothing of the sort.

3. THE COSMOLOGICAL ARGUMENT

There is rather more muddle and rather less penetration in Kant's discussion of the cosmological or first-cause argument. The argument as Kant presents it is a more economical version of the argument for the thesis of the fourth Antinomy, and runs as follows. 'If anything exists, an absolutely necessary being must also exist. Now I, at least, exist. Therefore an absolutely necessary being exists' (A604/B632). In more modern terms: if anything exists, it is contingent or causally dependent on something else, and that in turn on something else, and so on. Since the notion of an infinite series of contingent causes and effects yields an inadequate explanatory model, there must be a first, uncaused, cause in any series. At least one thing exists, so a first, uncaused, cause exists. As Kant observes, the argument is not entirely *a priori* and so presumably represents an advance on the wholly *a priori* ontological argument. For it begins with an actual event and attempts to explain its occurrence by appealing to some antecedent cause, and then to a further antecedent cause, and so on until we reach a first cause, *alias* God.

I would observe *en passant* that it is unfortunate that Kant addresses himself to a rather feeble version of the cosmological argument. Since he is engaged in exposing the illusions of rationalist metaphysics he might well have chosen the Cartesian version in the third Meditation, which goes as follows. I have an idea of perfection; there must be at least as much reality in the cause as in the effect; that is, there must be a perfect cause of this perfect effect; the only possible candidate is a perfect creator, namely God. Despite the references to perfection, it is a more difficult argument to handle, because it does not merely hinge on the claim that a causal series must have a first member, but rather on the claim that effects of an exceptional or striking kind must have causes of an exceptional or striking kind.

But let us return to Kant and to his chosen version of the cosmological argument. His main objection (A606–7/B634–5) is rather surprising and certainly wrong, for he suggests that the principal weakness of the argument is that it rests on the ontological argument, which is invalid. It rests on the ontological argument, since it needs to analyse the notion of an absolutely necessary being and needs to reveal that such a being has the properties we normally attribute to God, such as omnipotence, omniscience, moral awareness, and so on. And the ontological argument involved precisely the same kind of *a priori* analysis of the notion of an absolutely necessary being. The cosmological argument purports to be an argument from experience because it attempts to explain observed objects or events. To that extent it differs from the ontological argument, which is wholly *a priori* and merely analyses the notion of a God independently of any experience. 'But the cosmological proof uses this experience only for a single step in the argument, namely, to conclude the existence of a necessary being. What properties this being may have, the empirical premiss cannot tell us' (A606/B634). To identify the properties of the necessary being we must resort to the ontological argument.

This seems to me to be simply wrong. It is true that the ontological argument consists in a purely *a priori* analysis of certain concepts. Most notably it is supposed to reveal that divinity logically entails perfection, which logically entails existence. But it cannot prove that God exists, because it cannot prove that there is an instance of any of those concepts, that there really is anything answering to the descriptions 'divine', 'perfect', 'existing'. As we saw in the previous section, in its purest form the ontological argument consists merely of a series of analytic hypotheticals, and so cannot do the work required of it:

$(x)(Gx \rightarrow Px)$	Anything God-like is perfect
$(x)(Px \rightarrow Ex)$	Anything perfect exists
$\therefore (x)(Gx \rightarrow Ex)$	$\therefore$ Anything God-like exists

It may be valid, but it does not provide any reason for thinking that the hypotheticals are fulfilled.

But the cosmological argument is an entirely different kind of argument. It begins with an actual event, an instance of some concept. As Kant admits, it begins with a firm foot in experience. It then moves by way of a general causal principle to the conclusion that there must be a first cause:

$(y)(Oy \rightarrow \exists z Fz)$	If any event occurs, there is a first cause
$\exists y Oy$	At least one event occurs
$\therefore \exists z Fz$	$\therefore$ There is a first cause

Suppose, as Kant argues, we now employ some version of the ontological argument to discover the divinity of the first cause. That is, we argue that the concept of a first cause includes the concept of divinity. But if we add that result to the provisional conclusion of the cosmological argument we get what the theologian wants:

$\exists z Fz$	There is a first cause
$(z)(Fz \rightarrow Gz)$	Any first cause is God-like
$\therefore \exists z Gz$	$\therefore$ There is a God

In short, it is true that the ontological argument fails, and it may be true that the cosmological argument rests on part of the ontological. But it does not follow, as Kant would have us believe, that the cosmological argument is infected with the weaknesses of the ontological. For the cosmological already contains a crucial component missing from the ontological, namely an initial existential assumption, a reference to an actual thing or event. It does not consist in a 'proof from mere concepts'. It does not attempt to move from concepts to instances. Its conclusion does follow from its premises.

If the cosmological argument fails, it fails because one or more of its premises is false. For example Kant might have pressed the following objection, which is connected with the objection he actually presses. The provisional conclusion of the cosmological argument is that there must be a first cause. It is then claimed that the first cause has all the important properties normally attributed to the Christian God, such as omnipotence, omniscience, moral awareness, and so on. But the claim is false. Even if we concede that there is a first cause, there is no reason to attach any theological significance to it. It might have been an entirely inert first cause, a spontaneous movement of matter, a big bang, or something equally prosaic. We should not object to the cosmological argument's groping among mere concepts, but we should object very strongly to its groping ambitiously for the wrong concepts.

Kant also fails to press another central objection to the cosmological argument, even though he had expressed it eloquently in his observations on the antithesis of the third Antinomy (A449/B477). The argument starts with two important assumptions about causality, namely first, that every event is contingent or causally dependent on another, and second, that a causal series must have an 'absolutely necessary' first member. That is, the series of causes and effects must have started somewhere, and started with something pretty remarkable. The two assumptions are of course strictly incompatible as they stand, for if every event is contingent upon another there can be no first cause. But much more to the point, the assumption that there must be a first cause, that the series must have a beginning, is unacceptable. There is no reason *a priori* to insist that a causal series must have a beginning, that the world can only have existed for a finite length of time.

I suspect that the relics of Kant's rationalism prevented him from seriously entertaining the possibility of an infinite causal series, and made him prey to some of the 'dialectical illusions' he was attempting to expose. In the previous chapter I mentioned the thinly disguised reference to the principle of sufficient reason in the argument for the thesis of the third Antinomy: 'nothing takes place without a cause *sufficiently* determined *a priori*' (A446/B474). That is, every event must have an adequate explanation. The rationalist in Kant would not allow an infinite series of causes and effects, because he would be dissatisfied with the explanatory model it affords. He would want a complete explanation of any given event, a retreat to an 'absolutely unconditioned' which requires no further explanation. A retreat *ad infinitum* from one cause to another would not satisfy him because it would never yield a basic explanatory condition. In the words of the thesis of the fourth Antinomy, a causal series can only yield a completely satisfying explanation of a given event in one of two cases. Either we discover an absolutely unconditioned member of the series, a first cause, or more mysteriously we discover an absolutely unconditioned thing or event outside the series. We either insist on a first cause or support an infinite series of causes from outside the series.

As I have said already, I hold no brief for the language of conditions and the absolutely unconditioned. Nor do I think that the notion of an infinite causal series lacks explanatory force. But Kant must have been dissatisfied, for it is difficult otherwise to see why he should fail to pursue the possibility of an infinite causal series, why he should prefer instead to pursue the entirely misguided objection that the cosmological argument is infected by the diseases of the ontological.

4. THE PHYSICO-THEOLOGICAL ARGUMENT

The argument from design or physico-theological argument is probably the most impressive of the three arguments under discussion, since it reflects the very natural awe we sometimes feel when struck by the sheer complexity and beauty of the world around us. Unless we take refuge with Wordsworth in an ill-defined pantheism we may well seek an explanation of the order, beauty, and complexity of things in the form of the argument from design, as follows. The world around us is law-governed, systematic, ordered, and extremely complex, and it would be preposterous to write it off merely as a gigantic coincidence, as the result of an accidental conjunction of circumstances. The only plausible explanation is that the world is the work of a purposive intelligent creator, who fashioned it and sustains it.

It was common in the seventeenth and eighteenth centuries to express the argument in more homely and mechanical terms, terms which reflected the current fascination with mechanical things such as clocks, musical boxes, and marionettes.[1] If we found a clock in a deserted place, it was argued, we would naturally assume it had been made originally by a craftsman. We would not seriously consider the possibility that the pieces of the clock fell together in just that arrangement by accident. But the world is much more complicated than any clock, and by parity of reasoning we must suppose that originally it was made by an extremely skilled Clockmaker. The pieces of the world-clock could not possibly have fallen together in just this arrangement by accident.

Kant expresses the argument in the former, less homely, version (A622/B650) and offers two objections to it. The first objection is that the argument cannot support the strong conclusion required by traditional Christian theology, namely that there is an omnipotent creator, subject only to his own commands. 'The utmost ... that the argument can prove is an *architect* of the world who is always very much hampered by the adaptability of the material in which he works, not a *creator* of the world to whose idea everything is subject' (A627/B655). Presumably such a reduction in God's status would make him a correspondingly less worthy object of our admiration or worship. We reserve our fullest admiration and reverence only for a Creator who makes his own rules as he goes along, who really is omnipotent.

But is that a rational view? I would suggest that it is not, that Kant

---

[1] Cf. the reference to Vaucanson in the second *Critique*, Ak., p. 101; Abbott, p. 195.

fails to realize that his first objection is a very double-edged weapon. In one sense it demotes God from omnipotent creator to architect but in another it promotes Him in our estimation. Certainly an orthodox Christian seeks a God who is an omnipotent creator, who is able to create a world wholly according to his own wishes without any limitation by recalcitrant materials. A mere architect would not attract the same reverence and would be treated by Lady Bracknell as little more than a tradesman. But it has often been confidently and plausibly argued that a man can only be virtuous if he encounters obstacles to virtue. And Mark Tapley observed to Martin Chuzzlewit on many occasions that there is little credit in being jolly unless one's circumstances are difficult. By parity of reasoning, if I employ an architect to build my house, my admiration for him will undoubtedly increase if he manages to deal successfully with difficult geological conditions, perverse workmen, and a shortage of good materials. An architect who can decide exactly which geological conditions will obtain, when and how his workmen will work, and which materials will be available, deserves rather less credit. And the same should be true of God. There is no sense in worshipping an omnipotent God for the glory of his works, for an omnipotent creator ought to do a good job. We should reserve our praise and reverence for a divine architect who succeeds in creating and sustaining a world despite the restrictions imposed by the laws of physics and chemistry, the stupidity of human beings, and the viciousness of serpents.

Kant's second objection (A629/B657 ff.) to the physico-theological argument or argument from design is that it is only a more specific form of the cosmological argument, which rests in turn on the ontological argument. Thus the physico-theological argument suffers from the weaknesses of the other two arguments. It appeals at some stage to the main component of the cosmological argument, namely the move from evident effects to a non-evident first cause, and then to a vital component of the ontological argument, namely the *a priori* analysis of the properties of the first cause or absolutely necessary being.

I am not very impressed by this second objection. It is true that the argument from design is a more specific version of the cosmological argument and appeals from certain evident effects to a non-evident first cause, but it does not follow that it is therefore prey to all the weaknesses of the cosmological argument. Indeed as a general rule it is false that specific versions of general arguments are prey to the weaknesses of the general arguments. Quite the contrary, for a more specific version may have made important qualifications missing from the general argument, qualifications which make it stronger than the general argument. For example in the case under consideration the argument from design is a more specific version of the cosmological argument, for it attempts to explain evident effects by appealing to a non-evident first cause. But it is a much stronger argument. It does not merely claim that any effect must be explained eventually by reference to a first cause. It makes the much more specific and much more impressive claim that a particular kind of striking effect, namely the order and coherence of the universe, can only be explained by a particular kind of striking cause, namely the efforts of an intelligent and purposive creator.

If we are to demolish the argument from design we must part company with Kant and get to grips with the central claim that the order and coherence of the world cannot be dismissed as a gigantic coincidence. One objection is that the order and coherence might indeed be a gigantic coincidence. It is not good enough to say that such highly complex organ- ization is utterly improbable in the absence of divine intervention, for it is not clear how we could calculate the probabilities involved. Indeed as J. J. C. Smart observed in *Philosophy and Scientific Realism* (p. 54), if the world is infinite in space and time there must be an infinite number of cricket teams good enough to beat Australia. That is, we could argue that if the universe is sufficiently large and has existed for a sufficiently long time then a world very much like our own must appear from time to time.

Less speculatively and more seriously we might object that it is not at all clear that the world is particularly ordered or systematic. The fact that we make generalizations about it is not particularly significant, since we could always produce some trivial generalizations, however chaotic the world might be. It would be a simple mathematical matter. But even if we stop short of the trivial, it is not clear that the world is highly organized and systematic. After all, innocent people are killed and maimed in ghastly ways, the world's energy supplies run down quite quickly, and there are various living things (such as wasps) that have no apparent natural function at all. Such considerations might indicate that the world is a very ill-organised machine. Moreover we should be very wary of the sort of mechanical analogy I used earlier in expounding the argument from design. The purpose of a human clockmaker is certainly revealed in the systematic arrangement of parts in the clock. We know in outline how a clockmaker works and can imagine the kind of mess that results from his working badly or not at all. For example we can literally contrast a beautifully constructed clock with a heap of bits of metal dumped at random. But it is impossible to extend the analogy, to talk of the world as a very large clock. For we have no idea of how the Great Clock-maker works, or of the kind of mess that would result from his working badly or not at all. We are not in a position to contrast a beautifully constructed world-clock with a heap of bits dumped at random. As far as we can tell, our world may well be the heap of bits dumped at random.

5. FINAL THOUGHTS ON KANT ON GOD

Thus Kant's discussion of arguments for the existence of God is very much of a curate's egg. There are patches of devastating criticism, punctuated by passages of ill-digested and sometimes rather peripheral material. Kant's main claim, that the arguments are simply bad arguments, is for the most part sustained, although occasionally for the wrong reasons. I want to end our examination of the critique of rationalist theology by drawing attention to certain other main doctrines of the Dialectic which are to be found, but not always very prominently, in that critique. One is a general theme of the Dialectic, that speculative metaphysics gets into difficulties simply because it attempts to make claims about objects that are not objects of a possible experience. The theme is not very strident in the discussion of God, but it is certainly there: 'the question under consideration is obviously synthetic, calling for an extension of our knowledge beyond all limits of experience, namely, to the existence of a being that is to correspond to a mere idea of ours, an idea that cannot be paralleled in any experience' (A637–8/B665–6). We also find the normal Kantian counterpoint, the claim that the idea of God may none the less have an important regulative use (A616/B644 ff.). We cannot have knowledge of a God, but it may well be to our advantage to act as if there were a God.

Finally it is interesting to note the first intriguing glimpse of an important doctrine of the Dialectic of the second *Critique*, the doctrine that theology is logically dependent on ethics, not logically prior to it: 'the only theology of reason which is possible is that which is based on moral laws or seeks guidance from them' (A636/B664). That is, our theological concepts are wholly parasitic on our ethical concepts. We can only understand God as a perfect moral agent, as the giver of just rewards for virtue, and so on. The traditional view that theology is prior to ethics, that moral imperatives are the commands of God, turns things upside down. The basic, autonomous concepts are ethical, everything theological is secondary. Such heresy, developed at length in *Religion Within the Bounds of Reason Alone*, naturally attracted a great deal of hostile attention, including that of Friedrich Wilhelm II's censor, who asked Kant to refrain from any further attempts to undermine public morals. Kant's reply (Zweig, pp. 217–20) was masterly and combined a spirited defence of his right to express his views with all the respect conventionally due to his feudal superiors.

For a student of the first *Critique* the main point arising is that Kant obviously feels he can leave room for ethics and theology, despite the very rigid epistemological limits set by the Aesthetic and Analytic. Ethical and theological claims may not have the status of knowledge but none the less, he thinks, they may have another perfectly legitimate status. And one important device essential to that conjuring trick is transcendental idealism, and in particular noumenalism. Transcendental idealism is hardly mentioned in the discussion of arguments for the existence of God. But there are occasional references to 'the sensible world' and to 'the intelligible world', and hints of the view that the search for God is a search for a noumenal agent. After all, we cannot avoid reading the whole section in the light of the noumenalism of the solution of the fourth Antinomy, a solution which purports at the very least to show 'that the thoroughgoing contingency of all natural things ... is quite consistent with the optional assumption of a necessary, though purely intelligible, condition' (A562/B590).

6. CONSTITUTIVE AND REGULATIVE

Before leaving the Dialectic I want to discuss Kant's distinction between constitutive and regulative uses of the ideas of pure reason. The distinction is crucial to the whole of Kant's Critical philosophy and is discussed in an Appendix to the Dialectic at A642/B670 ff. Kant has already made one constitutive/regulative distinction, of little philosophical interest, in the Analytic (A179–80/B222–3) but the distinction to be made in the Dialectic is quite different and much more important. He thinks that he has shown that the concepts under discussion, the ideas of pure reason, have no constitutive use. That is, they cannot possibly yield knowledge-claims about Cartesian souls or the world as an absolute totality or God. Knowledge requires both concepts and intuitions, and there can be no intuitions or perceptions of souls, of the absolute totalities in question, or of God. But those concepts may well have another use, a *regulative* use, encouraging us to greater and more systematic scientific efforts. In particular it will unify our investigations in psychology, cosmology, and natural theology: 'we shall, *first*, in psychology ... connect all the appearances, all the actions and receptivity of our mind, *as if* the mind were a simple substance which persists with personal identity ... *Secondly*, in cosmology, we must follow up the conditions of both inner and outer natural appearances ... just *as if* the series of appearances were in itself endless, without any first or supreme member ... *Thirdly* ... in the domain of theology, we must view everything that can belong to the context of possible experience ... *as if* the sum of all appearances (the sensible world itself) had a single, highest and all-sufficient ground beyond itself, namely, a self-subsistent, original, creative reason' (A672/B700).

When I mentioned the constitutive/regulative distinction on previous occasions I suggested that 'regulative' could be interpreted to mean 'methodological'. That is, I suggested that Kant's considered view of the ideas of pure reason is that they have no knowledge-yielding use but that they may have a methodological use. Indeed if my interpretation is correct we may well break into applause for Kant's distinction between constitutive and regulative uses of a concept. For we do distinguish between substantive knowledge-claims, such as 'Dogs are quadrupeds' or 'The earth revolves around the sun', and methodological principles, such as 'Stop the engine before removing the valve-cover' or 'Point the chisel blade away from the body'. We might even draw nearer to Kant's own position by distinguishing between constitutive and regulative uses of one and the same concept. For example in 'Richard Burbage is a Danish prince' I am using the concept of a prince constitutively and making a substantive knowledge-claim. But in 'Behave as if Richard Burbage is a Danish prince' I am using 'prince' regulatively, issuing a methodological directive. It would not be difficult to formulate criteria for making such a distinction. Constitutive principles such as 'Dogs are quadrupeds' purport to make knowledge-claims and are true or false, whereas regulative principles such as 'Point the chisel blade away from the body' do not and are not. Regulative principles tell us what to do, issue instructions, whereas constitutive principles do not. One grammatical symptom of the distinction is that constitutive principles are often expressed in indicative sentences, whereas regulative principles are often expressed as imperatives.

But Kant is not making the distinction in that way. His own distinction between constitutive and regulative uses of concepts is at best foolish and at worst incoherent. He is making two claims, which may appear to knit together very neatly but which are in fact incompatible. He is claiming, first, that the ideas of reason have no constitutive use and, second, that they none the less have an important regulative use. We could not even in principle claim to know that there are Cartesian souls, that the world is infinite, that there is a God, etc., but none the less it is important that we should act as if there are Cartesian souls, as if the world is infinite, as if there is a God. One obvious objection is that Kant's second claim is simply false, that there is absolutely no reason to suppose that the ideas have any regulative or methodological function. Many psychologists work very well without behaving as if there are Cartesian souls, many modern cosmologists do not act as if the world is infinite, and many people live very cheerfully without ever acting as if there is an omnipotent and omniscient creator.

There is, however, a more profound and more important objection. Kant is trying to distinguish between knowing the world to be so-and-so, and acting as if it is so-and-so, between knowing that there are Cartesian souls and acting as if there are, and so on. I want to argue that for his general purposes in the Dialectic that distinction is spurious. Let us leave Kant for the moment and consider a related distinction, namely the distinction between knowing something to be red and acting as if it is red. Taking the first half of the distinction first, what is it to know that something is red? One very important thing involved in knowing that something is red is the ability to distinguish red things from non-red things. If I am to know that something is red I must at least have some way in experience of distinguishing between red things and yellow or green or blue. In Kantian language, if I am to make a genuine knowledge-claim about red things then red things must be possible objects of experience.

Now what of the other half of the distinction? What is involved in acting as if something is red? Matters are a trifle more complicated. For example if I am acting as if something is red then either I do not know that it is red, or I know that it is not and am pretending or supposing for some reason that it has another colour. Perhaps the dramatic society does not run to patrician purple for the production of *Julius Caesar* and our disbelief about the green substitute must be vigorously suspended. But one point is of vital importance: if I am acting as if something is red, I must at least know the meaning of 'red' or some equivalent term. But what is it to know the meaning of 'red'? Surely among other things it is to know how to distinguish red things from blue or yellow or green, to know how to pick out red strands of wool from an assorted bundle, to know how to pick out tomatoes from an assorted heap of fruit without any reference to taste, shape, smell, etc. Of course I may never encounter any red things, but if I know the meaning of 'red' I have a way in experience of picking out red things, should the situation arise. In Kantian terms, if I know the meaning of 'red' then red things are objects of a possible experience. In short, if I am to act as if something is red I must know the meaning of 'red', and if I know the meaning of 'red' then red things are objects of a possible experience.

The relevance of the example to Kant's use of a constitutive/regulative distinction should be obvious. He claims that the ideas of pure reason have no constitutive use, that they cannot be used to make genuine knowledge-claims, because the objects in question are not objects of a possible experience. He also claims that the ideas have an important regulative use, that we must act as if there are Cartesian souls, as if the world is infinite, as if there is a God. But if we are to act as if there are Cartesian souls, as if the world is infinite, as if there is a God, then at the very least we must know the meaning of 'Cartesian soul', 'infinite world', and

'God'. But if we know the meaning of such expressions then Cartesian souls, the extent of the world, and God must all be objects of a possible experience. That is, we must in principle have a way in experience of identifying Cartesian souls, the extent of the world, and God. But to say that those objects are objects of a possible experience is to say that the ideas of reason are constitutive after all, that they could in principle yield knowledge-claims. If Kant insists that the ideas are regulative he is forced to the conclusion that they are also constitutive. If they are to have any methodological function they must be capable of yielding genuine knowledge-claims.

Kant might reply that my objection proves too much, that I appear to be arguing that the whole strategy of the Dialectic is misconceived, that souls, the world as an absolute totality, and God are after all objects of a possible experience. But such a reply would be too hasty. I said that Kant is making two claims which appear to be compatible: first, that the ideas of pure reason, the ideas of a Cartesian soul, of the world as an absolute totality, and of God, are not constitutive, and second, that they are none the less regulative. All I have been concerned to show is that the two claims are incompatible. If the ideas are not constitutive, they are not regulative; if they are regulative, then they are also constitutive, can also yield genuine knowledge-claims. To put the point in more modern terms, Kant is right in general to insist that it is absurd or meaningless or vacuous to talk about objects such as souls, the limits of the universe, and God, which are not objects of a possible experience. But if the expressions 'soul', 'the limits of the universe', and 'God' are vacuous, so then are the sentences 'Act as if there are Cartesian souls', 'Act as if the universe is infinite', 'Act as if there is an omnipotent creator'. Let us agree that the general aims of the Dialectic are admirable, that the ideas have no constitutive use. But it follows that they have no regulative use either.

Why then should Kant have been so anxious to take up his position? Given that he gives us many reasons for thinking that the ideas have no constitutive use, that traditional speculative metaphysics is in a clear sense a vacuous enterprise, why should he go to such trouble to re-instate the ideas as methodological principles? The reason is simple and has already been mentioned several times. One of Kant's obvious debts to Hume was the central thesis of the Aesthetic and Analytic, that we can make genuine knowledge-claims only about objects of a possible experience. Knowledge requires intuitions as well as concepts. As we might say, we must in principle have some way of verifying knowledge-claims in sense-experience. But as Hume realized and as the logical positivists were delighted to point out, if we regard empirical verifiability as a necessary feature of any knowledge-claim, then at least two traditional areas of discourse, ethics and theology, start to look rather silly. The best we can do is to retreat to some form of naturalist theology and ethics, reducing all theological and ethical claims to claims about the ordinary observable features of human beings or other objects.

Kant appreciated the difficulty only too well. He saw quite clearly that on his own criterion of knowledge ethical and theological claims as traditionally understood could not count as knowledge. So the ideas of pure reason in which he is most interested, namely the idea of a soul, the idea of free causality, and the idea of God, are seriously threatened and can be rescued temporarily only by giving them some subordinate but none the less respectable status: 'even the *assumption*—as made on behalf of the necessary practical employment of my reason—of *God, freedom*, and *immortality* is not permissible unless at the same time speculative reason be deprived of its pretensions to transcendent insight. For in order to arrive at such insight it must make use of principles which, in fact, extend only to objects of possible experience, and which, if also applied to what cannot be an object of experience, always really change this into an appearance, thus rendering all *practical extension* of pure reason impossible. I have therefore found it necessary to deny *knowledge*, in order to make room for *faith*' (Bxxix–xxx). It would not be too cynical to say that in giving the ideas of a soul, free causality, and God a regulative status, indeed in attempting to give them any status at all, he is trying to prepare us for the ethical and theological doctrines to be developed in the *Groundwork* and second *Critique*. For in those later works he attempts to give more content to claims about wholly rational free agents, and even to take a peep into the world of noumena, without contradicting any of the main doctrines of the first *Critique*. Those attempts are unfortunately beyond the scope of this book.

7. BRIEF REVIEW OF THE DIALECTIC

The Aesthetic and Analytic defended in detail the thesis that knowledge requires both intuitions and concepts. We can, it seems, only make coherent knowledge-claims about objects that conform to the *a priori* intuitions of space and time and the *a priori* concepts of substance, causality, etc. The general programme of the Dialectic was to investigate the disastrous results of overlooking the fact that knowledge requires both intuitions and concepts. It examines a number of concepts to which no intuitions could correspond. It is no doubt inevitable that such metaphysical illusions should arise, because our faculty of reason searches constantly for more comprehensive, more complete, more basic explanatory conditions in an attempt to reach the absolutely unconditioned. It is inevitable that this admirable but vaulting ambition should o'erleap itself and fall on the other side of the limits of a possible experience.

As we have seen, the execution of the programme falls below those expectations. In particular the most important claim of all, that the objects of rationalist metaphysics are outside a possible experience, is not as prominent as one would wish. When it is prominent it is expressed in the language of transcendental idealism, almost as though the cardinal sin of rationalism was its rejection of idealism. Other features of Kant's programme are left in great obscurity. Kant never clearly explains what he means by saying that reason inevitably seeks a complete explanation, an absolutely unconditioned condition. Even in the Antinomies, where the language of conditions makes most sense and is pressed hardest, it is not clear what Kant means by the absolutely unconditioned. Indeed in the Dynamical Antinomies the distinction between conditioned and unconditioned collapses very swiftly into a distinction much more important for Kant's Critical purposes, namely that between phenomena and noumena.

The Dialectic also has a number of specific weaknesses. The various defences of transcendental idealism, notably in the discussion of the fourth Paralogism and in the Antinomies, are unconvincing. We are unprepared for the sudden appearance in the third Antinomy of certain sketchily explained ethical doctrines. We are sometimes not entirely clear which ideas of pure reason are being discussed. For example sometimes the 'cosmological idea' is described as the idea of an absolute totality and sometimes it is split into four separate ideas (A415/B443). In his discussion of the constitutive/regulative distinction Kant focuses attention on the cosmological idea of infinity (A672/B700) but his later ethical and theological works require him to concentrate on the ideas of free causality and necessary being. Finally, we should treat with scepticism the repeated claim that although the ideas of pure reason have no constitutive or knowledge-yielding use, they may well have an excellent regulative or methodological use. For I have argued that a concept has no possible constitutive use has no regulative use either.

PART V

THREE PROBLEMS

8

MATHEMATICS

1. THE PROBLEM

According to Kant's official account of the purpose and content of the first *Critique* mathematics is of paramount importance, because he wants to contrast the genuine synthetic *a priori* knowledge of mathematics and physics with the vacuous synthetic *a priori* speculation of rationalist metaphysics. The official account is misleading, for the references to mathematics are thinly scattered, even in the Aesthetic. But if we collect all the references together, we obtain an interesting and influential account of mathematics which is well worth discussing in its own right, whatever its strategic role in the Critical philosophy. I would suggest that the following passages are of particular interest: B14–17, Transcendental Aesthetic *passim*, A103, B154–5, A142–3/B181–2, A162–6/B202–7, A238–40/B298–9, A712–38/B741–66. There are also corresponding passages in the *Prolegomena*, notably §§6–13, and there is an interesting letter to Schultz, dated 25 Nov. 1788 (Zweig, pp. 128–31). By 'mathematics" Kant means principally Euclidean geometry and simple arithmetic. There is a brief reference to algebra at A717/B745 but it is not pursued. He is concerned to establish the logical status of mathematical 'judgements', and a mathematical judgement is virtually any proposition that can appear in a mathematical argument. Thus unfortunately Kant never distinguishes between mathematical theorems, such as 'the sum of the interior angles of a triangle equals two right angles', and mathematical axioms or postulates, such as 'between any two points a straight line can be drawn'. In the interests of clarity I shall concentrate on the most important class of mathematical judgements, namely mathematical theorems.

Although Kant never states the problem for discussion explicitly, his remarks on mathematics and on the analytic/synthetic distinction suggests that my own account of the problem in Chapter 1 is a reasonable account of the problem as he understood it. Expressed in those philosophically naïve and tendentious terms the problem is this. When trying to establish the logical status of mathematical theorems we have two contrary inclinations. One is to insist that the theorems are analytic/*a priori*/ necessary truths, while the other is to insist that they are synthetic/*a posteriori*/contingent truths. But neither alternative is very satisfactory. It is unsatisfactory to say that the theorems are analytic, because we suppose that analytic truths cannot enlarge our knowledge, that fundamentally they merely rearrange facts we already know. 'Red is a colour', 'bachelors are unmarried', and a 'cat is an animal' hardly enlarge our knowledge of red, of bachelors, or of cats. But mathematical theorems do seem to enlarge our knowledge. For example Pythagoras's theorem begins by constructing a comparatively simple figure, a right-angled triangle, and arrives eventually at a most striking conclusion about the relation between the squares on its three sides, a fact which had not occurred to us before. If mathematical theorems enlarge our knowledge they must be synthetic. But that alternative seems equally unsatisfactory, for synthetic truths are falsifiable. Although 'water boils at 100°C at sea-level' or 'dodos are extinct' happen to be true, we can easily imagine circumstances in which they might be false. The world might well have been such that dodos continued to thrive well into the twentieth century, and such that water boiled at 150 °C. But mathematical theorems are not falsifiable. We expect them to be true come what may. We are not prepared to allow the possibility that occasionally the angles of a triangle equal more than two right angles, or that two and two equal five or forty-two or five hundred. As Kant would say, we think we know mathematical theorems with 'apodeictic certainty'.

2. KANT'S MAIN DOCTRINES

Thus we are reluctant to say that mathematical theorems are analytic/ *a priori*/necessary, and we are also reluctant to say that they are synthetic/ *a posteriori*/contingent. Kant thinks he can relieve us of our embarrassment by refusing to regard the analytic/synthetic distinction as equivalent to the *a priori*/*a posteriori* distinction or the necessary/contingent distinction. He wants to argue that mathematical theorems are logically synthetic but *a priori* or necessary truths. He takes the analytic/synthetic distinction to be a distinction between those propositions that are logical truths or reducible to logical truths by appropriate definitional substitution, and those that are not. And he takes the *a priori*/*a posteriori* distinction to be a distinction between those propositions established independently of experience, and those established by experience. He argues that mathematical theorems are synthetic because they cannot be reduced to logical truths, and *a priori* because they are established independently of experience. He thinks he can avoid the disadvantages of the two alternatives I originally mentioned, for in arguing that the theorems are synthetic he allows them to enlarge our knowledge, and in arguing that they are *a priori* he explains why they cannot be falsified.

The general claim that mathematical theorems are synthetic and *a priori* can be broken down into a number of separate claims. The theorems are supposedly synthetic in two connected senses. First, they are logically synthetic, neither logical truths nor reducible to logical truths by appropriate definitional substitution. The claim that $2+2=4$ or that the interior angles of a triangle add up to $180°$ can be denied without self-contradiction. Second, they are the result of the mind's power of synthesis. It is an essential part of our mathematical thinking that we synthesize separate units into one whole. In geometry we synthesize a series of separate parts of space, such as the series of points which make up a straight line: 'I cannot represent to myself a line, however small, without drawing it in thought, that is, generating from a point all its parts one after the other' (A162–3/B203). In arithmetic we synthesize the separate units that together make up a certain number: 'Arithmetic achieves its concept of number by the successive addition of units in time' (*Prolegomena*, p. 283).

The claim that mathematical theorems are *a priori* is even more complex and can be taken on three distinct levels. On one level they are *a priori* in the sense that they are established independently of experience and are in no sense inductive generalizations. 'Such propositions cannot be empirical or, in other words, judgements of experience, nor can they be derived from any such judgements' (B41). Indeed, moving to a second level, it is a necessary feature of experience that objects conform to Euclidean geometry and simple arithmetic. We could not coherently describe an experience in which there were non-Pythagorean right-angled triangles, or in which $2+2=5$, or in which triangles sometimes had interior angles equal to three right angles. Although those propositions are logically synthetic, they are necessary conditions of a possible experience. Moving to a third level, Kant attempts to explain why mathematical theorems are necessary to experience by invoking transcendental idealism. Geometry and arithmetic are the mathematics of space and time respectively, and space and time are merely pure forms of human intuition, forms which we project on to our experience but which have no independent existence. The objects of experience must conform to Euclidean geometry and simple arithmetic because our minds construct the geometrical and arithmetical properties of the world in precisely that way. Indeed that is the only way in which we can guarantee the necessity, the 'apodeictic certainty', of mathematics. 'If ... space (and ... time) were not merely a form of your intuition, containing conditions *a priori*, under which alone things can be outer objects to you, and without which subjective conditions outer objects are in themselves nothing, you could not in regard to outer objects determine anything whatsoever in an *a priori* and synthetic manner' (A48/B66). The so-called necessity of mathematics is reduced to a certain psychological necessity.

So Kant's first main doctrine is that mathematical theorems are synthetic and *a priori*. Before moving to the second I would add two footnotes. First, although I have deliberately concentrated on Kant's account of mathematical theorems I should point out that he would also argue that mathematical postulates are synthetic and *a priori*. One of his examples of a synthetic *a priori* mathematical judgement at A239/B299 is the proposition that between two points there can be only one straight line. Second, although he explicitly says at B14 and elsewhere that all mathematical judgements are synthetic, he claims at B16–17 that certain analytic proportions may play a part in mathematical proof: 'for instance, $a=a$; the whole is equal to itself; or $(a+b)>a$, that is, the whole is greater than its part'. But he is anxious to point out that such analytic propositions are not particularly mathematical, that 'they serve only as links in the chain of method and not as principles'.

Kant's second main doctrine is that an essential part of mathematical thinking is what he calls the 'construction of figures'. For 'mathematical knowledge is the knowledge gained by reason from the *construction* of concepts. To *construct* a concept means to exhibit *a priori* the intuition which corresponds to the concept' (A713/B741). If I am to construct the concept of a straight line then I must (in principle) draw one (B16, A163/B204); if I am to construct the concept of a three-dimensional space I must in principle draw three lines at right angles to each other (B154); if I am to construct any numerical concept I must invoke the aid of my fingers or the beads of an abacus (B15), and so on. Kant is not making the fatuous claim that mathematics is impossible without any visual aids. He appears rather to be making a fairly superficial point which leads to a more profound and more puzzling point. The superficial point is that in mathematics we use particular examples which have a representative purpose, a universal significance. In geometry we draw lines, triangles, circles, and in arithmetic we contemplate fingers, oranges, and men digging trenches. But all those particular things have a universal purpose because they are only particular illustrations of general truths. 'The single figure which we draw is empirical, and yet it serves to express the concept, without impairing its universality ... Thus philosophical knowledge considers the particular only in the universal, mathematical knowledge the universal in the particular' (A713–4/B741–2).

But there is a more profound point buried under there, namely that mathematics is fundamentally the province of the faculty of intuitions rather than the faculty of concepts. The main feature that distinguishes mathematics from philosophy is that philosophy consists in analysing concepts and the relations between concepts, whereas mathematics consists in using intuition to pass from a premiss to a conclusion. 'Suppose a philosopher be given the concept of a triangle and he be left to find out ... what relation the sum of its angles bears to a right angle ... However long he meditates on this concept, he will never produce anything new ... Now let the geometer take up these questions ... through a chain of inferences guided throughout by intuition, he arrives at a fully evident and universally valid solution of the problem' (A716–7/B744–5). Mathematics is intuitive rather than discursive. There is a temptation to interpret 'intuition' very loosely, in the sense in which we might say metaphorically that we 'see' or 'intuit' that $2+2=4$. But Kant seems to use 'intuition' literally rather than metaphorically. That is, he wants to say that our awareness of mathematical truths is not merely analogous to our immediate perceptual awareness of the things around us, but is exactly the same kind of awareness. Exactly the same faculty is at work, namely sensibility, the faculty of intuitions. The intuitive method 'secures all inferences against error by setting each one before our eyes' (A734/B762).

I would not suggest that Kant's account of the relation between mathematics and the senses is intelligible. But it complements very neatly the claim that mathematical theorems are logically synthetic. Kant would say that an analytic proposition analyses one concept as contained in another. 'A cat is an animal' analyses the concept of an animal as contained in the concept of a cat. A synthetic proposition, on the other hand, merely records the coincidence of two logically independent concepts, the coincidence for example of the concept of water and the concept of boiling at 100 °C. in 'water boils at 100 °C.' Analytic truths do not enlarge our knowledge, synthetic truths do. Mathematical truths are synthetic and do enlarge our knowledge, for they consist in drawing attention to relations between concepts other than the relation of logical dependence. We are able to connect the concept of a triangle and the concept of interior angles equal to two right angles, even though there is no *logical* connection between them. And the synthetic string that connects them is 'intuition'. We do not see any logical relation between the meaning of 'triangle' and the meaning of 'interior angles equal to two right angles', for there is no such relation. But our intuition tells us that a triangle's interior angles are equal to two right angles.

The third main doctrine in Kant's account of mathematics can be stated very briefly. Since the Aesthetic is devoted to an examination of the faculty of intuitions, since mathematics is intuitive rather than discursive, and since the forms of intuition are space and time, Kant insists that geometry is the mathematics of space and arithmetic the mathematics of time. I think it is plausible to regard geometry as the mathematics of space, though I shall argue later that we should resist such an account of geometry. But it is not even remotely plausible to regard arithmetic as the mathematics of time. Yet plausible or not, Kant's views are quite clear. 'Arithmetic achieves its concept of number by the successive addition of units in time, and pure mechanics cannot attain its concepts of motion without employing the representation of time' (*Prolegomena*, p. 283).

Indeed it is very difficult to think of any arguments that might support such a view of arithmetic. It is not good enough to say that the concept of motion requires the representation of time, because it also requires the representation of space. Motion consists in being at different places at successive times. Nor would there be any point in saying—as Kant says—that arithmetic involves counting successive units and that counting takes time. For it would certainly not follow that we must explain numbers by referring to time. Although it is a necessary truth that $1 + 1 + 1 + 1 + 1 = 5$, it is only contingent that it takes me a certain time to count up to five. The concept of five does not involve the concept of counting up to five. Perhaps Kant might argue that arithmetic and time are connected for another reason, namely that the series of natural numbers and the series of instants are both ordered series, a series of units related by the relations 'successor of' and 'predecessor of', and a series of units related by the relations 'earlier than' and 'later than'. But that fact is hardly significant. By parity of reasoning we could prove that arithmetic is the mathematics of the English monarchy, which is an ordered series of kings and queens, or that arithmetic is the mathematics of space, which is an ordered series of points. I am strongly inclined to abandon these Kantian parallels between geometry and space, and between arithmetic and time, with the comment that they are merely further examples of a misguided passion for a systematic presentation of the Critical philosophy.

3. OBJECTIONS

There are many objections to Kant's account of mathematics. One objection to which I shall return in the next chapter is that Kant confuses logical with psychological necessity. He is too ready to rest the necessity of mathematics on certain psychological claims about the way in which our minds construct the spatial and temporal features of the world. Another objection is that he gives too prominent a place to the 'construction of figures', that there are many mathematical terms that do not and could not yield appropriate constructions in intuition. For example constructions are very contrived and artificial in any geometry of more than three spatial dimensions, and it is difficult to think of any intuitive figures that could assist complex calculations in the differential calculus. A third objection is that Kant's claim that mathematical inference proceeds intuitively, that it is the province of sensibility, is vague if interpreted metaphorically and incomprehensible if interpreted literally. I expressed a fourth objection in the previous section, namely that although it is plausible to regard geometry as the mathematics of space, it is not at all plausible to regard arithmetic as the mathematics of time.

All those objections are no doubt of interest but I want to concentrate on two objections to the doctrine that is most important to contemporary philosophers, the doctrine that mathematical theorems are synthetic but *a priori*, that they are not reducible to logical truths but are none the less established independently of experience. The first objection is that the doctrine rests on a very muddled account of the analytic/synthetic distinction, an account to be found principally at A6–7/B10. 'Either the predicate B belongs to the subject A, as something which is (covertly) contained in this concept A; or B lies outside the concept A, although it does indeed stand in connection with it. In the one case I entitle the judgment analytic, in the other synthetic. Analytic judgments (affirmative) are therefore those in which the connection of the predicate with the subject is thought through identity; those in which this connection is thought without identity should be entitled synthetic.' So far in this book I have charitably summarized Kant's account of the distinction as follows: analytic propositions are logical truths or reducible to logical truths by appropriate definitional substitution; synthetic propositions are those that are not so reducible. The first part of the quoted passage and the references to the 'principle of contradiction' at B14 f. would appear to justify my charity. (More charity would have to be extended to disguise the fact that Kant's account only applies to affirmative subject–predicate propositions.) But the latter part of the quotation introduces a psychological tone into the discussion, and seems to suggest that analytic propositions are those in which the predicate is *thought* to be contained in the subject. Now to say that a predicate is contained in the subject is by no means the same as to say that it is thought to be contained. Kant is simply wrong when he says that 'the question is not what we *ought* to join in thought to the given concept, but what we *actually* think in it' (B17). If we attend to what is thought then many logical truths will have to be regarded as synthetic. For example my thought of '$\exists x(Fx \,\&\, Gx) \,\&\, \exists x(Fx \,\&\, (y)(Gy \rightarrow \sim Hxy))$' contains no thought of '$\exists x(Fx \,\&\, \sim(y)(Fy \rightarrow Hyx))$', and yet I find from Lemmon's *Beginning Logic* (p. 134) that the latter follows analytically from the former. Indeed we often say that certain logical theorems are counterintuitive, that we are surprised to discover that the conclusion follows analytically from the premisses.

What we think is immaterial, for we may think all sorts of fatuous things when confronted with a certain proposition. Sadly, when talking about mathematics Kant insists on expressing his criterion of analyticity in the psychological idiom. He claims that mathematical theorems are synthetic because in thinking the subject we do not think in any way of the predicate: '. . . the concept of the sum of 7 and 5 contains nothing save the union of the two numbers into one, and in this no thought is being taken as to what that single number may be which combines both. The concept of 12 is by no means already thought in merely thinking this union of 7 and 5' (B15). Indeed if we express our criterion of analyticity in the psychological idiom it is difficult to avoid the conclusion that mathematical theorems are synthetic. For example a thought about right-angled triangles does not necessarily involve a thought about triangles with Pythagorean properties. Many schoolchildren have had the first thought but not the second. Conversely if we express our criterion of analyticity in the more rigorous logical idiom the way is then open to treat mathematical theorems as analytic. An analytic proposition is a proposition that is a logical truth or reducible to a logical truth by appropriate definitional substitution, and it follows logically from the definition of a Euclidean right-angled triangle that it has Pythagorean properties.

So much then for the first objection, that Kant's account of mathematics rests on a muddled account of the analytic/synthetic distinction. But since there might be other reasons for thinking that mathematical theorems are synthetic, we must press on to a second objection, which invites us to contemplate an important distinction entirely absent from Kant's account of mathematics, the distinction between uninterpreted and interpreted calculi. An *uninterpreted* calculus consists of a set of symbols, together with formation and transformation rules. That is, there are rules for forming strings of symbols and rules for transforming one string of symbols into another. It may also contain 'axioms' or 'postulates', that is, strings of symbols that occupy a privileged position in the calculus because they are not derived from any other strings of symbols. For example the uninterpreted propositional calculus consists of a set of symbols, 'p', 'q', 'r', '$\rightarrow$', 'v', '&', '$\sim$', etc. There are formation rules, which decree for example that '$p \text{ v } q$' is a well-formed string of symbols and that '$v p \text{ \&}$' is not. There are transformation rules, which allow us to move from 'p' to '$p \text{ v } q$', or from 'q' to '$p \rightarrow q$', or from '$p \text{ \& } q$' to 'p', and so on. There are certain axioms or postulates, such as '$\sim(p \text{ \& } \sim p)$' or '$p \text{ v } \sim p$', strings of symbols that have a privileged position in the calculus because they are not derived from any other strings of symbols. In an uninterpreted calculus there are no propositions and nothing is asserted. There is no truth and no falsehood, and therefore neither analytic nor synthetic truth. For example regarded solely as a formula in an uninterpreted calculus '$(p \,\&\, (p \to q)) \to q$' is neither true nor false, neither analytic nor synthetic, for it is not a genuine proposition. Similarly in the uninterpreted predicate calculus there is no referring and no describing. For example regarded as a formula in the uninterpreted calculus '$\sim(y)\sim Fy$' is merely a string of symbols which we are permitted to derive from '$\exists y Fy$', another string of symbols.

An *interpreted* calculus is a calculus in which the symbols have been given a meaning or interpretation. To give an interpretation is to give a further set of transformation rules, which enable us to translate symbols or strings of symbols from the calculus into expressions or sentences of a natural language. For example we interpret the propositional calculus by substituting propositional sentences of English (or French or German or Swahili) on 'p', 'q', 'r', etc., propositional sentences such as 'the cat is on the mat', 'Socrates is a man', 'I met an aged, aged man a-sitting on a gate'. And we treat '$\sim$' as 'not', '$\&$' as 'and', 'v' as 'or', and so on. Thus in an interpreted calculus we may well have genuine propositions, strings of symbols that make true or false claims. *A fortiori* there will be analytic and synthetic truths: some interpreted sentences of the calculus will be true in virtue of the rules and axioms of the uninterpreted calculus and the rules of interpretation, and other interpreted sentences will be true for other reasons. For example 'if p and p implies q, then q' is an analytic truth when regarded as a sentence in the interpreted propositional calculus, because it is true in virtue of a transformation rule of the uninterpreted calculus (that 'q' can be derived from '$p \,\&\, (p \to q)$') and in virtue of the rules for interpreting 'p', 'q', etc., as propositional sentences, '$\&$' as 'and', and so on. Similarly in the interpreted predicate calculus there can be genuine reference and description, for in interpreting the calculus we substitute referring terms on 'a', 'b', 'x', 'y', etc., predicate terms on 'F', 'G', etc., and quantifiers on '$\exists$', '$\forall$'. And in an interpreted calculus we can have proper arguments, systematic moves from one set of interpreted symbols to another, from one propositional sentence to another. We argue validly as long as we obey the transformation rules of the calculus and our rules of interpretation.

It is easy to overlook the distinction between uninterpreted and interpreted calculi because the calculi with which we are most familiar were developed with particular interpretations in mind. The propositional and predicate calculi were developed with a view to being interpreted as calculi of propositions and of reference, predication, and quantification. And the calculus of Euclidean geometry was originally developed as an interpreted calculus for the surveying and measurement of physical space. But regarded simply as uninterpreted formal calculi they could in principle be given any interpretation. We could in principle substitute natural numbers on 'p', 'q', 'r', etc., in the propositional calculus, and expressions for addition, multiplication, and subtraction on the logical connectives. We might for example interpret 'p & $(p \rightarrow q) \vdash q$' to mean '$2+(2\times 3)=3$'. The only objection to such a highly original plan would be the practical objection that our calculations would have no predictive value. In my example the interpreted theorem would lead us to expect that adding a pair of oranges to three pairs of oranges would yield three oranges. We cannot even guarantee that a more sensible interpretation of the propositional calculus will rule out all possible absurdities. Prior argued in 'The Runabout Inference Ticket' that we have to formulate the rules of the uninterpreted calculus very carefully if we are to avoid embarrassing consequences when it is interpreted, however reasonable the interpretation may appear. For example we could not interpret the propositional calculus as a calculus of propositions if it contained the 'tonk' rule, the runabout inference ticket, namely the rule (i) that 'p' implies 'p tonk q' and (ii) that 'p tonk q' implies 'q'. For we would then be able to derive any proposition from any other, and so would be able to derive false conclusions from true premisses.

So we must maintain a distinction between uninterpreted and interpreted calculi and must remember that a calculus can in principle be given any interpretation, even though in practice the calculi with which we are most familiar were developed with particular interpretations in view. Let us now concentrate on the calculi of arithmetic and Euclidean geometry. We must distinguish clearly between the uninterpreted and interpreted calculi. The uninterpreted calculi yield no propositions, nothing true or false, analytic or synthetic. There are no genuine referring terms and no genuine predicate terms. For example in the uninterpreted Euclidean calculus 'straight line' does not refer to any straight line, 'parallel' to any parallel, 'angle' to any angle, or indeed to anything at all. Indeed the uninterpreted Euclidean calculus is no more geometrical than any other calculus. It consists merely in a set of symbols, rules for forming strings of symbols, rules for transforming one string into another string of symbols, and axioms or postulates, that is, strings of symbols that have a privileged position because they are not derived from any other strings of symbols. When we interpret the calculus we give a certain meaning of significance to the symbols of the calculus. For example we may interpret Euclidean geometry as a geometry of physical space, by interpreting 'line' to refer to physical lines, 'parallel' to parallels, 'angle' to angles, and so on. Similarly we may interpret the calculus of arithmetic as an arithmetic of objects, by using '2' to refer to pairs of things, '3' to trios of things, '+' to the addition of one set of things to another, and so on.

So the interpreted calculi will yield propositions about physical lines, angles, plane figures, or about pairs of oranges and apples, men digging trenches, and so on.

What then is the status of mathematical theorems such as that $7+5=12$, or that $2\times2=4$, or that the sum of the interior angles of a triangle is two right angles, or that the square on the hypotenuse of a right-angled triangle equals the sum of the squares on the other two sides? If by 'theorems' we mean theorems in the *uninterpreted* calculus, then they are not genuine propositions, are neither true nor false, neither analytic nor synthetic. They are merely strings of symbols which can be derived from the axioms or postulates of the calculus according to its transformation rules. But if by 'theorems' we mean—as Kant meant—theorems in the *interpreted* calculus, then the theorems are analytic truths in this sense: if the interpreted axioms or postulates of the calculus are true then the interpreted theorems are true. For the interpreted theorems follow analytically from the interpreted axioms or postulates according to the formation and transformation rules of the calculus and the rules of interpretation. For example we might interpret the Euclidean calculus in the conventional way as a geometry of physical space, by taking 'line' to mean 'line', 'angle' to mean 'angle', 'parallel' to mean 'parallel', and so on. And if the interpreted axioms or postulates are true as statements about physical space, then it must be true that the interior angles of a physical triangle add up to two right angles, or that a physical right-angled triangle has Pythagorean properties. For the theorems follow analytically from the axioms or postulates according to the formation and transformation rules of the Euclidean calculus and the rules of interpretation.

Thus strictly speaking the theorems are not themselves analytic truths but are rather the consequents of analytic hypotheticals whose antecedents are the interpreted axioms or postulates of the calculus. The analytic truths of the interpreted calculus are of the form 'if p, then q', where 'p' refers to the interpreted axioms or postulates of the calculus and 'q' to the interpreted theorems. Obviously we can detach the interpreted theorems from the hypotheticals and obtain synthetic propositions about the world, about physical space or sets of physical objects. For example, although the interpreted theorem that right-angled triangles have Pythagorean properties may follow analytically from interpreted Euclidean axioms or postulates, detached from the axioms or postulates it stands as a synthetic claim about right-angled triangles in physical space.

We can now attack a problem that puzzled Kant considerably, namely that of showing to what extent the theorems of geometry and arithmetic apply or must apply to the world. What should we say for example when we discover that the interior angles of even the best-behaved triangles muster more or less than two right angles? There are four main possibilities. First, in attempting to derive interpreted theorems, propositions about physical space, we may have broken one of the transformation rules of the calculus. That is, we may have argued invalidly, and the interpreted theorem does not follow analytically from the interpreted axioms or postulates. Second, we may have interpreted the calculus perversely, for example by allowing 'straight line' to refer to any physical line, whether straight or not. Third, the interpreted theorems may be incompatible with certain physical theories and can only be maintained at the cost of those physical theories. For example, as Carnap argues in Chapters 15 and 16 of *Philosophical Foundations of Physics*, certain Euclidean theorems appear to be false when interpreted as claims about physical plane figures in strong gravitational fields. But that is only because we assume that light rays do not bend, and that rigid measuring rods do not expand and contract, in strong gravitational fields. If we were prepared to revise that assumption and thereby make our physics extremely messy, we could maintain Euclidean theorems, interpreted as claims about physical space. 'Euclidean geometry can be preserved if we introduce new physical laws, or the rigidity of bodies can be preserved if we adopt a non-Euclidean geometry. We are free to choose whatever geometry we wish for physical space provided we are willing to make whatever adjustments are necessary in physical laws' (op. cit., p. 157). Einstein chose to retain a simple physics and to adopt a non-Euclidean geometry.

The fourth and most important possibility is that the theorems are false when interpreted as claims about the world because at least one of the axioms or postulates of the calculus is false when interpreted as a claim about the world. For example certain Euclidean theorems are false when interpreted as claims about physical space because they rest on the parallels postulate, which is false when interpreted as a claim about physical space. The interpreted theorems no doubt follow analytically from the interpreted postulates but at least one of the interpreted postulates is false. And of course there is nothing surprising in the fact that one may move analytically from falsehood to falsehood.

Let us apply all my remarks directly to Kant's main doctrines. He argues that mathematical judgements in general and mathematical theorems in particular are synthetic *a priori*, that they are in no sense reducible to logical truths but that they are established independently of experience and must apply to objects of experience. I have in effect argued that he is mistaken in three respects. First, he neglects the very important distinction between uninterpreted and interpreted calculi, and so fails to appreciate that we can in principle choose one interpretation of a calculus rather than another. He treats Euclidean geometry and simple arithmetic as interpreted calculi and does not realize that there can be no guarantee that such interpretations will be the only interpretations or even the best interpretations available.

Second, he claims that mathematical theorems are synthetic in the sense that we can never derive them analytically from the axioms or postulates of the (interpreted) calculus; we can only derive them synthetically with the aid of intuition; we can offer no logical guarantee that they are true, but can see that they are true. I have argued that the interpreted theorems follow analytically from the interpreted axioms or postulates of the calculus. Given the formation and transformation rules of the calculus and the rules of interpretation, if the interpreted axioms or postulates are true then the theorems must be true. It is often said that Kant can be forgiven for invoking the aid of intuition in mathematical proofs, for insisting that the (interpreted) theorems do not follow analytically from the (interpreted) axioms or postulates. For the Euclidean postulates with which he was familiar were technically incomplete and did not entail the theorems. It is only comparatively recently that mathematicians have attempted to complete Euclid's set of postulates and so to give Euclidean geometry the logical rigour I have attributed to it. But such sympathetic remarks reveal a complete misunderstanding of the *Critique of Pure Reason*. Kant thought that logic is the province of our intellectual faculty (known as understanding in certain contexts and as reason in others) but that mathematics is the province of sensibility. That is, according to Kant it is only by constructing figures in intuition that we construct our mathematical concepts. 'Thus philosophical knowledge considers the particular only in the universal, mathematical knowledge the universal in the particular' (A714/B742). Intuition for Kant is not the paper that conceals the cracks of a logically defective calculus, but an essential part of any mathematical thinking.

Third, Kant regards mathematical theorems as unfalsifiable. Objects must be such that two objects and two objects always equal four objects, and physical space must be such that the interior angles of a triangle add up to two right angles. His main reason for thinking so would seem to be transcendental idealism: objects must conform to the theorems of arithmetic and Euclidean geometry because our faculty of sensibility constructs objects in time and space with precisely those properties. I have argued that although the interpreted theorems of arithmetic and Euclidean geometry follow analytically from the interpreted axioms or postulates, detached from the axioms or postulates they stand as synthetic and falsifiable claims about physical objects. Interpreted as a statement about the addition of one pair of objects to another, and detached from the axioms of arithmetic, '2+2=4' is a synthetic and falsifiable claim. We cannot guarantee that by adding two objects to two objects we will always obtain four objects. Similarly and more obviously, interpreted as a statement about physical space and detached from the postulates of Euclidean geometry, 'the interior angles of a triangle add up to two right angles' is synthetic and falsifiable. Indeed if Einstein is correct it has been falsified. As I pointed out earlier, that is not a surprising or disturbing result. Assuming that our proofs of Euclidean theorems are rigorous, that our interpretation of the Euclidean calculus is reasonable, and that Einstein's physical theories are to be accepted, it merely follows that at least one of Euclid's postulates is false when interpreted as a statement about physical space, and we must adopt a non-Euclidean calculus as the geometry of physical space.

4. A SPECIAL PLACE FOR LOGIC AND ARITHMETIC?

According to the objection I have just examined, we should treat the calculi of geometry and arithmetic just as we treat logical calculi such as the propositional calculus and the predicate calculus. Just as the interpreted theorems of a logical calculus follow analytically from the interpreted axioms of the calculus, so the interpreted theorems of geometry and arithmetic follow analytically from the interpreted axioms or postulates of the calculi. We can of course detach the theorems from the axioms or postulates, and regard them as falsifiable claims about physical objects. Detached from the interpreted postulates of Euclidean geometry, the interpreted theorem that right-angled triangles have Pythagorean properties is a synthetic claim about physical space; and detached from the interpreted axioms of arithmetic, the interpreted theorem that $7+5=12$ is a synthetic claim about the result of adding seven physical objects to five physical objects.

But it might be argued that there is an important difference between geometry on the one hand, and logic and arithmetic on the other. For we do not regard the interpreted theorems of logic and arithmetic as falsifiable. We do not expect to find circumstances in which we would want to say something of the form 'p, $p{\rightarrow}q$ but $\sim q$' or of the form '$\sim p$, $p \vee q$ but $\sim q$'. And we do not expect to find circumstances in which we would want to say that two and two are five, or that seven and twelve are thirteen. In contrast we are quite content —unlike Kant—to regard interpreted Euclidean theorems as falsifiable and in certain cases falsified. We are prepared to admit that the interior angles of a physical triangle do not add up to two right angles, and that the circumference of a physical circle does not equal πd. It might be said therefore that Kant was right to insist that arithmetic cannot be falsified, even though he was wrong to insist that geometry cannot be falsified.

But it would be wrong to embrace such a conclusion. There may be differences between geometry, on the one hand, and arithmetic and logic, on the other, but they have nothing to do with falsifiability. It is true that interpreted logic, interpreted arithmetic, and interpreted geometry yield certain theorems that depend analytically on certain axioms or postulates. It is also true that Euclidean geometry has been falsified in the sense that its interpreted postulates generate false interpreted theorems, false claims about physical space. And finally it is true that we have no such grounds for thinking that arithmetic and logic have been or might be falsified. But those important facts do not constitute an asymmetry between geometry, on the one hand, and arithmetic and logic, on the other. The most that follows is that Euclidean geometry, interpreted as a geometry of physical space, contains at least one false postulate, whereas arithmetic, interpreted as an arithmetic of physical objects, does not, and logic, interpreted as a logic of natural languages, does not.

Two further points spring to mind. First, the question of interpretation is vitally important. As I pointed out earlier, one reason why the propositional calculus appears to be unfalsifiable is that it has been developed with a particular interpretation in view, namely interpretation as a logic of propositional argument in natural languages. We have been careful to exclude from the calculus any rules, such as Prior's runabout inference ticket, that would allow us to derive false conclusions from true premises in the interpreted calculus. Second, it might reasonably be argued that in the case of arithmetic we allow a certain looseness of fit between the interpreted calculus and the world. In asking 'Why are the Calculi of Logic and Arithmetic Applicable to Reality?' Popper argued that the interpreted theorem '$2+2=4$' is frequently falsified: for example if you put $2+2$ drops of water into a dry flask you rarely obtain four drops of water. And even if his example is unconvincing, it is still true that we can offer no absolute guarantee that the theorems of logic, arithmetic, and geometry will be true when we interpret them as claims about the world. The best we can do is to trim a calculus to suit a particular interpretation, as in the case of propositional and predicate logic, or to discard the calculus if its interpreted theorems are false, as in the case of Euclidean geometry. None of those remarks yield an important formal difference between simple arithmetic and logic, on the one hand, and Euclidean geometry, on the other.

5. EUCLIDEAN AND 'PHENOMENAL' GEOMETRY

Thus very little is left of the central Kantian claim that mathematical judgements are synthetic *a priori*. In the sense in which Kant regards them as synthetic, they are analytic; that is, the interpreted theorems follow analytically from the interpreted axioms or postulates according to the formation and transformation rules of the calculi and the rules of interpretation. In the sense in which he regards them as *a priori*, unfalsifiable, they are falsifiable; the theorems may be false when interpreted as claims about the physical world, for they may rest on postulates that are false when interpreted as claims about the physical world. Furthermore Kant is wrong to give a special status to Euclidean geometry, to regard it confidently as the only possible mathematics of physical space and as essential to our experience of the physical world. The development of non-Euclidean geometries more able to cope with the discoveries of modern physics puts a very firm end to that privileged position.

However, in Part Five of *The Bounds of Sense* Strawson attempts to cater in a less ambitious way for Kant's special interest in Euclidean geometry. He concedes for the reasons I have given that Euclidean geometry is not the only possible mathematics of physical space, and that it is not essential to our experience of the physical world. But he suggests that it may none the less have a special status in our experience because it consists of a certain generalizing and idealizing of the way the world looks to us. It is not an acceptable interpreted geometry of physical space, but it is a successful interpreted geometry of 'phenomenal' space. The world looks Euclidean and we picture or imagine spatial figures in Euclidean terms. For example 'we cannot, either in imagination or on paper, give ourselves a picture such that we are prepared to say of it both that it shows two distinct straight lines and that it shows both these lines as drawn through the same two points' (op. cit., p. 283).

Such a partial resurrection of Euclidean geometry has two main advantages. First, it does justice to the teaching and development of Euclidean geometry as a series of self-evident truths about actual or imagined objects. It might seem obvious to us that vertically opposite angles are equal, that the shortest distance between two points is a straight line, or that two straight lines cannot enclose a space. Whenever we draw or imagine geometrical figures we draw or imagine them in Euclidean terms. Second, Strawson's suggestion would justify Kant's attempt to connect geometry with the faculty of intuition. For if Euclidean geometry is a 'phenomenal' geometry of the appearances or looks of things, whether actual or imagined or pictured, then the faculty at work is indeed the faculty of sensing or perceiving, the Kantian faculty of sensibility. There would indeed be a connection between the *a priori* intuition of space that yields geometry and the *a priori* intuition of space that governs our perception of tables and chairs. And we would in turn be able to explain Kant's concern with the 'construction of figures', with the representation of the universal in the particular. 'Phenomenal geometry' would be concerned with the 'looks' of particular things such as triangles, whether on sports fields or in carpenter's shops, on pieces of paper or drawn on a blackboard, pictured on a blank wall or simply imagined 'in the mind's eye'. It would presumably be a central psychological fact about human beings that they see vertically opposite angles as equal, or the shortest distance between two points as a straight line, and that they find it impossible to imagine two straight lines enclosing a space.

But the whole terminology of 'looks' is extremely vague. It is not at all clear what it means to say that the world looks Euclidean, or can only be pictured in Euclidean terms. And if the meaning of the suggestion is clear, its truth is not. I am not convinced that we see literally or metaphorically that only one line parallel to a given line can be drawn through a point not on the given line, or that vertically opposite angles are equal, or that a square ABCD is exactly twice the area of ABD. Indeed future generations, more practised in the use of non-Euclidean geometries, may find no difficulty in picturing or imagining all sorts of non-Euclidean figures. Finally, even if we were to concede that Euclidean geometry is psychologically central to our experience, that it is a 'phenomenal' geometry, it is difficult to see its philosophical significance. As Bennett argues in *Kant's Analytic*, 'even if it is true that nothing could "look non-Euclidean", this is irrelevant to the serious examination of spatial concepts, because single visual fields are only clues, by good luck rather reliable ones, to the spatial relations amongst things' (op cit., p. 31). I think we might reasonably go further than Bennett, for human senses are notoriously easy to deceive. Even when we understand the mechanisms involved, standard optical illusions such as the Müller-Lyer illusion continue to be illusions. The 'looks' of things are often wholly unreliable clues to the spatial properties of things. So even if it were true that the world looks Euclidean to us, we would be far from understanding either the actual structure of physical space or the relation between geometry and physical space.

9

TRANSCENDENTAL IDEALISM

I. POSITIVE IDEALISM

In my discussion of the first *Critique* so far, I have referred frequently to transcendental idealism, a set of doctrines that Kant weaves closely into his argument. As I have interpreted him the main four doctrines are these:

(a) There are two kinds of object, phenomena or appearances or things as they appear or the sensible world, and noumena or things in themselves or the intelligible world. We can and do have knowledge of phenomena, of things as they appear; we do not and cannot have knowledge of noumena, of things as they are in themselves. That is, with our human faculties, notably the human faculty of sensibility, we can only have knowledge of spatial and temporal phenomena; we cannot have knowledge of non-spatial and non-temporal noumena.

(b) Strictly the objects of experience or phenomena or things as they appear are 'nothing but a species of my representations', nothing but collections of perceptions. Their existence is wholly dependent on the perceiver.

(c) Experience is the result of complicated causal transactions between things in themselves and the self in itself: 'things as objects of our senses existing outside us are given, but we know nothing of what they may be in themselves, knowing only their appearances, that is, the representations which they cause in us by affecting our senses' (*Prolegomena*, p. 289). Strictly of course 'causal' and 'cause' should suffer the indignity of inverted commas, because things in themselves are non-spatial and non-temporal and we therefore cannot apply the category of causality to them. The complex psychological machinery involved is described in the theory of synthesis. The passive faculty of sensibility receives intuitions under the forms of space and time, and the active faculty of understanding organizes and unites the intuitions in one consciousness, brings them to the unity of apperception according to the forms of *a priori* synthesis, the categories.

(d) *A priori* knowledge of things in themselves or noumena is clearly impossible because we can only have knowledge of objects that could in principle yield intuitions, objects that are spatial and temporal. But we can certainly have *a priori* knowledge of things as they appear or phenomena. For example the Aesthetic examines our *a priori* knowledge of the mathematical properties of things as they appear or phenomena, and the Analytic examines our *a priori* knowledge of their physical properties. That kind of *a priori* exercise is perfectly legitimate because it begins with a careful examination of a possible experience, a series of possible intuitions or perceptions. In contrast the *a priori* metaphysics that is attacked in the Dialectic is unacceptable because it is concerned with objects as they are in themselves or noumena, objects that are not objects of a possible experience.

Intimately connected with the whole metaphysics of transcendental idealism is a distinction between the transcendent and the transcendental (cf. A11/B25, A296/B352-3). Kant frequently confuses the two halves of the distinction, especially in the Dialectic, but when he is on his best behaviour he uses it as follows. 'Transcendent' means 'not immanent', outside the limits of human experience. We can talk about transcendent objects or transcendent concepts or transcendent uses of a concept. For example according to Kant the ideas of pure reason are transcendent concepts, for they are concepts of objects outside the limits of a possible experience. Some of the ideas might of course have a perfectly respectable immanent use in another context. For example although the concept of substance is misused in the Cartesian Paralogisms and in references to God, it is used perfectly properly in the argument of the first Analogy, where it is applied to objects of a possible experience. 'Transcendental' is tied to '*a priori*' and means 'relating to *a priori* knowledge of objects'. For example the conclusions of the Aesthetic and the Analytic are transcendental because they articulate the *a priori* conditions of experience. The Aesthetic is Transcendental because it is devoted to the *a priori* contribution of sensibility to experience, the Analytic is Transcendental because it is devoted to the *a priori* contribution of understanding, and the Dialectic is Transcendental because it is devoted to the pseudo-science of *a priori* speculative metaphysics, a science which purports to give us access to transcendent objects. Transcendental idealism is transcendental because it appears to guarantee our *a priori* knowledge of objects. Objects must be spatial, temporal, causal, substantial, etc., because our faculties construct them in precisely that way: 'the objects are nothing but representations, the immediate perception ... of which is at the same time a sufficient proof of their reality' (A371).

For reasons that will become clear in the next section I shall call my interpretation of transcendental idealism the 'positive' interpretation. And as I pointed out in my discussion of the Antinomies, so interpreted transcendental idealism consists of two quite different doctrines, phenomenalism and noumenalism. Phenomenalism is the doctrine that objects of experience are and are only collections of perceptions or 'species of representations', and it is a characteristically empiricist doctrine. If one accepts that our knowledge comes directly or indirectly from sense-experience it is natural (though not essential) to reduce all claims about the external world to claims about actual or possible perceptions. Noumenalism is the doctrine that there are two kinds of object, phenomena and noumena, and it is a characteristically rationalist doctrine. For if one accepts that knowledge can only be acquired through the understanding, that the senses only yield a feeble and muddy approximation to genuine knowledge, it is natural (but again not essential) to suppose that the objects around us, the objects accessible to the senses, conceal or feebly reflect a world of objects accessible only to the understanding. A radical empiricism leads naturally (but not inevitably) to a Berkeleian world of perceivers and their perceptions, while a radical rationalism leads naturally (but not inevitably) to a search for Platonic forms or Leibnizian monads. Since Kant is both impressed by his recollection of David Hume and yet slightly drowsy from his dogmatic slumber, he is led in both directions at once.

Kant's noumenalism plays a comparatively minor role in the first *Critique* and I shall have little to say about it until in section 4 I discuss its important role in Kant's ethics. But his phenomenalism is both prominent and important in the first *Critique*, and I must make a determined effort to support my claim that Kant is a Berkeleian, that he wants to reduce objects to collections of perceptions. I would offer two main considerations in favour of my 'positive' or Berkeleian interpretation. The first is the purely textual consideration that there are many passages, particularly in the Aesthetic, that could easily be mistaken for transliterations of Berkeley: 'if the subject, or even only the subjective constitution of the senses in general, be removed, the whole constitution and all the relations of objects in space and time, nay space and time themselves, would vanish' (A42/B59); 'not only are the drops of rain mere appearances, but ... even their round shape, nay even the space in which they fall, are nothing in themselves, but merely modifications or fundamental forms of our sensible intuition' (A46/B63).

The second consideration is that at least two of Kant's arguments in the Dialectic rest squarely on a Berkeleian reduction of objects to collections of perceptions. The first is his criticism of Descartes's causal theory of perception, in the discussion of the fourth Paralogism in the first edition. According to Descartes external objects are the unobservable but inferred causes of our perceptions. Kant argues that the inference from observed perceptions to unobservable objects is extremely shaky, and suggests transcendental idealism as a more acceptable alternative. 'By *transcendental idealism* I mean the doctrine that appearances are to be regarded as being, one and all, representations only' (A369). 'External objects (bodies) ... are mere appearances, and are therefore nothing but a species of my representations, the objects of which are something only through these representations. Apart from them they are nothing' (A370). Not merely are the Berkeleian tones unmistakable, but Kant has to reduce objects to collections of perceptions if he is to make his point against Descartes. For his point is that if we regard perceptions and objects as two kinds of thing, we are committed to inferring the existence of objects from the occurrence of perceptions. And the inference cannot possibly guarantee the existence of objects. We can only guarantee their existence if there is no inference, if we dismantle the distinction between perceptions and objects. Objects then become as immediate to me as any of my experiences, and I can no more doubt the existence of the external world than I can doubt the occurrence of my sensations. 'In order to arrive at the reality of outer objects I have just as little need to resort to inference as I have in regard to the reality of the object of my inner sense ... For in both cases alike the objects are nothing but representations' (A371).

The other argument of interest is to be found in Kant's solution of the Mathematical Antinomies. He claims that in each case we arrive at a contradiction, despite arguing rigorously from true premisses. There must therefore be an implicit and false premiss, namely that the world exists as a whole, in itself, quite independent of our perceptions. Since the premiss generates contradiction it must be discharged. In other words, Kant argues, the Mathematical Antinomies prove indirectly that there is no world as a whole, in itself, independent of our perceptions. 'The objects of experience ... are *never* given *in themselves*, but only in experience, and have no existence outside it' (A492/B521). 'Nothing is really given us save perception and the empirical advance from this to other possible perceptions' (A493/B521). It is difficult to avoid comparing Kant with Berkeley unless one reads perversely between or behind the lines, for the lines themselves are unequivocal: 'this space and this time, and with them all appearances, are not in themselves *things*; they are nothing but representations, and cannot exist outside our mind' (A492/B520). But much more to the point, it is difficult to understand Kant's solution of the Mathematical Antinomies unless he is a Berkeleian phenomenalist. For he wants to contrast the concept of a world in itself, which generates Antinomies, with the concept of a world as 'mere representations', which does not. It is difficult to give any content to the contrast unless it is a contrast between a world quite independent of any

perceivers and a world of Berkeleian perceptions. He repeatedly reminds
us that 'appearances' exist only in the regress of observation and that
the only coherent task for the scientist is the acquisition of more and
more remote observations. 'The series are not things in themselves, but
only appearances, which, as conditions of one another, are given only
in the regress itself. The question, therefore, is no longer how great this
series of conditions may be in itself . . . but how we are to carry out the
empirical regress, and how far we should continue it' (A514/B542).

2. NEGATIVE IDEALISM

So I want to argue that Kant is a 'noumenalist' in the sense that he distinguishes between two sets of objects, non-spatial and non-temporal noumena and spatio-temporal phenomena; and that he is a 'phenomenalist'
in the sense that he reduces objects of experience or phenomena to collections of perceptions. But there is at least one other interpretation available, which attributes to Kant neither genuine noumenalism nor genuine
phenomenalism. Indeed Kant himself would probably repudiate my
interpretation, at least to the extent of repudiating any comparison with
Berkeley. After all, the Refutation of Idealism was inserted in the second
edition precisely because many critics of the first edition had accused
Kant of holding Berkeleian views. A convenient way of approaching an
alternative or 'negative' interpretation of transcendental idealism is to
contemplate the chapter on Phenomena and Noumena at the end of the
Analytic of Principles (A235–60/B294–315), for it contains an important
distinction between a positive sense of 'noumenon' and 'phenomenon',
and a negative sense.

   To talk of noumena and phenomena in a *positive* sense is to talk of
two sets of objects. Noumena are non-spatial and non-temporal objects
and are therefore inaccessible to human beings, whose faculty of intuitions, the faculty of sensibility, is spatial and temporal. Noumena
would only be accessible to beings with a different faculty of intuitions,
beings which were capable of 'intellectual' intuition, capable of perceiving things non-spatially and non-temporally. Phenomena, on the other
hand, are spatio-temporal objects, the ordinary objects of human experience such as tables and chairs. I would argue that if Kant is using 'phenomenon' and 'noumenon' positively in the first *Critique* then my interpretation of transcendental idealism is substantially correct, and Kant
is both a noumenalist and a phenomenalist. He is a noumenalist in the
sense that he distinguishes between noumenal and phenomenal objects
and draws attention to certain 'causal' transactions between the two sets
of objects. He insists that the objects of human experience are phenomena
because they are spatial and temporal and because the forms of human

intuition are space and time. In the Aesthetic and Analytic he examines our knowledge of phenomenal objects and in the Dialectic he exposes the foolishness of any attempt to gain knowledge of noumena. Throughout the *Critique* his phenomenalism is revealed in frequent and frantic attempts to reduce phenomenal objects, tables and chairs, to collections of actual and possible perceptions.

So much then for the positive sense of 'noumenon' and 'phenomenon' and the corresponding positive interpretation of transcendental idealism. In contrast, to talk of noumena and phenomena in the *negative* sense is to talk of two kinds of access to the objects of experience. Not two kinds of object, but two kinds of *access* to objects. It is to distinguish between the noumenal or intellectual, the non-spatial and non-temporal, way of perceiving objects, and the phenomenal or sensible, the spatial and temporal, way. Since human beings perceive objects phenomenally, as spatial and temporal, we cannot say anything at all about noumenal access to objects, about non-spatial and non-temporal perception. Nor can we confidently say that human perception is the only kind of perception. We have to leave open the possibility of other kinds of perception even though we can say nothing whatever about them. In other words, negatively interpreted, 'the concept of a noumenon is ... a merely *limiting concept*, the function of which is to curb the pretensions of sensibility; and it is therefore only of negative employment ... it cannot affirm anything positive beyond the field of sensibility' (A255/B310–11).

The corresponding 'negative' interpretation of transcendental idealism is similar to an interpretation defended by H. E. Matthews in 'Strawson on Transcendental Idealism' and goes as follows. We perceive objects spatially and temporally, and indeed given our sensible faculty of intuition we could not perceive them in any other way. But we cannot confidently rule out the possibility of other, quite different, kinds of perception. To talk of noumena is only to draw attention somewhat elliptically to the peculiar limits of human knowledge and to expose the futility of trying to step outside them. Kant is only a 'noumenalist' in the feeble sense that he wants to remind us of the limits of our own perception, and to leave room for other kinds of perception even though we can say nothing whatever about them. And he is a 'phenomenalist' in the equally feeble sense that he wants to argue that the very general properties we attribute to objects depend on our having the faculties we have. We attribute spatial, temporal and causal properties to objects, for example, because we perceive objects as spatial, temporal, and causal. We say that the world is pink, as it were, because we all wear rose-coloured spectacles.

If the negative interpretation is correct, transcendental idealism is extremely innocuous and quite attractive. It consists in an attempt to restrict our metaphysical ambitions within the limits of human experience. It reminds us that our experience is of a certain kind and that it is in principle futile either to describe or positively to rule out any other kind of experience. We must be content merely to point out that we perceive objects in certain ways (e.g. spatially, temporally, causally, substantially). 'We know nothing but our mode of perceiving them—a mode which is peculiar to us, and not necessarily shared in by every being, though, certainly, by every human being. With this alone have we any concern' (A42/B59).

But such an interpretation will not do, for two reasons. First, it fails miserably to explain certain passages I quoted above, in which Kant appears to say quite literally that objects are collections of representations. The quotation in the previous paragraph probably disposes of one of the passages I used but there are many others which resist such treatment. And the chapter on Phenomena and Noumena certainly does not give unqualified support to the negative interpretation of transcendental idealism. For example in the first-edition version Kant makes a decidedly positive remark about the existence of noumena: 'the concept of appearances, as limited by the Transcendental Aesthetic, already of itself establishes the objective reality of *noumena* and justifies the division of objects into *phaenomena* and *noumena*' (A249).

Second, the negative interpretation does no justice to the important psychological component of transcendental idealism. Kant is not merely arguing that we attribute certain properties to the world because we perceive it so; he wants to make the stronger point that the world has those properties because we construct it in precisely that way. We experience a spatio-temporal world because our sensibility presents a manifold of spatial and temporal intuitions, and we experience a world that is causal, substantial, etc., because we synthesize the manifold according to the concepts of cause, substance, etc. Indeed the essence of Kant's 'Copernican Revolution' is to make the phenomenal world dependent upon our own cognitive apparatus, since it is only in that way that we can guarantee *a priori* knowledge of objects. 'If intuition must conform to the constitution of the objects, I do not see how we could know anything of the latter *a priori*; but if the object (as object of the senses) must conform to the constitution of our faculty of intuition, I have no difficulty in conceiving such a possibility' (Bxvii). For example we can only guarantee the necessity of mathematics if the space of geometry and the time of arithmetic depend directly on the pure human intuitions of space and time. It is not good enough merely to say that we attribute certain mathematical properties to the world because we perceive the world mathematically. Kant's point is rather that we can only guarantee the necessity of mathematics by reducing the mathematical properties of objects to properties of the perceiver. 'If, therefore, space (and the same is true of time) were not merely a form of your intuition, containing conditions *a priori*, under which alone things can be outer objects to you, and without which subjective conditions outer objects are in themselves nothing, you could not in regard to outer objects determine anything whatsoever in an *a priori* and synthetic manner' (A48/B66).

3. FORMAL IDEALISM

The negative interpretation therefore leaves too much in need of explanation. Kant is not merely identifying the main features of human awareness of objects and leaving room for other kinds of awareness, such as the 'intellectual' or 'noumenal' kind. Nor is he merely arguing that humans regard the world as spatial, temporal, causal, substantial, etc., because they perceive it in precisely that way. But it might be argued that even if we reject the negative interpretation of transcendental idealism we are not compelled to return to my positive interpretation. That is, we are not compelled to attribute to Kant a clear distinction between phenomenal objects and noumenal objects, nor to accuse him of being a Berkeleian phenomenalist. As I have already observed, he would be particularly incensed by the comparison with Berkeley. Sadly many of his attempts to exorcize the spectre tend only to nourish it: 'I grant by all means that there are bodies without us, that is, things which, though quite unknown to us as to what they are in themselves, we yet know by the representations which their influence on our sensibility procures us. These representations we call "bodies", a term signifying merely the appearance of the thing which is unknown to us, but not therefore less actual. Can this be termed idealism?' (*Prolegomena*, p. 289).

We must resist the temptation to give the obvious answer and must consider a third interpretation of transcendental idealism, an interpretation which attempts to do justice to the important psychological component of transcendental idealism without forcing Kant into the arms of Berkeley. That is, it credits Kant with a certain kind of idealism but not Berkeleian idealism. Kant occasionally refers to his idealism as 'formal' (B519a) or 'critical' (*Prolegomena*, p. 294) and contrasts it with the 'material' idealism of Descartes or Berkeley, who hold 'the existence of objects in space outside us either to be merely doubtful and indemonstrable or to be false and impossible' (B274). Such references might suggest that Kant is using a distinction between form and matter, that his idealism is an idealism of form whereas Berkeley's is an idealism of matter. That is, Kant is perhaps only reducing the *form* of objects to properties of the perceiver, whereas Berkeley reduces *the objects themselves* to properties of the perceiver. Perhaps Kant is arguing that we project a certain number of formal properties upon the objects of experience. We mentally construct the objects around us only 'as regards their form' (A127), and the content of objects, their ordinary empirical character, is entirely independent of us. The world must be spatial, temporal, causal, substantial, etc., because our faculties of sensibility and understanding project such properties upon it. Our 'subjective constitution ... determine its form as appearance' (A44/B62). But objects also have certain 'material' properties such as colour or shape or mass, which are not dependent on our human faculties. Objects must be pink, as it were, because we see them through rose-tinted spectacles but the objects have an independent existence.

Thus according to this 'formal' interpretation the distinction between phenomena or things as they appear and noumena or things in themselves is not a distinction between two sets of objects. If Kant is a formal idealist it is a distinction between two kinds of *descriptions* of objects, between descriptions that refer to the formal features that our minds project upon objects, and descriptions that do not refer to those formal features. If we give the complete description of objects, which includes reference to such formal features as space, time, causality, substance, we are referring to things as they appear to us. In a Kantian phrase, we are describing them under one 'aspect' (A543/B571) or from one 'standpoint' (*Groundwork*, Ch. III). But to abstract the formal features and to describe objects in complete independence of human experience is to talk about things as they are in themselves. It is to describe them from a quite different 'standpoint', under a quite different 'aspect'.

Before discussing the 'formal' interpretation of transcendental idealism it will be helpful to set out the three interpretations. We can best appreciate the differences between them by reducing each of them to two main claims, as follows.

'*Positive*' *idealism*: (i) There are two sets of objects, spatio-temporal phenomena or things as they appear, and non-spatial and non-temporal noumena or things in themselves.

(ii) Objects of experience or phenomena are and are only collections of perceptions.

'*Negative*' *idealism*: (i) There are two kinds of awareness of objects, spatial and temporal awareness (i.e. human awareness), and non-spatial and non-temporal awareness (e.g. 'intellectual' awareness). Although we cannot coherently rule in the possibility of non-spatial and non-temporal awareness, we cannot reasonably rule it out.

(ii) We attribute space, time, causality, substance, etc., to objects because we perceive them spatially, temporally, causally, substantially, etc.

'Formal' idealism: (i) We may describe objects in two ways. We may describe things as they appear to us, by referring to the central formal features of human experience, or we may describe things as they are in themselves, independently of any characteristic formal features of human experience.

(ii) Objects must appear to us as spatial, temporal, causal, substantial, etc., because our faculties of sensibility and understanding give precisely that formal structure to our experience of objects.

Thus although the formal interpretation is similar in certain respects to the negative interpretation, it is much more promising because it does much more justice to the central psychological doctrines of transcendental idealism. Indeed formal idealism is clearly a version of idealism whereas negative idealism is not: formal idealism is clearly a version of the general thesis that statements about objects of experience must be reduced in some non-trivial way to statements about the perceiver. And there can be no doubt that formal idealism will serve Kant's central Critical purposes very well. He wants to demolish much of traditional speculative metaphysics but also wants to pull up short of Humean scepticism. Although he wants to dismiss as vacuous certain synthetic *a priori* claims about souls, the nature and extent of the universe, and God, he none the less wants to guarantee some substantive *a priori* knowledge of the world. Formal idealism will do the trick. For if the basic formal features of objects are projected on them by our faculties of sensibility and understanding then we have a guarantee that, as objects of experience, they will have those features. We will be able to guarantee that objects do conform to the synthetic *a priori* principles of mathematics and physics. There is a sense in which objects must be pink if we are wearing rose-coloured spectacles. If the form of objects must conform to the constitution of our faculty of intuition, as Kant would say, we have no difficulty in guaranteeing knowledge of objects *a priori*.

Despite its Critical advantages formal idealism is extremely eccentric, represents very little advance on Berkeleian idealism, and with minor qualifications is open to the objections I shall consider in section 5. But most importantly for our present purposes, I am not at all convinced that Kant is a formal idealist in the sense defined. Certainly he refers to his own idealism as 'formal' and contrasts it with the 'material' idealism of Berkeley or Descartes. No doubt it is tempting to suppose that he is using a clear distinction between the form and the matter of experience; that whereas Berkeley is arguing for an idealism of objects Kant is only arguing for an idealism of the formal features of objects; that Kant does not want to reduce all properties of objects to properties of the perceiver, but only such very general properties as space, time, causality, substance.

It may also be true that formal idealism will fulfil Kant's main Critical purposes because it will guarantee some substantive *a priori* knowledge of the world. None the less I would still argue that Kant is not a formal idealist but a positive idealist and, more specifically, that he is a Berkeleian idealist. I am reluctant to do so, for we are all to some extent influenced by the Great Man Argument, which turns on the compelling but false assumption that Great Men cannot say Silly Things. But I see no other possible interpretation of many of the passages I quoted in section 1. 'By *transcendental idealism* I mean the doctrine that appearances are to be regarded as being, one and all, representations only' (A369). 'External objects (bodies) . . . are mere appearances, and are therefore nothing but a species of my representations, the objects of which are something only through these representations. Apart from them they are nothing' (A370). Moreover, as I also argued in section 1, two of Kant's arguments make little sense unless Kant is a Berkeleian idealist—namely his attack on Descartes's causal theory of perception, in the discussion of the fourth Paralogism in the first edition, and the solution of the Mathematical Antinomies. In short, we should not be confused by Kant's distinction between 'formal' and 'material' idealism, for his own 'formal' idealism is indistinguishable from the 'material' idealism of Berkeley.

4. NOUMENALISM AND ETHICS

So far I have concentrated on one part of transcendental idealism and have argued that the positive interpretation is correct in one respect, for Kant is indeed a Berkeleian phenomenalist. But what of his alleged noumenalism, the distinction between non-spatial, non-temporal noumena and spatio-temporal phenomena? Is this really a 'positive' distinction between two kinds of *object*, or a 'negative' distinction between two kinds of *awareness* of objects, or perhaps even a 'formal' distinction between less and more comprehensive *descriptions* of objects? Much of the evidence in the first *Critique* is inconclusive, principally because Kant did not need the concept of a noumenon for most of his argument. There is however the foolish observation in the Preface to the second edition, that we must at least be able to think of things in themselves, since 'otherwise we should be landed in the absurd conclusion that there can be appearance without anything that appears' (Bxxvi–xxvii). Furthermore it is clear from the context that it is the self in itself that is of most interest, because it is to play an important role in Kant's later ethical works. There are many references to the 'practical interest' of pure reason in the discussion of the Paralogisms and of the third Antinomy. Kant tries hard to avoid referring to noumena as objects, to avoid making any positive claim about their existence or properties. But occasionally he lapses. 'Man ... who knows all the rest of nature solely through the senses, knows himself also through pure apperception; and this, indeed, in acts and inner determinations which he cannot regard as impressions of the senses. He is thus to himself, on the one hand phenomenon, and on the other hand, in respect of certain faculties the action of which cannot be ascribed to the receptivity of sensibility, a purely intelligible object' (A546–7/B574–5).

As the ethical doctrines are developed in the *Groundwork* and the second *Critique*, the distinction between noumenal reason and phenomenal sensibility becomes crucial. For Kant wants to guarantee the autonomy and universality of ethics, to ensure that our moral principles are principles for any rational being, whether or not he is a human being with peculiarly human wants and interests. They are not merely principles for Prussians or for Western Europeans or indeed for human beings. They are not 'hypothetical' principles, principles which are to be followed if one has a certain desire or is in a certain situation or in a particular social class. They are not even conditional on a desire for happiness, whether it be our happiness or someone else's. Happiness is to be regarded as a fortunate but accidental consequence of virtue: 'The principle of happiness may, indeed, furnish maxims, but never such as would be competent to be laws of the will, even if *universal* happiness were made the object' (*Critique of Practical Reason*, Ak., p. 36; Abbott, p. 125). Moral principles must be 'categorical', must make demands that are unqualified, that are not conditional upon our own desires or the desires of anyone else or even the desires of human beings in general. They are universal principles for any rational being, whether he be a human being or an angel or a Martian.

Therefore human phenomenal sensibility can yield no moral principles. It is the faculty of wants, desires, interests, the faculty which embraces everything Plato might have called appetite and Hume might have called a passion, everything from primitive desires for food, shelter, and sex to sophisticated desires for books, lectures, and gramophone records. If moral principles depended on sensibility they would not be genuinely universal, for they would only make demands on human beings. They must be the unadulterated offspring of the faculty common to all rational beings, the faculty of pure practical reason, and the promptings of pure practical reason are revealed as the 'free causes' of the third Antinomy: 'the moral law expresses nothing else than the *autonomy* of the pure practical reason; that is, freedom' (ibid., Ak., p. 33; Abbott, p. 122).

There are obvious and devastating objections to such an elevated view of ethics. For example it is difficult to see how any choice can be rational if it is logically independent of any wants or interests or desires. Surely I cannot make moral choices or offer moral advice without making essential reference to what I or other people want, without choosing between competing desires. If practical reason is indeed pure when it makes moral choices, it is difficult to see how it makes them, and we can understand only too well the desperation of the unfortunate Maria von Herbert: 'If I hadn't read so much of your work I would certainly have taken my own life by now. But the conclusion I had to draw from your theory stops me—it is wrong for me to die because my life is tormented, and I am instead supposed to live because of my being ... I read the metaphysic of morals and the categorical imperative, and it doesn't help a bit' (Letter from Maria von Herbert to Kant, August 1791; Zweig, p. 175). We may well feel that her subsequent suicide was a fitting comment on Kant's ethical philosophy.

The important point for our purposes is that Kant's ethical views rest squarely on noumenalism *positively* interpreted. He does want to talk of noumenal objects in general and noumenal people in particular. Of course many of his remarks are superficially innocuous. We have seen that in his solution of the third Antinomy he tries to avoid any direct reference to noumenal objects, and in the third chapter of the *Groundwork* he talks of phenomenal and noumenal causality as 'two standpoints', two ways of describing the world in general and human beings in particular. But careful examination of detail reveals noumenalism positively interpreted. For example it seems that free causality 'refers to an object that cannot be determined or given in any experience' (A533/B561). And Kant explains that the distinction between free noumenal cause and natural phenomenal effect is irretrievably connected with the phenomenalist reduction of objects of experience to collections of representations. For objects of experience, understood as collections of representations, are 'appearances' and appearances presuppose things that appear: 'if they are viewed not as things in themselves, but merely as representations, connected according to empirical laws, they must themselves have grounds which are not appearances ... they must rest upon a transcendental object which determines them as mere representations' (A537/B565, A538/B566).

In the second *Critique* Kant throws all caution to the winds. The most important noumenal causes for his purposes are the autonomous promptings, or free acts of will, of pure practical reason. The moral man is the man whose actions are generated wholly by his noumenal faculty of reason, completely independently of his phenomenal faculty of sensibility. And it is his awareness of his freedom, of the noumenal causality of reason, that gives him access to a supersensible world of noumenal objects: 'that unconditioned causality ... is no longer merely indefinitely and problematically *thought* ... but is even *as regards the law of its causality* definitely and assertorially *known*; and with it the fact that a being (I myself) belonging to the world of sense, belongs also to the supersensible world, this is also positively *known*, and thus the reality of the supersensible world is established' (op. cit., Ak., p. 105; Abbott, p. 200). Not even the frantic and puzzling assurances that such knowledge is only knowledge 'from a practical point of view' can repair the damage. We seem to have stepped beyond the limits of experience, to have been offered access to a world of noumena positively interpreted, a world of non-spatial and non-temporal objects.

I would close this section with a cautious historical observation. One may wonder why Kant should want to defend noumenalism, to leave room for non-spatial and non-temporal objects which according to the first *Critique* are not possible objects of human experience. I have just examined an important philosophical reason, namely that noumenalism supports a rigidly autonomous system of ethics. If we are to obtain universal or categorical moral rules, rules which are logically independent of any contingent wants or interests, we must sever any link with the contingent phenomenal faculty of sensibility. Moral principles must be the thoroughbred offspring of the noumenal faculty of pure practical reason. By grounding ethics firmly on something so divorced from human experience Kant avoids every form of naturalistic fallacy, avoids all the toils of 'heteronomy'.

But that explanation only pushes our problem one stage further back, for one still wants to ask why Kant should want to defend such bleak ethical doctrines. It may be true that noumenalism is an essential part of his attempt to guarantee the autonomy of ethics, to make moral principles the province of pure practical reason alone, but why should he want to guarantee that degree of autonomy? Why should he so easily cast off the central doctrines of the first *Critique* and seek the illicit delight of a supersensible world in the second *Critique*? I would suggest that the only plausible explanation is historical, that Kant never fully freed himself from his rationalist origins. The superficial empiricism, nay even the occasional positivism, of the first *Critique* was powerless to eradicate the lingering influence of Kant's dogmatic slumber. The general thesis of noumenalism and the specifically ethical doctrines it supports are the direct descendants of two classically rationalist claims. The first is the general claim that knowledge through the reason or understanding alone is the very paradigm of knowledge, that knowledge through the senses is at best a muddy and miserable approximation to the real thing. Kant's discussion of moral awareness, our awareness of the free causality of pure

practical reason, suggests that such awareness has a dignity and an eleva-
tion far superior to our ordinary perceptual awareness of tables and
chairs. After all, in the second *Critique* Kant argues for the 'primacy'
of practical reason, claims that practical reason gives us access to supersensible realms denied to theoretical reason. The second and more specific rationalist view that clearly inspires Kant's noumenalism is Leibniz's
account of monads, the non-spatial, non-temporal, and non-causal
('windowless') basic elements of the universe. Leibniz never successfully explains how non-spatial, non-temporal, and non-causal monads
should yield to human beings a picture of spatio-temporal objects
in causal interaction. Similarly Kant never successfully explains how
non-spatial, non-temporal, and non-causal noumena should yield
human experience, experience of objects that are spatial, temporal,
causal, substantial, etc.

5. OBJECTIONS TO TRANSCENDENTAL IDEALISM

The *Critique of Pure Reason* is inspired by a profound respect for empiricist criteria of knowledge. Kant insists that knowledge requires both concepts and intuitions, and therefore that much of what passes for *a priori*
metaphysical knowledge is spurious. Yet in the *Groundwork* and second
Critique we see him toying with some of the forbidden objects of rationalist metaphysics. The difficulties of transcendental idealism are only the
difficulties of the whole Critical philosophy writ small. Kant wants to
be a phenomenalist, to reduce objects of experience to collections of actual
and possible perceptions, and he wants to be a noumenalist, to distinguish
between the phenomenal objects of experience and unknowable noumenal objects. And he is struggling with limited success to reconcile two
distinct philosophical traditions. His phenomenalism shows the strong,
even excessive, influence of an empiricist account of knowledge, of the
view that all substantive knowledge depends directly or indirectly on
sense-experience. His noumenalism shows a profound reluctance to
abandon a rationalist preference for knowledge obtained through the
reason or the understanding alone, and reveals a connected interest in
a world of supersensible or intelligible objects, which lie beyond the ordinary, confused, inferior objects of sense-experience.

I have argued that the positive interpretation of Kant's idealism is
correct, that he does distinguish between noumenal objects and phenomenal objects, and does reduce phenomenal objects to collections of perceptions. Although I have taken a rather patronizing attitude towards
Kant's idealism so interpreted, I have not yet expressed any very clear
objections to it. I must now attempt to remedy the omission. The objection to noumenalism, to the distinction between unknowable noumena

and spatio-temporal phenomena, is simple and straightforward and is expressed eloquently by Kant on many occasions. If knowledge requires both concepts and intuitions, if noumenal objects are non-spatial and non-temporal, and if human intuition or perception is spatial and temporal, then we cannot say anything whatever about noumena. We cannot even think of them or entertain their possibility. For to entertain their possibility entails being able to describe them in general terms, to say what would count as finding them, perceiving them, having appropriate intuitions of them. But if they are non-spatial and non-temporal, and if objects of human experience are necessarily spatial and temporal, we logically cannot say what would count as finding them. The notion of noumena, whether actual or possible, is entirely vacuous on the best Critical assumptions.

Kant's phenomenalism is open to many of the objections normally levelled at Berkeley but I shall not discuss them here, for I prefer to concentrate on the difficulties that are peculiar to Kant's position. One might say that his phenomenalism is not merely superficially disappointing but is fundamentally incoherent. The most obvious disappointment is that phenomenalism seriously undermines the central argument of the Analytic against scepticism with regard to the senses. We are strongly persuaded that we must distinguish between ourselves and external things, that we must regard external things as logically independent of us, as spatial, temporal, causal, substantial, etc. But we are then invited to dilute those admirable claims and to dismantle the distinction between perceiver and object by reducing objects to collections of perceptions. Of course if we obliterate the external world we cannot have sceptical doubts about it, but one would prefer to leave the central argument of the Analytic in its literal and pristine condition.

Furthermore the attempt to combine a superficial realism with a Berkeleian phenomenalism is very definitely incoherent, because phenomenalism entails a radical solipsism and according to the Transcendental Deduction solipsism is incoherent. That is, if all objects consist in species of my actual and possible representations then everything and everybody consists of me and my representations. If the idealist Kant is right, then everything and everybody consists in collections of Kant's actual and possible perceptions. At the same time, according to the Kant who wrote the Transcendental Deduction, a series of experiences is possible only if someone is aware of them as his and can distinguish between himself and other things. Kant must be able to distinguish between himself and other things. But if every possible object of experience is a collection of Kant's actual and possible perceptions, if everything and everybody consists of Kant and his perceptions, then Kant will lose all sense of his own identity, will lose the distinction between himself and other things. A solipsist cannot even know that he is lonely.

That specific disappointment and specific incoherence can be generalized, for Kant's transcendental idealism is part of a persistent conflation of the logically and psychologically *a priori*. Kant intends in the *Critique of Pure Reason* to articulate the necessary conditions of a possible experience, to list the crucial synthetic *a priori* truths of mathematics and physics. But his execution of the intention in the Aesthetic and Analytic yields two entirely separate theses, which for obvious reasons I shall call the logical thesis and the psychological thesis. The *logical* thesis is that experience logically must be of external objects, which are spatial, temporal, causal, substantial, etc. Any description of a possible experience that neglects any of those conditions will be unintelligible, logically absurd. The *psychological* thesis is that the self in itself is affected by various other things in themselves, in such a way that the faculties of sensibility and understanding, aided by imagination, construct a picture of external objects (or phenomena or things as they appear) which are spatial, temporal, causal, substantial, etc. Thus when we refer to the objects of experience we are referring to collections of actual and possible perceptions, 'species of representations', the fruits of the constructive work of sensibility and understanding.

The two theses are entirely separate. The logical thesis is supposed to be a necessary truth whereas the psychological thesis is a contingent truth. The logical thesis entails that an account of experience of objects that are non-spatial, non-temporal, non-causal, non-substantial, etc., is absurd or unintelligible, whereas the psychological thesis merely entails that such a strange experience would be different from our own. The logical thesis can only be established by careful analysis of the notion of a possible experience, while the psychological thesis must be established *a posteriori* or experimentally, despite Kant's impression to the contrary. No doubt the theses are easily conflated, for the conditions mentioned are the same in each case, namely space, time, causality, substance, etc. But in one case the conditions are claimed to be logically necessary for experience, and in the other they are claimed to be psychologically necessary. As it stands the psychological thesis does not rule out the possibility that such psychological necessities are logically contingent.

Of course Kant does not distinguish clearly between the two theses and travels cheerfully back and forth from one to the other in the same breath. Whenever his transcendental idealism is being pressed very hard we find him arguing for the hybrid thesis that experience must be of external objects which are spatial, temporal, causal, substantial, etc., because our minds make them so. For example in the Analytic he is not content merely to conclude that we must have experience of external objects which are substances and which obey causal laws. He feels it necessary to offer a psychological analysis of his conclusion: the notion of an external world of causal substances is necessary to experience precisely because the faculty of understanding synthesizes intuitions in that way. His account of mathematics follows the same dismal pattern. Having reached the interesting conclusion that mathematical judgements are synthetic but necessary truths, he feels he must interpret the conclusion psychologically: the judgements are necessary truths precisely because the faculty of sensibility constructs the spatial and temporal properties of objects and so yields geometry and arithmetic. Objects must have certain features because we have made them so.

Thus the first *Critique* suffers from a constant tension between Kant's realism, his attempt to guarantee knowledge of a world outside us and independent of us, and his idealism, his attempt to describe the psychological origins of our experience and to reduce the objects of experience to collections of actual and possible perceptions. With misguided enthusiasm he even boasts frequently that he is both an 'empirical realist' and a 'transcendental idealist' (cf. A28/B44, A35–6/B52, A369). But to justify the boast he must have things both ways, because he is arguing both from within and from outside the limits of human experience. His realism keeps him firmly within the limits of human experience. Knowledge requires both concepts and intuitions, and if we are to make any intelligible claim about the world we must have some way *in experience* of establishing or refuting it. Thus we must ask, and can only ask, what must the world be like, if I am to make sense of it? What grounds are there in experience for making this distinction or using that concept? What are the main features of any experience intelligible to a human perceiver? The realist Kant suggests that the perceiver must distinguish between himself and external things, must regard the external things as spatial, temporal, causal, substantial, etc. He must have a way *in experience* of identifying and re-identifying objects of that kind, objects like tables and chairs.

That is all very salutary, but at the same time Kant is trying to step outside the limits of experience. Instead of asking questions about experience intelligible to human beings he wants to ask questions about the real structure of the world. He wants to investigate the noumenal origins of our experience and wants to reduce objects such as tables and chairs to collections of perceptions. But since knowledge requires both concepts and intuitions such desires should be resisted. No feature of our experience could either establish or refute any of those noumenalist or phenomenalist claims. No feature of our experience could establish that there are two sets of objects, noumena and phenomena, and no feature of our experience could establish that objects of experience are strictly collections of perceptions. Thus in claiming that there are two kinds of object and that objects of experience are strictly collections of perceptions, Kant is committing the same sort of mistakes as his opponents in the Dialectic, for he is attempting to make substantive knowledge-claims that could not even in principle be established or refuted in experience.

10

TRANSCENDENTAL ARGUMENTS

1. THE PROBLEM

In this final chapter I want to discuss a problem that is slightly peripheral to our systematic discussion of the *Critique of Pure Reason* but is none the less of enormous importance both to our understanding of Kant and to our modern philosophical endeavours. One way of approaching the problem is to consider the main argument of the Analytic in its sympathetically reconstructed form, which went as follows. There is a series of experiences, temporally ordered. Someone must be aware of them as his and so he must be able to distinguish himself from other things. That is, he must be aware of external things. And he can be aware of them only if they are spatial, temporal, substantial, and obey some laws of change.

Kant would call it a 'transcendental' argument because it purports to guarantee *a priori* knowledge of the world (cf. A11–12/B25). Many modern philosophers, particularly those influenced by Wittgenstein, have used arguments of a similar kind, arguments that purport to establish certain *a priori* truths about the world. For example Strawson argues in Chapter 2 of *Individuals* that experience must be of spatial objects, or objects in a dimension analogous to space. In the following chapter he claims that I can ascribe experiences to myself only if I can ascribe them to others. Bennett claims in *Rationality* that using language presupposes the ability to use a concept of time. Wittgenstein argues in the *Investigations* that I can refer to a sensation as '*S*' only if I can publicly check my use of '*S*'. And Malcolm argues in *Dreaming* that we can intelligibly talk of dream experiences only if we have some public criterion of dreaming other than the avowals of people after they have woken up.

Those are all typical modern examples of transcendental arguments. There are of course differences between them. Some are good and some are not. The rhetorical frills vary from case to case, and sometimes the arguments are described as articulating 'conceptual necessities' or 'criterial necessities' rather than *a priori* truths. In some cases the arguments are technically not arguments at all, but general hypotheticals: 'it is a necessary condition of experience that there is one space and one time'

or 'it is necessary to experience that most of our memory-claims be true'
or 'if we are to use sensation-words they must have public criteria of
application', and so on. But since the hypotheticals and the arguments
yield the same philosophical problem I shall continue to talk loosely of
transcendental arguments, arguments that purport to establish certain
a priori or necessary truths about the world.

The problem arising is this. In the arguments mentioned we encounter
a number of logical expressions such as '*a priori*', 'only if', 'necessary
condition of ... that ...', 'requires', etc., which connect each step to the
following step. But how should we analyse such expressions? What sort
of arguments are transcendental arguments? Are they formally deductive, at least in intention, and distinguished from other deductive arguments only by their striking content? That is, could we expect in each
case to move from premises to eventual conclusions armed only with
definitions of the vital expressions and the laws of deductive inference?
Or are they heavily disguised inductive arguments, yielding at best conclusions that are strictly *a posteriori* or empirical? Are the arguments
proper arguments, or are they rather apologies for general rules of philosophical method such as the verification principle? When we see the
magic words '*a priori*' or 'necessary' in the arguments, what sense of '*a
priori*' or 'necessary' is being used? Are we to think of strict logical
necessity or of causal necessity or of something else?

We must offer a general analysis of transcendental arguments, discover
which brand of logical cement is supposed to bind premises to conclusions. Of course it would be absurd to claim that they are all good
arguments. But many certainly are good and it is important to give an
account of their logical form. For if the transcendental style turns out
to be philosophically worthless in principle, many modern philosophical
discussions will be severely undermined. We must ask and answer a very
Kantian question about philosophical method, about the nature and
extent of *a priori* or transcendental speculation.

2. ANALYTIC NECESSITY

The first and probably the most obvious suggestion is that valid transcendental arguments are deductively valid, that their conclusions follow analytically, by the laws of deductive inference, from their premises. For
example the Kantian argument with which we began should be expressed
as follows. The occurrence of a series of experiences logically entails their
belonging to someone who is aware of them as his. Such self-awareness
logically entails his being able to distinguish between himself and other
things, his using concepts of external objects. And that in turn entails
that such objects are spatial, temporal, causal, substantial, etc. Or to take

other examples, using sensation-words entails their being words in a public language, experience of space and time entails that there is only one space and one time, and so on. In all the arguments we are trying to move from premisses to conclusions with the help solely of the laws of deductive inference and appropriate definitional assumptions. The arguments may not be as obviously analytic as 'x is a cat, so x is an animal' or 'y is a four-sided plane figure, so y is a quadrilateral'. They will usually be so complicated that, as Bennett suggests in *Kant's Analytic* (p. 42), they will at best be 'unobviously' analytic.

I want to insist that they are nothing of the sort. Some of the examples I have used are certainly not analytic, because they are not valid by any standard. For example I argued in Chapter 2 that it is in no way necessary that we experience one and only one space. But much more to the point, even the very impressive transcendental arguments, such as the reconstructed argument of the Analytic, are not analytic, do not move from premisses to conclusion according to the laws of deductive inference. A good case could be made for saying that Kant's argument begins with an analytic truth, since it is analytically true that a series of experiences must belong to someone and that he must be aware of them as his. Indeed, as we saw in Chapter 3, Kant makes precisely that point by arguing that the principle of the necessary unity of apperception is 'an identical, and therefore analytic, proposition' (B135). But the rest of the argument is not analytic, not deductively valid. For example it is no part of the meaning of 'object' that objects are spatial, temporal, causal substances. One of the very striking features of Kant's argument is that it begins with a premiss about a series of experiences and finishes with a conclusion about external things. It moves very plausibly from one 'distinct existence' to another by *a priori* argument. Yet for familiar Humean reasons it is difficult to accept any analytic connection between distinct existences.

But it might be suggested that there is a hidden premiss which guarantees the deductive rigour of the argument. And one candidate immediately springs to mind, for Kant stresses frequently that his argument is an investigation of a possible experience. So although we begin with one explicit premiss, that there is a series of experiences ordered in time, perhaps we should expose an implicit premiss, that the series of experiences constitutes a possible experience. Whenever the argument threatens to break a rule of deductive inference, that implicit premiss should be exposed, for it will bear us in deductive triumph to the next step. We will deduce all the conclusions we require.

Unfortunately the proposal suffers from severe weaknesses which arise from the interpretation of the phrase 'possible experience'. Suppose for example 'experience' means 'experience of outer things'. Then we can certainly deduce one important conclusion of the Analytic, that my experiences must be experiences of objects outside me. But that is both too much and too little. It is too little because we are no nearer deducing that the objects must be spatial, temporal, causal substances, etc. It is too much because we have eliminated scepticism about the external world by a stipulative definition. That is, we have stipulated that 'experience' means 'experience of outer things' and have then derived the footling conclusion that experience must be of outer things. We might avoid those difficulties by interpreting 'possible experience' in another way. We might weaken the definition so that 'experience' means 'series of experiences, states of consciousness'. But that will merely reduce our implicit premiss to the trivial observation that a series of experiences is a series of experiences, and that will hardly entail any of the conclusions Kant wishes to draw. Or we might strengthen the definition, so that 'experience' means 'experience of external things which are spatial, temporal, causal substances, etc.' But the consequent deductive rigour of Kant's whole argument is achieved at the cost of utter triviality. The important and striking conclusions of the Aesthetic and Analytic will be the simple and obvious consequences of a tendentious stipulative definition.

Another way of looking at the matter is this. It may well be tempting to import a further premiss in an effort to make Kant's argument logically rigorous, to make premisses logically entail conclusion. But our problems reappear in a different place. For what is the status of the further premiss that a given series of experiences constitutes a possible experience? If it is to generate the required degree of deductive rigour it has to be interpreted to mean 'the series of experiences in question constitutes an experience of external objects which are spatial, temporal, causal substances, etc.' Presumably it is meant to be some sort of *a priori* truth rather than an interesting observation on the contingent oddities of our chosen series of experiences. But if it is some kind of *a priori* truth, what kind? It does not appear to be a logical truth, logically analytic. In other words, although we may have avoided talking of a synthetic transcendental argument, we seem to be left with a synthetic transcendental premiss. The problem about the status of transcendental arguments merely turns into a problem about the status of transcendental premisses.

3. SYNTHETIC NECESSITY

So little is to be gained from insisting that valid transcendental arguments are deductively valid, that their conclusions follow analytically from their premisses. They might be strengthened by the addition of a further premiss but we will then be left with questions about the status of the premiss. The next suggestion to be examined is that transcendental arguments are logically synthetic but none the less necessary. They purport to state necessary truths but those truths are logically synthetic. That is, if we are to use and appreciate transcendental arguments we must admit that there may be synthetic *a priori* relations between propositions, for example between the premiss and the conclusion of Kant's argument. We might begin by recalling my remarks at the end of the previous chapter, on the tension in the first *Critique* between Kant's realist account of a possible experience from *within* experience and his idealist account from *outside* experience. I said that only the realist account can be of any interest. We want an account of experience that is intelligible to the person who is having the experience. We want to be able to check any claim about the world within experience, to show how in experience we can make certain distinctions, use certain concepts. We are not interested merely in the claim that there might be a perceiver with various experiences, but want to know what grounds he might have for discovering his condition. We are not interested merely in the claim that there might be external things, but want to know what grounds we could have for thinking so and for attributing certain properties to them. Generally we want to know which conditions are *sufficient* for our having certain concepts, sufficient for my self-awareness, sufficient for my identifying external objects, sufficient for my using sensation-words, and so on.

And we might use our newly discovered idiom of sufficient conditions in an attempt to understand the reconstructed Kantian argument. Although according to Kant step 2 is an analytic truth, a statement of the many-layered principle of the necessary unity of apperception, the rest of the argument can be expressed in the idiom of sufficient conditions as follows.

1. There is a series of experiences, temporally ordered.

2. Someone must be aware of them as his.

3. His distinguishing himself from external objects is sufficient for his being aware of experiences as his.

4. His applying concepts of objects is sufficient for his distinguishing himself from external things.

5. His perceiving a world of objects that are spatial, temporal, causal, substantial, etc., is sufficient for his applying concepts of objects.

I suspect that various qualifications need to be made if the notion of sufficiency is to be useful. For example we probably have to insert '*ceteris paribus*' here and there, because our alleged sufficient conditions will only be sufficient with the aid of a number of general background conditions. But there is something still more important to be added, something implicit in Kantian talk of the 'necessary' conditions of a possible experience. Suppose that on Mars the existence of purple fungi is sufficient for the Martians' using the concept of an omnipotent creator. We may suppose that a Martian Kant has argued that it is a necessary condition of any theological experience intelligible to a Martian that there are purple fungi. But such hypotheses make no sense to us. Even if purple fungi are sufficient for the Martians' using the concept of an omnipotent creator, we could not understand why. Thus we cannot take an interest in absolutely any conditions sufficient for our using this or that concept. We can only take an interest in those conditions we can understand or make intelligible to ourselves. Given our limited conceptual resources we are simply incapable of understanding or thinking of certain possibilities.

If we thread all those considerations together, the proposal for discussion is this. The relation between the premisses and conclusion of a valid transcendental argument is a synthetic but *a priori* relation. And when a sentence of the form '*A* is a necessary condition of *B*' occurs in a transcendental argument it means (i) that *A* is sufficient for *B* (*ceteris paribus*) and (ii) that we cannot conceive of any other conditions that would be sufficient for *B*. For example to say that my using concepts of objects is necessary for my self-awareness is to say (i) that my using concepts of objects is sufficient for my self-awareness (*ceteris paribus*) and (ii) that we are incapable of thinking of any other conditions that are sufficient for my self-awareness.

If the proposal is acceptable it enables us to distinguish between successful and unsuccessful transcendental arguments. For example Strawson claims in Chapter 3 of *Individuals* that I can ascribe experiences to myself only if I can ascribe them to others. Translated into our novel canonical form his claim is (i) that my being able to ascribe experiences to others is sufficient (*ceteris paribus*) for my being able to ascribe them to myself and (ii) that we cannot conceive of any other conditions that would be sufficient for my being able to ascribe experiences to myself. We might reject his argument by pointing out certain other conditions that would be sufficient, by arguing for example that the existence of other *things*, not necessarily other persons, would be sufficient for my being aware of myself and my experiences. Strawson's transcendental argument is unsuccessful because we can easily sever the close connection between self-ascription and other-ascription of experiences.

Thus the suggestion is that all transcendental arguments are deductively invalid but that some are none the less 'valid' on other grounds, for they succeed in establishing certain synthetic *a priori* truths about the world. However, this heroic attempt to resurrect the notion of synthetic necessity is open to several objections. One objection is that it rests on a parochial view of human experience, because it refers to our ability to conceive this or that. It may well be true that there are peculiar connections between some of our concepts and others, but we are absurdly parochial if we believe that all kinds of possible experience must share precisely the same features, that the so-called necessities of our own view of the world are necessary to any possible view of the world. To take an analogy, it may be true that every social system so far described is hierarchical, that the concept of a social system is used only where the concept of a hierarchy is used. But it does not follow that every possible social system must share the same features.

I am inclined gladly to embrace the charge of parochialism, to this extent. It may be true that there are fairies at the bottom of my garden but as long as they remain in an entirely alien conceptual parish, as long as I am unable to describe any possible way in which I might identify them, might relate their activities to events in the world around me, it is worse than pointless to speculate about them. As Kant would say, knowledge requires both concepts and intuitions. Even in our attempts to establish *a priori* truths about the world, in our transcendental arguments, we are bound by the limits of human knowledge and human imagination. It is pointless to say merely that we can or cannot use certain concepts. We must ask rather how we could use them, what grounds we might have in experience for using them, how we might establish in experience that the world has certain features. To fabricate logically consistent fairy stories is not enough; we must be able to understand the activities of the fairies. Transcendental arguments do not merely establish certain synthetic *a priori* truths about the world. They establish synthetic *a priori* truths which we can understand and which must reflect the limits of our knowledge and imagination.

The objection might be pressed more strongly however. For the references to what we can understand, what we can imagine, what we can conceive, are very worrying. As our culture and especially our scientific culture changes, we may find we can conceive rather more or rather less than before. Transcendental arguments will be exposed as little more than exercises in the history of ideas, a patently *a posteriori* exercise. For Kantian reasons we may be justified in confining our attention to what we can make intelligible to ourselves, but there is a great danger of being historically parochial, of committing the sort of mistake that Kant committed when he claimed a special necessity and finality for Euclidean geometry and Newtonian physics. There is a great danger of our defending transcendental arguments that express the conceptual idiosyncrasies of twentieth-century Europeans.

Even if we could defend the proposal from the first objection it is impossible to defend it from a second. I have so far argued that transcendental arguments are in some sense *a priori* arguments, that although they are not deductively valid they purport to establish *a priori* truths about the world. But the crucial notion in the proposal under discussion, that of sufficiency, looks very much like a causal notion, and specific causal connections are established *a posteriori*, empirically. Transcendental arguments will certainly lose their charm if they rapidly degenerate into *a posteriori* arguments. One might insist that sufficiency is rather different from causal sufficiency, that 'sufficient' does not suggest the occurrence of two successive events but rather a relation between two conditions or states of affairs. Unfortunately, if sufficiency is not the same as causal sufficiency it is very difficult indeed to see what it is. More generally it is difficult to see how one could refute the Humean claim that any relation between 'distinct existences' is *a posteriori*, not *a priori*. The alleged investigation of certain synthetic *a priori* truths collapses on examination into an account of fairly abstract synthetic *a posteriori* or causal generalizations.

4. THE VERIFICATION PRINCIPLE

So little progress is to be made by reflecting on the notion of synthetic necessity or on the limits of human imagination. Nor, as we saw earlier, is there any point in trying to force transcendental arguments into a deductive mould. But one important Kantian thought is worth pursuing, namely the thought that knowledge requires both concepts and intuitions, that even when we speculate about the world *a priori* we must confine our attention to a possible experience. We must always ask how *in experience* we could find a use for this or that concept. It is that thought which inspires a third suggestion. In 'Transcendental Arguments' Barry Stroud suggests that on close examination transcendental arguments prove to be specific applications of the verification principle: 'the use of a so-called transcendental argument to demonstrate the self-defeating character of scepticism would amount to nothing more and nothing less than an application of some version of the verification principle, and if this is what a transcendental argument is then there is nothing special or unique, and certainly nothing new, about this way of attacking scepticism' (op. cit., pp. 255–6; Penelhum and MacIntosh, pp. 68–9). Presumably one might also say that there is nothing *a priori* about transcendental arguments in any interesting sense of '*a priori*'. For since the verification principle is a regulative or methodological principle, it is neither true nor false, and so is not an *a priori* truth. It is as best *a priori* in the uninteresting sense that it is a methodological principle that many philosophers are very reluctant to abandon.

How exactly should we analyse transcendental arguments according to this proposal? Presumably they are all concerned with particular kinds of verification of given statements. For example Kant's argument is concerned to show how 'I have a series of successive experiences' may or must be verified. It is verified by identifying spatio-temporal objects outside me, by distinguishing them and their properties from me and my properties. Similarly Wittgenstein's private language argument is supposed to show how 'I have the same pain today as I had yesterday' may or must be verified. It is to be verified by reference to certain publicly accessible facts, such as my being injured, groaning, dabbing embrocation here and there, and so on.

All those remarks are unexceptionable but I do not think that Stroud has really got to the heart of the matter. I do not wish to discuss the verification principle as such, save to remark that Stroud seems to have in mind a rather weaker formulation of the principle than that which originally inspired logical positivism. That is, he seems to have in mind the weaker claim that any significant synthetic statement must have empirical criteria of verification, rather than the stronger claim that the meaning of a synthetic statement *is* its method of verification. Nor do I wish to deny that the verification principle in some form or other plays an important part in transcendental arguments, since, as I have already insisted, such arguments are concerned to show how certain statements may or must be verified, how in general I may or must verify 'I have a series of successive experiences' or 'I have a pain similar to the one I had yesterday' or 'I dreamt I saw an elephant getting on a bus' or 'I remember seeing the Coronation'. I would even concede that the verification principle is a necessary feature of any genuine transcendental argument. But it does not follow, nor is it true, that transcendental arguments are and are only applications of the verification principle.

To make the discussion less abstract let us consider one or two strands in the argument on which we have concentrated, the claim that I can have experiences only if I am aware of a world of external causally interacting objects. A sceptic will insist that I can have experiences whether or not there are external things, and that even if I am aware of external things they may well be acausal, chaotic. Now if Kant is to sustain his claim he must certainly deploy some version of the verification principle. Indeed one of the most important doctrines of the first *Critique*, that knowledge requires both concepts and intuitions, that knowledge is necessarily of objects of a possible experience, could be regarded reasonably as a version or a very near cousin of the verification principle. Kant will not merely concede but will insist that we must have empirical criteria of verification of such statements as 'I have a series of successive experiences'. But there is much more to the claim than that, for its sting lies in the suggestion that such criteria are yielded only by a world of external causally interacting material objects. That is, Kantians and sceptics are not arguing about the acceptability of the verification principle. The sceptic can certainly allow for the purposes of argument that statements such as 'I have a series of successive experiences' are meaningless without empirical criteria of verification. The question at issue is whether a chaotic and Berkeleian world yields such criteria, or not.

Or consider Wittgenstein's claim that one can use sensation-words only as part of a public language, only in so far as their criteria of application are public. Again he must rely on some version of the verification principle because he must at least be claiming that all sensation-words have empirical criteria of application, that there must be a way in experience of drawing the distinction between painful and pleasant sensations, between feeling hot and feeling cold, between feeling cheerful and feeling miserable, and so on. But that is not the central point at issue. What is at issue is whether purely private acts of attention to one's sensations and feelings yield such criteria, or not.

In short, transcendental arguments may rest on but do not consist in applications of some version of the verification principle. Indeed on purely historical grounds it is difficult to see why Stroud should have been tempted to say they were. For the fiercest modern opponents of Kantian and Wittgensteinian transcendental arguments are those such as Ayer in whom the fires of Humean scepticism and of logical positivism still burn more or less brightly. The Ayers of this world obviously believe that Kant and Wittgenstein hold views that are profoundly mistaken, but they would hardly attribute the mistake to a rigid adherence to the verification principle. They are much more likely to regard Kant's and Wittgenstein's attempts to restrict *a priori* our conceptual resources as betraying a certain lack of philosophical imagination.

5. PSYCHOLOGICAL NECESSITY

The final proposal I shall examine attempts deliberately to use some of the debris left from our demolition of previous proposals. I argued in section 2 that transcendental arguments are not deductively valid as they stand, and I made very uncomplimentary remarks about any attempt to add another premiss to do the deductive trick. But now I want to explore the possibility that we were talking about the wrong additional premiss, that there may be an implicit premiss or premisses which will guarantee that the conclusions of transcendental arguments follow analytically from their premisses. In section 3 I criticized attempts to rest transcendental arguments on certain psychological assumptions, claims about the contingent limits of human senses and understanding. But now I wish to reconsider that criticism in more detail. As I have already observed on a number of occasions, one very striking feature of many transcendental arguments is their constant reference to the possibility of experience, or to the unity of experience, or to what we can understand or make intelligible to ourselves. I wish to examine in detail the suggestion that the arguments are attempts to establish the *logical* consequences of certain *contingent* assumptions about the world and especially about human beings.

Let us consider several examples, some of which are new to our discussion. One very popular and lamentable kind of transcendental argument might be called the 'contrast' argument. For example Austin in *Sense and Sensibilia* (p. 11) used the following objection to sceptical doubts about the existence of the external world: the sceptic thinks that it is possible to suffer complete and perpetual hallucination; but perceptual mistake makes sense only against a background of perceptual success; therefore scepticism is incoherent. Now it is difficult to see how we could establish the crucial middle section of that argument as it stands. It is certainly not a logical truth that the occurrence of a hallucination entails the occurrence of a further, but veridical, perception, for there are no logical connections between distinct existences. Nor does the conclusion follow from the premises as they stand. The very most that follows is that we have no way of identifying complete and perpetual hallucination. But if we suppose that the argument contains a hidden, uncomplimentary, and false assumption about certain contingent human abilities, it tightens up considerably as follows: the sceptic thinks that it is possible to suffer complete and perpetual hallucination; human beings cannot identify Fs unless there are non-Fs within reach with which to contrast them; so they can only identify hallucinations if they also have veridical experiences with which to contrast them; so human beings cannot identify the total and perpetual hallucination envisaged by the sceptic. We obtain a refutation of the sceptic if we add my self-denying ordinance that we should only address our philosophical attention to the objects that humans can identify.

Austin's argument is of course a very poor argument. If it were true that humans cannot identify Fs unless there are non-Fs within reach with which to contrast them, we could never draw the distinction between unicorns and non-unicorns or between frictionless and non-frictionless bodies. We could also prove that veridical perception makes sense only against a background of hallucination. But there are other, more attractive, transcendental arguments. There are those which make assumptions about the discernible features of our psychological states. For example we might reasonably assume that careful introspective examination of my psychological states will not reveal that this sensation is similar to yesterday's toothache, or that that perception is illusory, or that that belief is false. Those are not introspectively discernible features of my psychological states. And such assumptions help to generate the claim that knowledge is not a special kind of psychological state, or that I cannot privately check my use of the word 'pain', or that there is no private way of distinguishing hallucination from veridical perception. The first argument might go as follows: knowing that p requires not merely believing that p but also the truth of p; but there may be no discernible psychological difference between a true belief and a false belief; therefore knowledge is not a special kind of psychological state. Or the second argument might go as follows: if I am to use the word 'pain', I must be able to check that I have used it correctly; but there may be no clearly discernible psychological difference between correct and incorrect uses of the word; therefore I cannot privately check my use of the word.

Transcendental arguments in a third group make certain assumptions about our notion of personal identity, especially our notion of memory. They attempt to generate a formal contradiction between certain philosophical claims and our assumptions about memory. For example we assume that a man who has a sense of his own identity over twenty years will remember the majority of his more striking experiences during that time, that his experience does not normally split into short chunks separated by attacks of complete amnesia. To talk of my sense of my own identity is to talk, in the Kantian phrase, of a unity of experience, and a unity of experience seems to require a fairly reliable memory. The assumption generated my main objection to the two times hypothesis in Chapter 2. I argued that if Nottingham time and jungle time really are quite distinct, if it is impossible to map the two times on to a single temporal series, then I can in principle 'visit' a jungle event any number of times. For example I can visit and revisit a particularly striking orgy many times. But if I take advantage of my opportunity, I will no doubt remember my first visit during my second, and my second during my third, and so on. But then a complete description of events in the jungle will contain a contradiction, for it will refer to my enjoying the orgy for the first and the second time, and as both remembering the orgy (for it is my second visit) and not remembering it (for it is my first visit). The purpose of the objection is not to show that the notion of there being two times is contradictory but rather that it contradicts certain assumptions about self-awareness and memory. Crudely, we can either retail the fantasy, or maintain our central assumptions about self-awareness and memory, but not both. In this very Kantian sense *experience* of two times is not possible.

Many other examples spring to mind but it would be tedious to pursue them. The general proposal for discussion should already have emerged fairly clearly. Transcendental arguments are not deductively valid as they stand, but can be made so if we uncover one or more implicit assumptions about the logically contingent limits of human experience. To argue transcendentally is to articulate the logical consequences of such contingent limits. The object of the exercise is emphatically not to show that certain claims about a certain world are consistent or inconsistent. The object is rather to show that *experience* of such a world is logically compatible or incompatible with our contingent assumptions about human abilities. This might in turn suggest that the philosophical merit of a given transcendental argument is largely a function of the merit of its contingent assumptions about human abilities. If the assumptions are plausible, as in the refutation of the two times fantasy, the argument will be philosophically attractive; if not, as in Austin's objection to scepticism about the external world, not.

However, I have three worries about the proposal and my application of it to a number of specific examples. The first and least important is that I am not confident that I have produced in every case an argument that is deductively valid. The second and more important worry is that the final products have a decidedly silly and stilted air which is missing from the originals. One might argue that the stiltedness can be attributed to my lack of experience in formalizing transcendental arguments, that the polish and sophistication of the originals is bound to be lost in translation into the severe idiom of deductive inference. But I suspect that a more plausible and embarrassing explanation would be that there is something fundamentally wrong in trying to make transcendental arguments hinge on contingent assumptions about human experience. Indeed it is extremely difficult to see how the proposal could be applied to the most important argument discussed in this book, namely the argument which yields the conclusion that experience must be of a world of external objects which are spatial, temporal, causal, substantial, etc. The argument is not deductively valid as it stands, for it consists in an inference from a premiss about a perceiver to a conclusion about the external world, a decidedly distinct existence. But it is difficult to think of a suitable claim which will strengthen it, a suitable claim about the general limits of human experience. After all, as I have constantly emphasized, the philosophical appeal of the argument consists in its starting originally with a very unambitious assumption, namely that there is a series of experiences, and in then making very plausible steps to a highly ambitious conclusion, namely that the experiences must all belong to someone who regards them in part as his perceptions of external objects which are spatial, temporal, causal, substantial, etc.

The third and most important worry is that the proposal is open to

an important objection I raised in section 3. In tightening up our transcendental arguments we have only pushed the problem one stage further
back. Instead of a problem about the status of transcendental arguments,
we now have a problem about the status of the vital implicit premisses,
the claims about the limits of human experience. I said that they were
logically contingent claims, for example that humans cannot identify Fs
unless there are non-Fs with which to contrast them, or that there may
be no discernible psychological difference between a true belief and a
false belief, and so on. It is very striking that such claims are extremely
general, that they refer only to very general limits of human experience.
We would not dream of offering a transcendental argument that hinged
on a highly specific claim, such as the claim that humans do not have
infra-red vision, or that they do not hear sounds of 40,000 c.p.s., or that
they perceive space as three-dimensional and Euclidean.

But why not? Why should we take a philosophical interest in the
general claims but not in the specific? One important answer has already
been given, namely that we are not interested in recording the history
of ideas. We are not interested in arguments that turn on the very specific
scientific theories of, say, the eighteenth century. That is why Kant's
obsession with Euclid and Newton tends to undermine his otherwise very
plausible transcendental arguments. We are interested rather in arguments that turn on more general, more universal, features of human experience. Euclidean and Newtonian assumptions are not common to all
men at all times but certain very general cognitive abilities are.

That answer is quite promising as far as it goes, since it reminds us
that transcendental arguments should not turn on humans' making certain *assumptions*, such as Euclidean and Newtonian assumptions, but on
their having certain *abilities*. The assumptions may change fairly frequently but the general abilities do not. But there is much more to be
said, for human visual and auditory abilities do not change, and yet we
would have no interest in a transcendental argument that turned on that
fact. We need some other explanation of our considerable interest in very
general human abilities and of our lack of interest in the highly specific.
The explanation surely is that the general abilities in question are those
to which we can conceive no alternatives. We can readily imagine our
eyes responding to infra-red light, or our ears to higher frequency sound.
But we cannot imagine what would serve as a discernible psychological
difference between a true and a false belief, or between a correct and an
incorrect use of a sensation-word. We cannot imagine a man's having
a sense of his own identity over twenty years unless he can remember
a large number of his experiences during that time.

But there is the rub. The point of the proposal was to offer a clear analysis of transcendental arguments, an analysis which *inter alia* would make it unnecessary to take refuge in such expressions as 'what we can conceive', 'what we can make intelligible to ourselves'. The arguments, I suggested, articulate the logical consequences of certain contingent assumptions about human abilities. But not every contingent claim will be of philosophical interest, and we must begin our transcendental arguments only with claims about those human abilities to which we can conceive no alternatives. But it is not at all clear what sense of 'can' is involved in claiming that we can conceive no alternatives. Is it a matter of logic that we can only conceive one set of alternatives rather than another? Or is it merely a matter of fact? If it is merely a matter of fact then transcendental arguments are not even exercises in the history of ideas, for they merely record highly general features of human psychology. Perhaps it is a synthetic *a priori* truth that we can conceive certain possibilities but not others? Even if we have solved the problem of the status of transcendental arguments, we are left with the problem of the status of transcendental premisses.

6. FINAL OBSERVATIONS

The fruits of our very complicated discussion are meagre indeed. I argued that valid transcendental arguments are not deductively valid, that their conclusions do not follow analytically from their premisses. I rejected the suggestion that there is a synthetic *a priori* connection between premisses and conclusions. I claimed that although transcendental arguments may exploit a version of the verification principle, they are not merely versions or applications of it. Finally I rejected the suggestion that transcendental arguments rest on certain assumptions about the psychologically *a priori* features of human beings, that they reveal the logical consequences of certain synthetic assumptions about the limits of human experience.

It would seem that the only conclusion to be drawn is that transcendental arguments are in principle and irretrievably mistaken, as Körner argues in his paper 'On the Impossibility of Transcendental Deductions'. I am extremely reluctant to draw that conclusion, even though such reluctance is strikingly reminiscent of the Vatican's refusal to peer through Galileo's telescope, or of Johnson's refutation of Berkeley. For the transcendental style of argument is very common in modern analytical philosophy, even among philosophers who have little respect for either Kant or Wittgenstein. In a clear sense the Kants, Strawsons, Bennetts, Wittgensteins, Malcolms of this world stand and fall together. If we refuse to allow any kind of transcendental argument in philosophy, then they all fall and philosophy is very much the poorer.

BIBLIOGRAPHY

M Y system of references is for the most part self-explanatory. But I should perhaps point out that references to the *Critique of Pure Reason* are to the pages of the first (A) and second (B) editions, references to the *Prolegomena* are to the pages of the Akademie edition, and references to the *Critique of Practical Reason* are to the pages of the Akademie edition and to the pages of Abbott's translation.

1. KANT'S WORKS IN ENGLISH

Kant: Selected Pre-Critical Writings, trans. G. B. Kerferd and D. E. Walford (University of Manchester Press, 1968).

Critique of Pure Reason, trans. N. Kemp-Smith (Macmillan, London, 1929).

Prolegomena to Any Future Metaphysics, trans. L. W. Beck (Bobbs-Merrill, Library of Liberal Arts, New York, 1950).

Groundwork of the Metaphysics of Morals, trans. H. J. Paton as *The Moral Law* (Hutchinson, London, third edition, 1956).

Critique of Practical Reason, trans. T. K. Abbott (Longmans, London, sixth edition, 1909).

Critique of Judgement, trans. J. H. Bernard (Macmillan, London, second edition, 1931).

Religion Within the Bounds of Reason Alone, trans. T. M. Greene and H. H. Hudson (Harper Torchbooks, New York, 1960).

Metaphysical Principles of Virtue (Part II of *Metaphysics of Morals*), trans. J. Ellington (Bobbs-Merrill, Library of Liberal Arts, New York, 1964).

Kant's Philosophical Correspondence 1759–99, ed. and trans. A. Zweig (University of Chicago Press, 1967).

2. LIST OF ALL THE WORKS MENTIONED IN THE TEXT, TOGETHER WITH A SELECTION OF IMPORTANT BOOKS AND ARTICLES ON THE FIRST *CRITIQUE*

AL-AZM, S. J., *The Origins of Kant's Arguments in the Antinomies* (Clarendon Press, Oxford, 1972).

ALSTON, W. P., 'The Ontological Argument Revisited' (*Philosophical Review*, 1960; reprinted in Plantinga).

AUSTIN, J. L., *Sense and Sensibilia* (Clarendon Press, Oxford, 1962).

BECK, L. W., 'The Second Analogy and the Principle of Indeterminacy' (*Kant-Studien*, 1966; reprinted in Penelhum and MacIntosh).

BELNAP, N. D., 'Tonk, Plonk and Plink' (*Analysis*, 1962).

BENNETT, J. F., *Kant's Analytic* (C.U.P., 1966).

—— *Kant's Dialectic* (C.U.P., 1974).

—— *Rationality* (Routledge and Kegan Paul, London, 1964).

BERKELEY, G., *Principles of Human Knowledge*.

CARNAP, R., *Philosophical Foundations of Physics* (Basic Books, New York and London, 1966).

CASTAÑEDA, H., ' "7+5=12" as a Synthetic Proposition' (*Philosophy and Phenomenological Research*, 1960–1).

CHIPMAN, L., 'Schematism' (*Kant-Studien*, 1972).

DESCARTES, R., *Philosophical Works*, ed. and trans. in two volumes by E. S. Haldane and G. R. T. Ross (C.U.P., 1911).

ENGEL, S. M., 'Kant's "Refutation" of the Ontological Argument' (*Philosophy and Phenomenological Research*, 1963–4; reprinted in Wolff).

FREGE, G., *Foundations of Arithmetic*, trans. J. L. Austin (Blackwell, Oxford, 1950).

HACKER, P. M. S., 'Are Transcendental Arguments a Version of Verificationism?' (*American Philosophical Quarterly*, 1972).

HEMPEL, C. G., 'Geometry and Empirical Science', in H. Feigl and W. Sellars (edd), *Readings in Philosophical Analysis* (Appleton Century Crofts, New York, 1949).

—— 'On the Nature of Mathematical Truth', in H. Feigl and W. Sellars (edd.), *Readings in Philosophical Analysis* (Appleton Century Crofts, New York, 1949).

HOLLIS, M., 'Times and Spaces' (*Mind*, 1967).

HOPKINS, J., 'Visual Geometry' (*Philosophical Review*, 1973).

HUME, D., *Enquiry Concerning Human Understanding*, ed. L. A. Selby-Bigge, with text revised and notes by P. H. Nidditch (Clarendon Press, Oxford, 1975).

—— *Treatise of Human Nature*, ed. L. A. Selby-Bigge (Clarendon Press, Oxford, 1896).

KEMP-SMITH, N., *A Commentary to Kant's Critique of Pure Reason* (Macmillan, London, second edition, 1923).

KITCHER, P., 'Kant and the Foundations of Mathematics' (*Philosophical Review*, 1975).

KÖRNER, S., *Kant* (Penguin Books, Harmondsworth, 1955).

—— 'On the Impossibility of Transcendental Deductions' (*Monist*, 1967).

—— 'On the Kantian Foundation of Science and Mathematics' (*Kant-Studien*, 1966; reprinted in Penelhum and MacIntosh).

The Leibniz-Clarke Correspondence, ed. G. H. Alexander (Manchester U.P., 1956).

LEMMON, E. J., *Beginning Logic* (Nelson, London, 1965).

LOCKE, J., *An Essay Concerning Human Understanding*.

MACINTOSH, J., 'Transcendental Arguments' (*PASS*, 1969).

MALCOLM, N., *Dreaming* (Routledge and Kegan Paul, London, 1959).

MATTHEWS, H. E., 'Strawson on Transcendental Idealism' (*Philosophical Quarterly*, 1969).

MELNICK, A., *Kant's Analogies of Experience* (University of Chicago Press, 1973).

MOORE, G. E., 'Is Existence a Predicate?' (*PASS*, 1936).

PARSONS, C. D., 'Infinity and Kant's Conception of the "Possibility of Experience"' (*Philosophical Review*, 1964; reprinted in Wolff).

PENELHUM, T. and MACINTOSH, J. J. (edd.), *The First Critique* (Wadsworth, Belmont, California, 1969).

PHILLIPS GRIFFITHS, A., 'Transcendental Arguments' (*PASS*, 1969).

PLANTINGA, A. (ed.), *The Ontological Argument* (Macmillan, London, 1968).

POPPER, K., 'Why are the Calculi of Logic and Arithmetic Applicable to Reality?' (*PASS*, 1946).

PRIOR, A. N., 'The Runabout Inference-Ticket' (*Analysis*, 1960).

QUINTON, A. M., 'Spaces and Times' (*Philosophy*, 1962).

REMNANT, P., 'Kant and the Cosmological Argument' (*Australasian Journal of Philosophy*, 1959; reprinted in Penelhum and MacIntosh).

SHAFFER, J., 'Existence, Predication and the Ontological Argument' (*Mind*, 1962; reprinted in Plantinga).

SMART, J. J. C., *Philosophy and Scientific Realism* (Routledge and Kegan Paul, London, 1963).

STRAWSON, P. F., *Bounds of Sense* (Methuen, London, 1966).

—— *Individuals* (Methuen, London, 1959).

STROUD, B., 'Transcendental Arguments' (*Journal of Philosophy*, 1968; reprinted in Penelhum and MacIntosh).

SWINBURNE, R. G., *Space and Time* (Macmillan, London, 1968).

WALSH, W. H., 'Categories' (*Kant-Studien*, 1954; reprinted in Wolff).

—— 'Schematism' (*Kant-Studien*, 1957; reprinted in Wolff).

WARNOCK, G. J., 'Concepts and Schematism' (*Analysis*, 1949).

WELDON, T. D., 'Schematism' (*PAS*, 1947-8).

WILKERSON, T. E., 'Things, Stuffs and Kant's Aesthetic' (*Philosophical Review*, 1973).

—— 'Time, Cause and Object: Kant's Second Analogy of Experience' (*Kant-Studien*, 1971).

WITTGENSTEIN, L., *Philosophical Investigations* (Basil Blackwell, Oxford, second edition, 1958).

WOLFF, R. P. (ed.), *Kant* (Doubleday, New York, 1967; Macmillan, London, 1968).

—— *Kant's Theory of Mental Activity* (Harvard University Press, 1963).

ZEMACH, E., 'Strawson's Transcendental Deduction' (*Philosophical Quarterly*, 1975).

INDEX